CP 7⁵⁰

Megaliths and Masterminds

Megaliths
and Masterminds

Peter Lancaster Brown

NEW YORK
CHARLES SCRIBNER'S SONS

1 3 5 7 9 11 13 15 17 19   I/C   20 18 16 14 12 10 8 6 4 2

Printed in Great Britain
Library of Congress Catalog Card Number 78–73050
SBN 0–684–15908–2

Contents

Line Figures in Text

Illustrations

ACKNOWLEDGEMENTS

The author and publishers gratefully acknowledge the following sources for certain illustrations: Crown Copyright, Ancient Monuments Branch, Ministry of Public Buildings and Works, Plates 1, 8, 16; British Museum, Plates 24, 29 (above right); The *Yorkshire Post*, page 100; Aerofilms Ltd, Plates 2, 3, 6.

The author is particularly grateful for the generous assistance rendered by his wife, Johanne.

1 Basics and Background

The word "Megalith" is compounded from the Greek *megas* (great) and *lithos* (stone) and is a term first applied to certain hoar-ancient monuments round about the middle of the nineteenth century. Nevertheless, in English-language literature the description "Megalithic" monument did not entirely displace older terms like "rude" or "rough" stone monument until after the second decade of the twentieth century. Indeed, in Sir Norman Lockyer's now classic work *Stonehenge and Other British Stone Monuments* (1906; 2nd ed. 1909), the term "Megalithic" only occurs a handful of times in the 500 pages of text.

Throughout the world there are many monuments and structures built of stone of widely differing ages that may rightly come under the heading "Megalithic". In the widest sense of its definition a Megalithic structure embraces any structure made of large stones. Thus Hadrian's Wall and other similar antiquities could be termed Megalithic. However, its modern *archaeological* usage has generally been restricted to a series of funerary and standing stone structures found chiefly in Western Asia, Africa and particularly in Europe. For the purposes here, the term "Megalithic" is also extended to include the stone pyramids of Egypt and Mesoamerica.

First, what are we really talking about when we refer to a Megalithic monument? Disregarding for the moment the temples and pyramids of Egypt and the Mesoamerica, which will be discussed later, Megalithic monuments can be conveniently divided into broadly three categories:

single (isolated) standing stones,
grouped standing stones,
chambered tombs.

In the older literature, those in North-West Europe (and some-times elsewhere) were referred to under a Welsh-Breton nomen-clature which has largely fallen out of use in English-language publications, but not entirely. Single standing stones—the long-stones or monoliths—were known as menhirs (from *men* [stone] and *hir* [long]); grouped standing stones were known as crom-lechs (from *crom* [circle] or [curve] and *lech* [place]); and cham-bered tombs were known as dolmens (from *dol* or *tol* [table] and *men* [stone]). The names menhir and cromlech still have cur-rency in France.

The trouble was that these descriptions were frequently inter-changeable and confusion resulted. No one nowadays (in English-speaking countries at least) would refer to Stonehenge or other grouped stones forming a circle as a cromlech, but this term was frequently applied to all stone circles in the nineteenth century. In Britain, just to confuse matters, "cromlech" and "dolmen" were terms often used as alternative descriptions to the same object (Plate 1). Nowadays the term "cromlech" is usually re-stricted to certain grouped standing stone monuments found in France and are quite unlike the British stone circles.

The Megalithic chambered tombs have recieved much atten-tion from archaeologists, and in specialist literature they are usually found divided into their various architectural sub-divisions. Types of chambered tomb differ from region to region. For example, in France the most familiar form of Megalithic chambered tomb is the *allée couverte* (Fig. 1).

Chambered tombs are very significant indeed to the study of Megalithic science, for some of them appear to be (solar) orien-tated, and in addition they provide more positive evidence than stone circles and single standing stones do about social and cul-tural practices locally in vogue.

Some of the most intriguing Megalithic monuments are grouped standing stones which were erected to form long 'aven-ues', often in multiple parallel or semi-parallel rows. The most spectacular of these are found in Brittany round Carnac (Plate 3) where they extend cross-country for several kilometres.

Sometimes associated with stone avenues, but containing no stones themselves, are earthwork features known under the name Cursus (Latin for "racecourse"). Whether they were in fact race-courses is highly conjectural. This name was first given them in the eighteenth century by the British antiquarian William Stukeley, who is one of the key historical figures in the (often fanciful) interpretation of British Megalithic monuments.

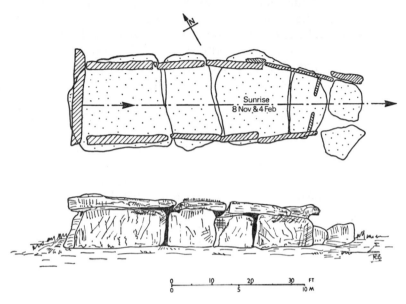

Figure 1   Plan view and south elevation of the *allée couverte* at Bagneux near Saumer, France. The erection of this structure is dated before the Egyptian pyramids, and Boyle Somerville (*see* Chapter 12) claimed it was purpose-orientated to sunrise on 8 November or 4 February—ancient calendar dates about midpoint between the winter solstice and the equinoxes (half-quarter day).

Closely associated with Megalithic (stone) monuments are the so-called Megaxylic (made-of-wood) monuments. The best known example is Woodhenge situated some three kilometres east of Stonehenge. Because the great timbers that once formed its uprights have long rotted away in their postholes, Woodhenge was only discovered through the medium of aerial photography (Plate 2). Another outstanding "woodhenge" which again was first noticed from the air is at Arminghall near Norwich (Plate 4).

The general classification "henge" monument is a very confusing and unsatisfactory one. Although the name is derived from Stonehenge (probably Anglo-Saxon for "place of hanging stones"), only Stonehenge itself is known for certain to have been built with hanging stones carried in the form of lintels supported by stone uprights (Plate 8). Nevertheless, the term "henge" monument is official currency for upwards of a hundred sites scattered throughout Britain which usually have *no* stones and consist of circular or oval enclosures surrounded by a bank and ditch with entrances. Some have single entrances like the prototype monument Stonehenge (Fig. 4 *see page* 27); others, like Avebury (Fig. 5 *see page* 34), have two or more. A sub-class of henge have a surrounding bank with ditches both *inside* and *outside*.

In addition to the kinds of antiquities already cited, there are several important stone and non-stone monuments associated with the age of the Megalith builders. Many of the smaller stone circles found in Britain are classified as "hut" circles, others as cairn circles. Some of the most intriguing monuments are enigmatic earth-ring features, numbered in hundreds, which (like the woodhenges) can only be seen from the air. Lastly there are the various kinds of tumuli, or barrows, (long barrows, round barrows, bell-shaped barrows, etc.) built to contain remains of the dead or to commemorate the dead. Barrows made of earth, turves, wood or rock extend over a long time-span. They preceded the age of the Megalith builders and continued to be built by different peoples right into the modern era up to Saxon/Viking times.

Because of the inference that Megalithic monuments were either "stones of the Devil" or "pagan altars", the Christian Church in its early days made several attempts to suppress the cult of stone worship two thousand years after the last monuments had been erected and their builders long forgotten. The councils of Arles in A.D. 452, of Tours in A.D. 567 and Nantes in A.D. 658 all condemned the cult of stones along with the cults of trees and springs. In Spain the council of Toledo in A.D. 681 and 682 also condemned "Worshippers of Stones". In many areas "pagan" monuments were Christianized. In Britain the church instructed that pagan sites should be obliterated by building over them. A direct reference to this practice is found in the Venerable Bede's *Ecclesiastical History* which cites a letter from Pope Gregory instructing that pagan temples ought not to be destroyed but sanctified and then converted to churches. Evidence of converted

French and British Megalithic/Christian sites can still be seen
in various places (Plate 19).

Especially among peasant populations Megalithic monuments
have acquired a special mystique. Throughout Europe particularly,
names given to monuments have very fanciful associations. Frequently encountered are names like Druid Stones, Pagans' Altar,
Sorcerers' Stones, Wizard Stones, Witches' Rocks, Fairy Stones,
Stones of the Barbarians, etc. In France it is common to find
the use of saints' names such as Saint Cornely's Soldiers (Plate
3), and again in Switzerland we find Saint Martin's Stones,
while in Britain folklore names are frequently encountered such
as King Arthur's Stone (or Quoit), Arthur's Table or Merlin's
Rocks. In Northern Britain we find Odin's Stones, while all
over Britan there are colourful names given to entire stone circles,
for example, Meg and her Daughters at Penrith.

Dolmens especially seem to attract many names associated
with Old Nick—names like Forges of the Devil or the Druids'
Kitchens; while dolmens found in India (of a later date than
those in Europe) are often locally referred to as Stones of the
Monkeys.

In Spain and North Africa we find Graves of the Gentiles or
Tombs of Idolaters. In France local names for *allées couvertes*
may be referred to as various kinds of prisons or Shops of the
Saracens; while dolmens there sometimes become Wolves' Altars
(or Tables) or Wolves' Houses.

In Holland and Germany we find the *Hünenbetter*—giants'
beds. Not surprisingly, some examples are of large size. Typical
is the chambered grave at Mecklemburg which measures 46 x 10
metres (150 x 36 feet) and rises to a height of 1.5 meters (5 feet);
round it stand 48 tall Megalithic blocks. Local folk tradition
throughout their distribution attribute the *Hünenbetter* to a prehistoric race of giants who employed dwarfs to build them. When
they were completed, the unfortunate workers were supposedly
devoured by their masters. The French *allées couvertes* may also
have associations with giants and carry names like Gargantua's
Tomb, while a nearby standing stone (a menhir) may be referred
to as Gargantua's Little Finger.

Megalithic monuments were also utilized to evoke their supposed magic for the benefit of the crippled, sick or infertile. One famous dolmen in Northern France was said to be a sure cure for rheumatism for those who passed under it. One special kind of intriguing combination monument, the Men-an-tol (Fig. 2), was

Figure 2　Men-an-tol. The middle stone has a pierced centre and is aligned between two upright monoliths, and the arrangement is suggestive of an involvement in some kind of fertility cult.

said to have special powers of healing the various ills of the sick if the afflicted was passed through the central hole. In nineteenth-century literature the tall menhirs of Brittany (Plate 5) were frequently cited as fertility stones, round which childless couples, preferably naked, danced. The exact number of times a couple had to gyrate to evoke its supposed fertility powers varied according to the local formula.

Stonehenge too has many early folk-medicine stories associated with it. The earliest reference to this dates back to Geoffrey of Monmouth's *History of the Kings of Britain* written about 1136, in which he says its stones possess "a healing virtue against many ailments". The infamous Geoffrey and his apocryphal tales figure very largely in Stonehenge history as we shall see later.

Stonehenge, standing on Salisbury Plain in Southern England, can now claim—excepting perhaps the Great Pyramid of Cheops in Egypt—to be the most famous of all the classical Megalithic monuments. Stonehenge is unique on several counts, and few monuments—again excepting the Great Pyramid—have been studied as frequently or intensively as Stonehenge or, for that matter, have raised more contentious steam among the pundits . . . As far back as 1876, a learned reviewer of Stonehenge theories commented ". . . that more books have been printed about that much frequented Stonehenge than about all the megalithic structures, collectively, which the world contains; and the literature of this . . . would fill the shelves of a small library". Since then the bibliography of Stonehenge has perhaps expanded ten-fold.

It was round the beginning of the twentieth century that the modern contentious debates about Stonehenge really took fire. Earlier contentions in the seventeenth and eighteenth centuries had been chiefly concerned with three main points : who had built the monument; was it pre- or post-Roman; and was it involved in Druid rites? The early twentieth-century contentions were now more concerned with the purpose of the monument.

Although vague astronomical theories had been attached to Stonehenge since 1740, it was not until Sir Norman Lockyer published his classic *Stonehenge* that astronomical theories gained a surer footing. Lockyer's work, however, was in for a stormy passage and received a strong rebuff at the hands of dissenting archaeologists. In hindsight some of this criticism was deserved, for while Lockyer's attack on the Stonehenge problem was pioneering and praiseworthy, his methodology was suspect and of such a nature it frequently embarrassed his supporters.

Following Lockyer's death in 1920, the astronomical theories about Stonehenge gradually fell out of fashion. In the decades which followed, the archaeologists repossessed the monument as some kind of barbarian Neolithic sanctuary *c*.2000 B.C., *and* believed they had soundly dismissed for all time any ideas that the monument was an observatory, staffed by an astronomical-

priestly incumbency of near geniuses that had received its knowledge from one of the great civilizations of the Near East as
Lockyer's theories would have it.

But the archaeologists were in for a surprise. In the early 1960s,
two men quite independently and totally unknown to each other
re-examined the Stonehenge problem yet again, and the mystery
surrounding the Stonehenge Megaliths suddenly became deeper
and more mysterious than ever. . . .

One of these investigators was the British-born American
astronomer Gerald Hawkins, working at the Smithsonian Observatory at Cambridge, Mass. In 1963, after a programme of
field-work at Stonehenge, he published the results of his computer-
laboratory findings in the premier science magazine *Nature*
under the provocative title "Stonehenge Decoded". Hawkins indeed made the bold claim to have solved the long-standing riddle
of Stonehenge. His general conclusion was that while Lockyer's
methodology and several of his assumptions were suspect, he had,
nevertheless, been on the right track.

In his article Hawkins set out to demonstrate that whatever
else the monument might be, his computer-findings had shown
it also to represent a sophisticated ancient observatory built by
Neolithic man in several stages (spanning the period *c*. 2000 B.C.)
in order to keep track not only of the seasonal shift of the Sun
(a view that had been held since 1740) but also the shift of the
much more complicated vagaries of moonrise and moonset.

This article by Hawkins, plus several others which followed
it, was to trigger one of the most intriguing on-running scientific
debates in the modern era.

But unknown to Hawkins, a British amateur astronomer C.
A. ("Peter") Newham, a retired utilities engineer, had a little
earlier been working on the same problem but without the aid
of a computer. Although Newham's work had been mentioned
in an article in a provincial North-Country paper a good eight
months before *Nature* published Hawkins's article, it passed without comment and raised not a ripple of interest. Indeed, when
the great Megalithic debate began echoing round the world,
most interested scientists were totally unaware of Newham's
earlier work.

But others too had been quietly working away on the astronomical thesis—visiting sites and gleaning information to prove

that British Megalithic monuments were observatories of a kind. With the academic dust raised by Hawkins's first article, their work now also came to light. One man in particular in this category was the Scot Alexander Thom, Emeritus Professor of Engineering Science at Oxford. Thom's work was known to a few cognoscenti, but this too had raised little comment. It was now revealed that for many years Thom had been surveying hundreds of Megalithic monuments—mostly little-known stone circles and standing stones in forgotten and remote moorland locales; he had not then included Stonehenge which he was to cover later.

Thom had derived many clues from earlier British investigators, some of them like A. L. Lewis and others who had published many accounts round the time of Lockyer's work, but whose findings had been summarily dismissed. But Thom had gone much further than anyone before him, for he claimed he had rediscovered an old and long-forgotten geometric unit that he named the "Megalithic Yard" which he believed to be the standard unit used by the Neolithic astronomer-priests to set out and construct their stone monuments. Consequently, if Thom's work was to be taken at face value, he had discovered the key to the whole problem of the stone circles that abound up and down the British countryside and whose sometimes odd designs and shapes had taxed the speculative reasoning-powers of past investigators.

What finally provided the impetus to the whole subject—now firmly labelled in some quarters as 'Megalithic astronomy" or "astro-archaeology"—was Hawkins's second article in *Nature* entitled "Stonehenge : A Neolithic Computer". This indeed was an original and revolutionary article which described with great verisimilitude how the various circle features at Stonehenge could have been utilized by ancient men as a kind of computer to predict eclipses. If Hawkins's theory could be substantiated, it implied, as others had earlier foreshadowed, that the ancient Britains before 2000 B.C. were not only the earliest founders of scientific astronomy, but that the history books had got it all wrong about the intellectual level of the people who inhabited Britain, and neighbouring North-West Europe, 2000 years before the Roman armies set foot there.

It was now that a well-known controversial figure threw his hat into the scientific ring to air his own views. This was Fred

Hoyle, better known for his work on cosmology as the chief propounder of a theory of the Universe known as the Steady State. Hoyle, as an original thinker, applied his genius to studying Hawkins's paper and suddenly realized he could improve upon it with an eclipse-predicting *modus operandi* of his own without ever visiting the monument.

However, not everyone was prepared to jump on the bandwagon and agree about the revolutionary astronomical ideas now fostered on Stonehenge. The foremost dissenters were the archaeologists, who, as a corporate body even before Lockyer's time, had been inherently hostile to all astronomical inferences at Stonehenge. Now with the spate of new theories not only applied to Stonehenge but to many other British (and later French) Megalithic monuments, they were overwhelmed.

Lockyer had begun his astro-archaeological studies in Egypt in the 1890s by trying to prove some astronomical significances built into Egyptian temples. His co-worker F. C. Penrose had earlier attempted to do the same for Greek temples. Consensus opinion for both Lockyer's and Penrose's work in Greece, Egypt and Britain could be fairly summed up as "interesting speculation but not proven". While Lockyer's and Penrose's work was often slipshod and relied heavily on some doubtful mythological evidence, the work of the new investigators of the 1960s was immaculately presented in hard mathematical numbers in a form difficult for the largely non-numerate archaeologists to grasp— or in some instances even to begin to comprehend. Here indeed lay a good part of the trouble.

The chief archaeologist dissenter, but subsequently the most constructive, came forth in the guise of R. J. C. Atkinson, recognized as one of the greatest living authorities on Stonehenge. Atkinson had done much field-work at Stonehenge, and his book *Stonehenge* (1956) was judged to be definitive. Atkinson, provocatively, threw down the gauntlet for the archaeologists by stating in a review that Hawkins's work was "unconvincing, tendentious and slipshod". These indeed have become famous epithets in the Stonehenge debate. Yet, ironically, Atkinson himself was not a *total* dissenter, for earlier he had given much encouragement to Newham. Newham had in fact sought out Atkinson's advice about his own astronomical theories, and it was Atkinson who had advised Newham to seek pubication in the magazine *Antiquity*. Atkinson was also soon convinced by some of Thom's ideas which he believed could not be dismissed out of hand as some of his non-mathematical and less-numerate archaeologist colleagues were inclined to do. Atkinson wrote that Thom must be considered seriously if for no other reason than he had now provided ingenious solutions to some of the perplexing problems that long had confronted archaeologists about the odd geometric shapes of some of the old stone circles.

Nevertheless, many archaeologists were not prepared to be as open-minded as Atkinson, their spokesman. Stonehenge, they believed, was nothing more than a pagan religious centre or sanctuary—pure and simple. They could dismiss at once all that glib hypothetical nonsense about the British Isles being inhabited by a race of geniuses in the days of yore. They asked, and indeed it is a fair question: how could a barbarous, primitive and preliterate people, as was indicated in the archaeological field evidence for the period, have acquired specialist knowledge that only the Babylonian astronomers acquired some 1500 years later?

2 Scratched Bones and Speculations

One of the stumbling-blocks confronting modern prehistoric researches is that by tradition those who study prehistory—such as historians and archaeologists—are usually arts-trained people. While many would now agree that modern archaeology is fast becoming a science, not all would agree it is a science—or indeed that it should be—including not a few archaeologists.

As a consequence of their background and training, archaeologists of the old school, with some exceptions, are not able to offer constructive criticism to the new astro-archaeological ideas. It is an undisputable fact that prehistorians, anthropologists and archaeologists are much less numerate people than astronomers, physical scientists, engineers, architects and land surveyors, who are strongly attracted to astro-archaeological studies because *it involves using numbers and exact measurement*. R. J. C. Atkinson himself recognised the dilemma facing archaeologists when confronted with the hard-number "evidence", and during the contentious Megalith debates of the "sixties", he readily admitted that, in his experience, archaeologists are by no means as numerate as they should be.

Sir Norman Lockyer—a true polymathic scientist if ever there was one—was much vexed by the sometimes hostile negative attitude of his archaeologist critics. What annoyed Lockyer was the archaeologists' narrow-minded attitude in telling astronomers to stick to astronomy and they in turn would stick to archaeology. This head-in-the-sand attitude was frequently voiced by archaeologists in the Megalith debates of the 1960s. Lockyer himself was a self-trained astronomer as well as a land surveyor; and because of the intransigence of some of the archaeologist critics, he delighted in catching them out in debate when he tempted them out of their depth, and they tried to quote figures back at him across the floor.

Nowadays it has largely been recognized that astro-archaeological studies cannot be pursued by a single-discipline body ever-jealous of its own preserves. To be successful as a modern science, astro-archaeology needs to be much more than a simple amalgam of astronomy and archaeology. Its scope is far reaching and needs from time to time to draw on the coffers of specialized disciplines including geology, anthropology, mythology, folklore, philology, paleography, ethnology, prehistoric and neoprimitive art, prehistoric and classical scholarship, biology, botany, geochemistry, nuclear physics—and even at times pseudology—plus a host of other 'ologies and arts. The snag, of course, is that specialists are still only human. Each branch of learning may have a strong emotional bias towards its own narrow interests, and this is what inevitably brings about the conflicts of ideas in the solution of a particular problem.

When dissenting archaeologists to the new Stonehenge theories pointed out that the earlier inhabitants of North-West Europe c. 2000 B.C. were certainly illiterate, barbarian peoples as compared to the enlightened men of the recognized great literate civilizations of Sumer, Egypt, Asia Minor, Shang China and the Indus Valley, and could therefore not possibly have evolved a truly scientific astronomy, they posed a question that sooner or later needed a sensible answer.

This was partly answered by *Nature* which had first published the authors of the claims for the high intellectual abilities of ancient Britains. In an editorial, *Nature* remarked that it admitted it was the very cleverness of the new ideas attributed to designers of Stonehenge that was going to be the most difficult part to accept. Rightly the editorial posed the question whether it was likely that preliterate peoples who had not yet invented enduring houses as domestic abodes could possibly have been clever enough to build instruments in crude stone with crude tools of such intricacy at Stonehenge as implied by the astronomers. But the same editorial added, significantly, that archaeology was usually *only* able to describe the mundane, lower limits of the degrees of sophistication of any society, and *if* archaeolo-

gists knew more than they did about life (in Britain) around *c.*
2500-2000 B.C., the archaeologists might be in a better position to
show positively that the astronomers' ideas were quite implaus-
ible.

"Civilization" as used by the archaeologists is an arbitrary term.
It is generally used to define a society in antiquity that possessed
at least two of three things: towns of more than 5,000 inhabitants, a system of writing, and complex "ceremonial" centres.
For this reason for the period round 2000-1500 B.C. it is usual
to restrict recognized civilizations to Sumer, Egypt, Asia Minor,
Shang China and the Indus Valley. Under the above definition,
North-West Europe in the millenniums before the modern era
is totally excluded, for although the criterion of the possession of
complex "ceremonial" centres is well satisfied (e.g. Stonehenge
and Avebury in Britain, Carnac in France, etc.), there is no
evidence which has come down to us through the archaeological
record in this period for permanent towns of more than 5,000
inhabitants and for an established system of script writing.

There can be little doubt, however, that the largest "ceremonial" centres such as Stonehenge, Avebury and Carnac on
occasions must have attracted crowds in excess of 5,000 people.
One has only to visit Avebury in particular and study its massive
"amphitheatre" layout (Plate 6) to realize that the claim that this
monument *has* room enough to hold *upwards of a quarter of a
million people* is no idle boast. Whether in antiquity it did hold
such large numbers of people is conjectural.

Traditionally, in North-West Europe, script writing is supposed to have diffused there by Roman and possibly earlier
Greek influences. Nevertheless, because of the exciting inferences
that North-West Europeans *c.* 2000 B.C. were not the barbarian
peoples once believed, it is certainly not stepping beyond the
bounds of reasonable speculation to suppose that some kind of
earlier writing or recording was in existence at this time—and
perhaps, if truth be known, many millenniums before this.

One thing *is* certain. Man in Europe *c.* 3000-2000 B.C. was
by then a pretty sophisticated product of genus *Homo.* It is now
known that man has been around in various parts of the world
for a much longer period than pre-nineteen-sixties' archaeologists
and paleontologists would ever readily have admitted to. For

example, in East Africa the evolution of man has been traced back in the fossil record to a period at least $3\frac{1}{2}$ to 4 million years before the present—to a period before the onset of Pleistocene when at least six major ice sheets (and several intervening lesser ones) in turn advanced and then retreated.

Thus Stone-Age man developed over a time-span measured in millions of years rather than the time-span of a few thousand which the Victorians once believed. It was suddenly, however, during the last great ice advance that Stone-Age man in Europe and Australia seems to have achieved new cultural peaks in the period known as the Upper Paleolithic (Upper Old Stone Age) which began about 35,000 B.C. and lasted until the onset of the Mesolithic (Middle Stone Age) about 10,000 B.C.

But the archaeological record from the Upper Paleolithic is anything but complete. At best those human artefacts of durable materials which have survived must be considered as highly selective evidence. It is the record of ancient man's surviving "art" from this period that now provides us with many of the tantalizing clues about man's cultural level at this time and in particular about his possible early interest in the heavens which was to blossom fully several millenniums later in the age of the Megalith builders at the climax of the Neolithic.

In what has been considered as Upper Paleolithic represent-ational art we can see star asterisms depicted unambiguously at La Lileta in Spain and at Fratel in Portugal. In a picture at Los Buitres there is a representation of the Sun, while at Pala Pinta de Carloa there is a picture of two suns set on a starry background. In the Upper Paleolithic period we also come across enigmatic lozenge-shaped motifs which then haunt the archae-ological record in several cultures right up to the present day—they frequently turn up on Megalithic monuments, and they are also common on seals from Sumer *c.* 3000 B.C. Whether in Upper Paleolithic times these lozenge motifs were crudely exe-cuted stellar asterisms is conjectural. They might also depict the two "eyes" of the day and night—the Sun and the Moon.

Nevertheless, none of the astronomically motivated art-repre-sentations so far discussed can even claim remotely to show that Upper Paleolithic man had any concept of *scientific* astronomy —which is usually defined as attempts, no matter how crudely executed, to predict or follow the cyclic movement of a celestial body such as a sequence of monthly lunar phases (repeated over $29\frac{1}{2}$ days) or the apparent annual journey of the Sun back and forth across the horizon (in $364\frac{1}{4}$ days). Indeed, until very recently archaeologists, if asked, would have considered it a fruitless exercise for astronomers to look for any kind of astronomical representations, scientific or otherwise, in artefacts before or outside the period of the classical civilizations of Egypt and Babylonia.

It is not surprising then that the man who began such a search in dim prehistory was neither an archaeologist nor an astronomer in any accepted sense of the word—or for that matter any kind of traditional scholar of the old school, cossetted away in some ivy-clad tower of a distinguished university.

The man who did begin such a search—the American Alexander Marshack—was by training a journalist of many talents. Marshack had travelled widely in Europe and Asia and made no bones about having been employed in turn as a book and drama reviewer, an art reporter, a photographer, a script-writer, a producer and director of plays and—to archaeologists perhaps the most heinous crime of all—a popular science writer. These qualifications for serious study are not the kind calculated to endear him to any traditional academics. But in the 1960s several others like him emerged to do open battle with academic specialists.

Marshack began his own researches into man's intellectual past when he was engaged in writing a popular book about the path which led man to make his first attempts at a landing on the Moon. Marshack was soon surprised to find how difficult it was to root out the origins of science and civilization, and quite soon he arrived at the conclusion that there *must* be 'something missing' from the archaeological record.

By coincidence he began browsing through a copy of the *Scientific American*—the June 1962 issue. By chance this issue carried an intriguing article about a small scratched bone that had been found at Ishango—a site of the Mesolithic period— near the headwaters of the Nile. The article had been written by the Belgian Jean de Heinzelin who described the bone and discussed the various plausible interpretations which might be put to the scratches. Similarly scratched bones dating from the European Upper Paleolithic were well-known artefacts that pre-

viously had always been supposed by prehistorians and archaeologists to represent inscribed abstract decorative patterns—or
by a very tiny minority some elementary numeration system such
as tally-marks representing the numbers of beasts a hunter had
killed in the chase.

The Ishango bone was dated *c.* 6500 B.C. or some two or
three thousand years before the first dynasty in Egypt and the
appearance of the first known hieroglyphic writing there. In his
article de Heinzelin believed the bone to be the handle of an
implement used for engraving or perhaps even tattooing. But
the pattern of scratches, or notches, was the most interesting
feature. These were arranged in distinct columns. De Heinzelin
was first inclined to dismiss them as decorative motifs, but he
later changed his mind and believed they *might* possibly show
an arithmetical game devised by prehistoric people who likely
had evolved a number system based on 10 as well as possibly
having some knowledge of prime numbers and duplication
(multiplying by 2).

Marshack, after reading de Heinzelin's article, relates that he
then studied the photographs and drawings of the bone for
perhaps an hour or so. They engrossed him; they intrigued him;
they puzzled him. He took a break for coffee. While he drank
the coffee, his thoughts went back time and time again to that
bit of dull, blackened bone with its odd scratches. There seemed
something wrong with the accepted interpretation. Then suddenly he had an idea. Since Marshack was then deeply immersed
in writing his popular book about the Moon, the Moon was
also paramount in his thoughts, subconsciously vying with that
bit of scratched bone for his attention. He wrote afterwards: "I
decided to try a hunch." Fifteen minutes later, after carefully
re-examining the drawings and photographs of the puzzling
scratch patterns, he claimed to have "cracked the code". He felt
he was looking at a lunar notation—a man-inscribed system
which could be read unambiguously to show the simple day-to-
day cycles of the Moon's period round the Earth reflected by
the lunar phases.

If this sudden inspiration was correct, he was looking at the
oldest known evidence for man's scientific interest in the sky.
If it did prove correct, it was a break-through to the understanding of the mind of ancient man—as important a discovery per-

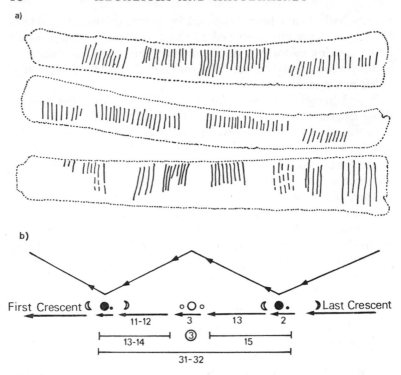

haps as Young's and Champollion's break-through in unlocking the secrets of Egyptian hieroglyphs and maybe as far-reaching.

As a consequence of this seminal inspiration, Marshack travelled to Europe to search out and examine more artefacts which had been gleaned from known sites of the Upper Paleolithic. First stop was the Musée des Antiquités Nationales at Saint-Germain-en-Laye, near Paris, to examine their collection of twenty or so exhibition cabinets of engraved Upper-Paleolithic material—and double this number of objects stored away in various rooms and drawers.

When Marshack arrived in Europe to begin his museum pilgrimage, he was keyed up in anticipation of making significant discoveries. His later account—sometimes written in evocative, dramatic prose—reflects his state of mind at this time. When he entered the museum's main exhibition room, he writes he experienced "...the sudden chill feeling of an intruder in an

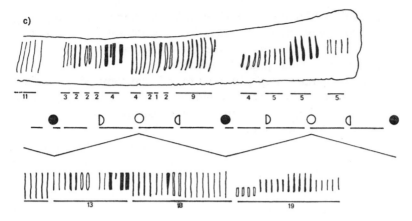

Figure 3   The Ishango Bone and lunar notations. (a) Engraved marks on the three faces of the bone (based on a photograph). (b) Standard lunar template devised by Alexander Marshack to show observational divisions of the lunar month: waxing period is reckoned 13 days; Full Moon 3 days; waning period 11–12 days; invisible (conjunction) period 1–2 days. In practice the count for one lunar month may work out as three periods of 15; 3; and 13–14 days, giving an anomalous lunar-month count of 31–32 (as against a true period of 29½ days). (c) Top face of the Ishango Bone as interpreted by Marshack against the template model (simplified) showing possible sets and subsets of a lunar-phase notation.

abandoned graveyard ...". And "... there was a huge silence in the musty air of the high-ceilinged stone chamber".

Almost straightway he found several bones which he was soon persuaded showed characteristic lunar notations similar to the Ishango bone. But patterns were often different; yet they were not random as others who had studied them had previously supposed. He was convinced that the marks inscribed had been made sequentially. To test out the various patterns he compared each one with a standard lunar notation as he had earlier done with the Ishango bone (Fig. 3). When he matched them, he was convinced they provided a reasonable, if not always an exact, fit. He was further encouraged and now firmly believed he was on the right track.

The search was intensified. He armed himself with a pocket-microscope to help him pick out minute marks and dots he had discovered inscribed on some of the bones not readily discernible with the unassisted eye. He toiled daily among the dusty Upper-

Paleolithic exhibits of the various museums he visited, comparing their bones with those of others—ever watchful for an artefact containing rows of dots and/or incisions that might match up to his standard lunar-phase template.

Under the microscope, he now found that some of the incised bones showed faint traces of red ochre lodged in the grooves. This set Marshack wondering whether the red oxide had been purposely added to each notational sub-group as it was inscribed —to act as a printers' ink to make sure that the grooves or pits would stand out against the stark white of fresh bone. But he was not wholly convinced that this idea was correct. He learnt that ancient man used red ochres for many purposes—to redden corpses, graves and even his habitations. This tradition of ochre decoration was carried from the Upper Paleolithic into contemporary times by the Australian Aborigines and other neoprimitives.

To fully appreciate the significant patterns that Marshack was searching for among the dusty, scratched and incised bones, one needs to be aware of how the Moon moves round the Earth in relation to time (and the Sun). The lunar month of about $29\frac{1}{2}$ days as shown by the phases of the Moon has no direct connection with the year as determined by the Earth's movement round the Sun in $364\frac{1}{4}$ days. Had there been a connection, the whole history of man's effort in using the Moon as a calendar would have been much simpler. No amount of juggling will allow multiples of the short lunar-month calendar to fit neatly as a smaller unit into the longer solar one. This must have been a lesson that ancient man soon learnt in his study of the heavens, but it must have sorely exasperated him. The time interval between the occurrences of two New Moons represents on average 29 days 12 hours 44 minutes 2.98 seconds. This period is called the *synodic month* and is the true lunar month (there are other important lunar periods, but discussion of these will be left until later). Twelve lunar months (12 x $29\frac{1}{2}$ plus a bit) give about 355 days which falls short of the calender year expressed by the Sun by 10 to 11 days.

But although it is impossible to mesh neatly the lunar month with the solar year, the month (from *moonth* or Moon-time) nevertheless became the convenient subdivision of the year. However, it must be born in mind that the modern calendar months —ranging in length from 28 to 31 days—are quite independent of the lunar months.

In spite of the difficulty in trying to fit the lunar month into the solar year, the use of the Moon must be one of the oldest forms of time-reckoning. Its comparative rapid revolution round the Earth and changing appearance from night to night from wafer-thin crescent at New Moon to full-face illumination and then back to a thin crescent before the next New Moon provides an easily recognizable and remembered time unit and represents the most natural intermediate step between the short-day unit and the long-year unit.

So far so good. But one of the chief difficulties in using the Moon as a timekeeper is the very practical problem of visually keeping track of it from day to day. Apart from the obvious meteorological effects such as cloud and fog when the Moon might be rendered invisible for days, or even weeks, on end, there are several other factors to consider which include the seasonal variation in the path of the Moon as seen by an observer and the position of the Moon in its orbit round the Earth.

To understand Marshack's approach to the problem and his difficulties, one first needs to appreciate that to an observer (discounting meteorological effects) no two consecutive reappearances of the thin crescent of the *visible* New Moon after the Moon's brief invisible period at the time of *actual* New Moon (when the Moon is in conjunction with the Sun) are ever separated by more than 30 days or less than 29 days. Because of the $29\frac{1}{2}$-day odd-number period of the lunar month, an observer inscribing marks on a bone would in practice have found that he had a different number for each lunation. To complicate matters, the Moon is lost from visibility near the Sun (at the time of actual New Moon) for one, two or maybe three days each lunation—before the first thin crescent reappears in the western sky after sunset. In this way an observer keeping tally after sighting the first slender crescent in the west might inscribe 27 or 28 marks before the last slender crescent is lost in the east in the morning sky. But all things being equal, the next notation period will leave him with a count of 29 or 30 marks. Thus, if one takes into account realistic weather conditions, consecutive tallies will in practice be highly variable. If, for example, the observer does not see the Moon after the invisible conjunction period and continues his day-notation scratches past the last visible crescent towards the next first, the number of tallies in a cycle might sometimes be as high as thirty-three.

It is the appreciation and recognition of the existence of these problems which gives Marshack's ideas some flexibility. If the lunar phases could be noted *exactly*, it would be easier to draw firmer conclusions about Marshack's claims for inscribed bones. As his results stand at the present time, he is persuasive, but not *wholly*. The tally sequences he has cited for the various scratched bones and similar artefacts frequently involve the student in playing a numbers game that sometimes appears to be rather arbitrary. Nevertheless, Marshack's cited sequences over longer periods of two lunations, or 59 days, do help iron out inconsistencies found in the single periods. His work so far *has* provided a unique pioneering study, but whether he has proved beyond doubt that Upper-Paleolithic man had a "scientific" interest in the Moon is still an open question. From some quarters his claims have drawn strong criticism—particularly from those who claim specialized knowledge of Upper-Paleolithic art rather than from astronomers. Many of these critics dispute the whole idea that such scratch marks are notational and dismiss them (but not very convincingly) as man's first primitive efforts in abstract decoration.

Marshack's examples of single lunar notations vary in period from 27 to 33 days. There are variations of 5 to 8 days between First and Last Quarters and 1 to 4 days in periods between Full Moon and New Moon—give or take 1 day for errors in observation. The difficulty, even for the student sympathetic to Marshack's ideas, is that all the examples he has studied and published seem to require an assumption to be made about "cloud-outs" or they require some other niggling adjustments to account for inconsistencies. For this reason some critics (not too unreasonably) have considered his ideas to be a trifle too glib and that they allow for too much arbitrary juggling with numbers to suit circumstances.

Although Marshack's investigation into attempts to find traces of lunar-calendar notations in the Upper Paleolithic was an original piece of research, primitive lunar calendars from elsewhere had long been recognized before Marshack began his own investigation. Marshack himself has looked closely at these *proven* examples in relation to his own ideas. Among these perhaps the least ambiguous examples are near-contemporary lunar calendar sticks from the Nicobar Islands. These consist of notched sticks shaped to appear as a knife or scimitar with notches both on the edge and the flat. Lunar months are recorded by chevron marks, and when all the available space is used, further marks are engraved across earlier ones, resulting in cross-hatch pattern. The pattern of inscribed marks on these sticks is made so as to distinguish the days of the waxing Moon towards Full Moon and then the days of the waning Moon towards New Moon.

Lunar calendar-stick devices were also well known to the Indians of North America, who used notches cut in a stick for computing nights, months and sometimes years. Primitives in New Guinea used a system where the months were recorded by notch-cuts in trees. Not far removed from the principle of sticks was the widespread use among primitives of knotted cords used for counting days. The Peruvians with their mysterious quipus —"the recipes of the Devil", as the Conquistador priests called them—are supposed to have been able to record much other astronomical information this way. The Australian Aborigines also used notched sticks to carry messages and convey time by citing the number of Moons.

In the context of these examples, it can be appreciated that Marshack's claims for notched artefacts found from the Upper Paleolithic is no whimsical or idle speculation. Nearer our own time, mnemonic devices using notches or scribed marks on wooden batons had a wide currency among illiterates. In Britain, nineteenth-century bakers' roundsmen used such devices; and a century earlier, during the great canal-and-railway-building projects, illiterate cooks contracted to supply food to large gangs of navvies kept tally of individual ownership of victuals by nicks in wooden slats.

Going further back into Celtic times, we come across the strange oghamic inscriptions which in appearance are sometimes highly reminiscent of tallied artefacts from the Upper Paleolithic.

No one can be sure how oghams originated, but they are believed to have been peculiar to the Celtic populations of the British Isles. Some believe it was a criptic script imported from the East or from Iberia. Others believe that it was a script invented (or utilized) by the Druids as a secret code for private signalling. There does indeed appear to be some affinity between oghams and the telegraphy system used by Roman armies, and oghams also appear to be closely allied to the later runes of North-West Europe. It is of interest that the use of rune characters for calendar sticks was maintained in Scandinavia until comparatively recent times.

Oghams were employed for writing messages and letters—usually on wooden staves, occasionally on shields, and for carvings on tombstones. Both oghams and the later derivative runes were frequently involved in a kind of "number magic" which so far has remained incomprehensible to modern epigraphists.

Whether indeed the Celtic-cum-Druid oghamic writing can rightfully trace its roots to a distant prehistory many millenniums earlier—to those strange scratched bones of the Upper Paleolithic—is an intriguing thought. In the light of Marshack's inspired researches, perhaps some enterprising student of epigraphy might again look into the still unanswered question of whence came the oghams.

3 Megaliths and Mistletoe

While Megalithic monuments like the Great Pyramid in Egypt had been known and commented on since the fifth century B.C., it was not until the twelfth century A.D. we find the first mention of Stonehenge in Henry of Huntingdon's *Historia Anglorum* where the author includes it as one of the four wonders of England and—surprisingly—as one of the "natural" features of the landscape.

This late mention and the apparent earlier omission in the various chronicles is still a puzzle. Many considered that Stonehenge was a relatively late addition to the English landscape—likely to have been contemporary with, or later than, Romano-British times. Many antiquarians certainly believed that the dolmens and chambered passage graves throughout Europe were of Roman period or post-Roman vintage.

In the nineteenth century, Sven Nilsson, the influential Swedish archaeologist, had suggested that Megalithic funerary chambers were copies of the actual dwelling houses of their builders. Others taking up the same theme had gone further, claiming that most of the so-called funerary chambers were really domestic abodes pure and simple. What obscured the issue was that many of the *allées couvertes* in Brittany—judging from the recognizable miscellany of domestic refuse found inside them—did appear to be abodes of the living in Gallo-Roman times. What influenced this dwelling-theory was the practical use some of the French *allées couvertes* had been turned to in the nineteenth century. Until recently many were used as cowsheds and farm buildings, and the great *allée couverte* at Saumer (Fig. 1) served for years as a barn, a garage and a café!

C

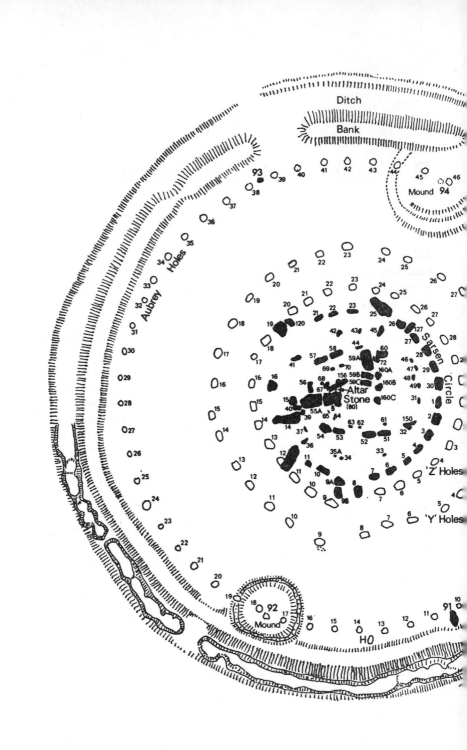

Ditch

Bank

Mound 94

Aubrey Holes

Sarsen Circle

Altar Stone (80)

'Z' Holes

'Y' Holes

Mound 92

Mound

H

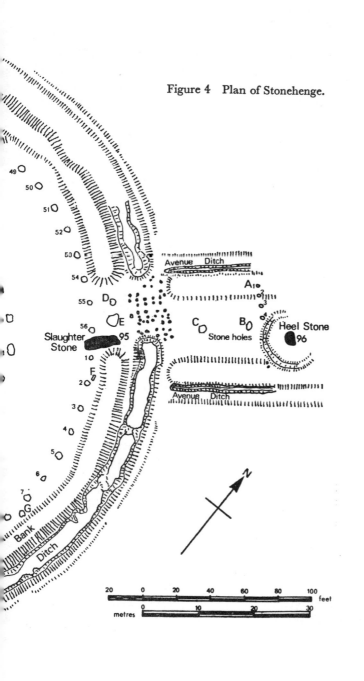

Figure 4   Plan of Stonehenge.

Although the pyramids had been known from antiquity, the first really "scientific" book about them was not published until 1648, the year Cromwell won at Naseby. This book, *Pyramidographia,* was written by the Englishman John Greaves, Professor of Astronomy at the University of Oxford. Greaves dismissed several of the then current more fanciful ideas—that the pyramids were astronomical observatories of a kind, that they were granaries built to store the abundant corn of Egypt for the years of famine, or that they were refuges for priests when the Nile flooded. Yet, in spite of Greaves, these fanciful ideas were to dog the pyramids right into contemporary times.

Stonehenge received its own fanciful mythology with the publication of Geoffrey of Monmouth's apocryphal *History of the Kings of Britain (c.* 1136). According to Geoffrey, Aurelius Ambrosius, King of the Britains, desired to have a monument erected to commemorate the death of 460 British nobles slain by the men of Hengist the Saxon. Hengist is the man supposed to have spearheaded a Saxon invasion of England in the fifth century.

According to Geoffrey, Ambrosius summoned his court prophet and magician, the famous Merlin, to seek his advice in the matter. Merlin is reported to have said :

> If you want to grace the burial-place of these men with a work that shall endure for ever, send for the Giants' Dance that is on Killare, a mountain in Ireland. For a structure of stones is there that none of this age could erect, unless he combined great skill and artistry. For the stones are big, nor is there stone anywhere of more virtue; and, so they be set round this plot in a circle, even as they be now there set up, there shall they stand for ever ... Giants of old did carry them from the farthest ends of Africa, and did set them up in Ireland when they lived there.

A plan was hatched. Ambrosius sent to Ireland his brother, Uther Pendragon, backed by an army of fifteen thousand. Although the Irish are said to have hotly defended the stones under the leadership of the legendary King Gillomanius, whose name is allegedly interpreted to mean "servant of the stones", they were defeated, and the stones duly captured by the Brits. But a problem arose. Try as they would, Uther Pendragon's men could not shift a single stone. Then Merlin intervened, and, as Geoffrey relates, "using his own devices" caused the stones to be moved to the coast and then hauled aboard a vessel and finally transported to Salisbury Plain where they now lie fixed—immoveable for all time. Commemorating this tale is an early illustration of Stonehenge, dated round the mid-fourteenth century, showing Merlin at work with two aides transfixing (by magic?) one of the famous lintels.

In spite of the recognized apocryphal nature of Geoffrey's famous tale, there are still those who believe the story may have a grain of truth; except that Geoffrey got his facts wrong. It was not the large (sandstone) sarsens that came from Ireland, but the even more mysterious so-called bluestones—a knotty issue we shall return to later.

Exploration of Stonehenge as a genuine antiquity is said to have begun in 1620 when King James I—once nicknamed the wisest fool in Christendom—was staying as a guest of the Earl of Pembroke. On an outing the King was taken to view the neighbouring wonder of Stonehenge and was so impressed that he later instructed his surveyor-general, the architect Inigo Jones, to study the monument and make a plan of it.

Inigo Jones probably started his work at Stonehenge in 1621. Even then the monument was in considerable ruin. The central trilithon (Plate 8) had fallen, and several important stones were missing. Jones compiled notes, made measurements and drew up several illustrations, but his work was never published in his lifetime. However, the material was not lost, and after his death it was collected by his son-in-law, John Webb, and an edited version (by Webb) was published in 1655, including the now famous illustration showing Jones's version of Stonehenge restored as he believed it once stood (Plate 9).

In the first half of the seventeenth century, a controversy had arisen about the origin of Stonehenge. In 1624 a certain Edmund Bolton claimed it was the lost tomb of Boadicea. Many indeed had opted for a Roman-period origin if for no other reason than that the ancient Brits were considered far too bestial a people to have created such a splendid monument. Caesar had said they were bestial, and Caesar was then one of the principal influential sources of early British history.

When Inigo Jones's book *The Most Remarkable Antiquity of Britain, vulgarly called Stone-Heng, Restored* appeared in 1655, its author dismissed the Geoffrey of Monmouth legend and other current prehistoric claims and ascribed Stonehenge to the Roman period. In 1663, Walter Charleton, physician to King Charles II, published his *Chorea Gigantum* in which he claimed Stonehenge to be a ninth-century Danish monument. However, two years later John Webb returned to the attack and published his *Vindication of Stone-Heng Restored* [to the Romans].

Jones's and Webb's conclusions were unduly influenced by Jones's architectural approach to studying the subject. After ridiculing the Geoffrey story as "an idle conceit" he wrote:

> Considering what magnificence the Romans in prosperous times anciently used in all works and their knowledge and experience in all Arts and Science : their powerful means for effecting great works : together with their Order in building, and the manner of workmanship accustomed among them, Stoneheng in my judgement was a work, built by Romans, and they the sole Founders thereof...

Continuing, Jones posed the question: when was it built? Then he explained:

> ... Happily, about the times, when the Romans having settled the Country here had reduced the naturall inhabitants of this Island unto the Society of Civil life...

He then suggested an explanation that it was actually a temple where sacrifices were offered to the sky-god Coelus in the form of "Buls or Oxen, and severall Sorts of beasts".

Jones, as the antiquary John Aubrey who followed him, sometimes had a picturesque and engaging turn of phrase and was free with the metaphor. For example, he wrote:

> Whether in this adventure, I have wafted my Barque into the wished Port of Truths discovery concerning Stoneheng, I leave to the judgement of Skilfull Pilots. I have endeavored at least, to give life to the attempt, trending perhaps to such degree, as either may invite others to undertake the Voyage anew, or prosecute the same in more ample manner, in which, I wish them their desired Successe, and that with prosperous Gales they may make a more full and certain discovery...

John Aubrey's voyage of discovery was soon in his wake.

With John Aubrey (1626-97) we arrive at one of the greatest and most colourful of the early antiquaries who studied Stonehenge. He was born at Easton Piercy only a short distance from the monument and relates to us in one of his books that from an early age he had a love of antiquarian pursuits and in particular "Salisbury-Plaines and Stonehenge". It was Aubrey who first discovered the outer circle of holes, or pits, which now bears his name and is a feature very much involved with theories that Stonehenge is a possible eclipse predictor.

Like many of the seventeenth-century researchers at Stonehenge, he was an influential figure in contemporary society—a friend of the King and a Fellow of the Royal Society. Today he is probably best remembered for his book *Brief Lives* which contains brilliant sketches of notable characters like Shakespeare, Hobbes, Milton, Bacon, etc.—but his magnum opus was *Monumenta Britannica*, never published in his lifetime.

At court, because he found favour with the King, his enemies accused him of being a hanger-on of the great and an incorrigible gossip-monger to boot. Whatever his failings, he was a rare breed of antiquarian and never happier than when poking about Stonehenge which he revisited in 1663 at the expressed wish of Charles II for the King's further edification.

Aubrey relates: "There have been several books writt by learned men concerning Stoneheng, much differing from one another, some affirming one thing, some another. . . ." He submitted that Stonehenge and other circle monuments he had inspected "were Temples of the Druids". Inigo Jones had mentioned Druids earlier but had dismissed the idea, explaining: "Stoneheng was no work of the Druid's, or the ancient Britans; the learning of the Druid's consisting more in contemplation than practice, and the ancient Britains accounting it their chiefest glory to be wholly ignorant in whatever Arts. . . ." Aubrey, however, believed Jones was mistaken. Exploiting an early usage of the comparative method, he develops his argument, writing:

When a traveller rides along the Ruines of a Monastry, he knows by the manner of building sc. Chapell, Cloysters &c : that it was a convent but of what order [sc. Benedictine, Dominican &c.] it was he cannot tell by the bare View. So it is cleer, that all the Monuments, which I have here recounted, were Temples : Now my presumption is . . . that these ancient Monuments [sc. *Aubury,*

Stonehenge, Kerring y Druidd &c.] were Temples of the Priests of the most eminent Order, viz, *Druids,* and it is strongly to be presumed, that Aubury, Stoneheng &c : are as ancient as those times.

Nevertheless, Aubrey did admit his theory was conjectural. With a nice turn of phrase he concludes: ". . . although I have not brought it into a clear light; yet I can affirm that I have brought it from utter darkness to a thin mist, and have gonne further in this Essay than any one before me." He then remarks : "These Antiquities are so exceedingly old that no Bookes doe reach them, so there is no Way to retrieve them but by comparative antiquitie, which I have writt upon the spott, from the Monuments themselves. . . ."

Later in life, revealing his wry humour, he writes that his first draft of his Stonehenge text "was worn out with time and handling"; and he continues: ". . . and now, methinks, after many years lying dormant, I come abroad like the Ghost of one of these Druids."

It was Aubrey who brewed up several colourful Druidical fancies at Stonehenge. For example, he noted that birds frequently nested in the natural cavities contained in some of the weathered sarsens. As a consequence he proposed the idea that the hollowed out mortises used by the builders to hold the sarsen lintels in place might indeed have been purpose-built nesting-boxes for the holy birds of the Druids ("the *Aves Druidum* of the *Templa Druidum*").

There can be little doubt that through the years the shadowy Druid priesthood has caught public imagination in much the same way as have the apocryphal legends concerning folk heroes like King Arthur, Merlin and Robin Hood. Part of the growth of Druid myth stems from the reason that few *hard* facts are known about them. It seems probable that they were not established in Britain until La Tené phase of the Iron Age *c.* 300 B.C. at the earliest. It is generally not widely appreciated that there is not a single native account of the old Celtic nations that flourished in Britain and France. Few realize that no Celtic language has any literary remains earlier than the seventh century A.D. (usually glosses), and the oldest manuscripts of connected works cannot be traced back beyond the eleventh century.

From where then came knowledge of the Druids?

It is to Roman and Greek classical writers we have to turn. These left contemporary accounts of Celtic history, religion, and customs and, it now appears, often *a very prejudiced view of the so-called "barbarous" northern races*. Most accounts are very scrappy and are usually restricted to generalized statements about the Celtic peoples, frequently putting them in poor light against the favoured races of Rome and Greece.

Among classical references are those in Caesar's *De Bello Gallico*, book six, in which (borrowing from the Stoic Posidonius *c*. 135-51—who was somewhat of an astronomer himself) he attributed much knowledge to the Druids. Caesar relates that the Druids taught "many things concerning the stars, and their motions; the size of the world and its countries; the nature of things; and the force and power of immortal gods".

In Pliny's very influential account we learn that mistletoe was sacred if it "vegetated from the oak". The Druids selected groves of oaks and thought everything was sent from heaven which grew on this tree. Pliny says that on the sixth day of the Moon—which began the Druids' months and years and their "long count" period of thirty years—they came to the oak "on which they observed any of the parasitical plant which they called all-healing". Under the venerated tree they prepared a sacrifice and feast. Two white bulls were brought forth, whose horns were first tied. The officiating Druid in a white robe climbed the tree and with a golden knife pruned off the mistletoe, which was received in a white woollen cloth below. The victims were then sacrificed, and the Druids addressed their gods to make the mistletoe prosperous for those to whom it was given. Pliny says that they believed it "caused fecundity" and was an amulet against poison. He remarks that the Druids were superior in knowledge to the rest of the nation; they were present at all religious rites; they obeyed one chief who had supreme authority over all; and it was said that some Druids took twenty years to acquire their education. It was conceived unlawful to commit their knowledge to writing (hence no native accounts). As a font of Druidical knowledge and customs, Pliny recounts they taught that the soul never perished but passed at death into other bodies—thus all fear of death in them was removed. J. G. Frazer was later to make much of Druids, mistletoe and oak groves in his classic study *The Golden Bough*.

If John Aubrey was enamoured by the Druids, the next major

investigator of Megalithic monuments, William Stukeley (1687-1765), was positively beset by them. Aubrey couched his ideas in somewhat cautiously worded remarks like "...This Inquiry I must confess, is a gropeing in the Dark...'. Stukeley, however, showed none of Aubrey's reticence. In his opinion it was beyond doubt that the Druids had worshipped at Stonehenge, Avebury and at similar sites—and, furthermore, the object of their worship had been the serpent. The serpent theme in the hands of Stukeley was to obsess him as much as the Druids themselves.

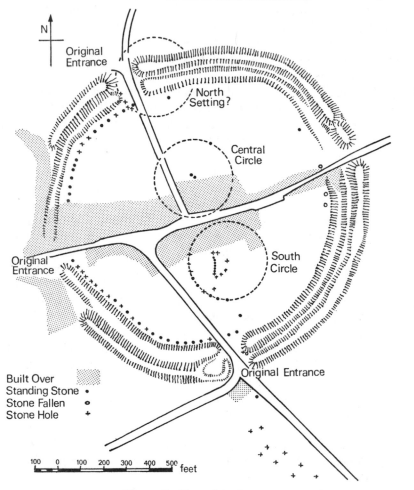

Figure 5   Plan of Avebury.

Stukeley's serpent temples of "Dracontia" were based on a mythical story, via Pliny, which told of the Druids of Gaul having used as a charm a certain magic egg made by a snake. In this way he conceived the Druids to be serpent-worshippers, and evidence of this he supposed lay in the winding snaked Megalithic avenues approaching Avebury from the south-west and south-east (Plate 10) and in avenues found elsewhere.

Stukeley became so obsessed by his snake-egg theory that at one stage he went so far as to alter his own survey of part of the Avebury complex from circles to egg-shaped structures so as to fit the theory more convincingly. Little wonder he soon earned the title of the Arch-Druid.

In his classic British Megalithic thesis, Stukeley began with the solid and respectable biblical figure of Abraham and wove his tale round the early Phoenician voyagers to Britain—introducing a classic exposition of the hyperdiffusionist migration theory that provided an architype model for others to follow.

Nevertheless, in spite of his obsession, he was also the finest field-archaeologist of his period in all England, and this great reputation was maintained until the close of the eighteenth century. In common with many romantic characters of his time, he possessed a strong underlying vein of mysticism in his make-up which became more manifest as he grew older. In 1721 he joined the Free-masons, and in the garden of his house he laid out a Druidical grove and temple where in 1728 he buried a still-born child.

He lived to the age of 78, unshaken in his Druid beliefs. Although unorthodox, he was strongly religious (in 1729 he took orders and in 1747 became a London rector). He claimed that all pagan religions, particularly that of the Druids, had in many of their concepts forshadowed the tenets of Christianity—including the doctrine of the Trinity. This concept of the doctrine of the Trinity was to raise its head again in the Stonehenge theories of the 1960s when the cosmologist Fred Hoyle stepped in to present his opinions.

Stukeley made some excellent surveys of both Stonehenge and Avebury. Without his field-work—particularly that at Avebury—we should now know a great deal less about either monument. His work called attention to features which had apparently gone unnoticed.

One of the most significant claims—which has subsequently

triggered many like it—was his belief that the builders of Stone-henge, Avebury and other stone monuments had used in their design a unit of measurement that he said he had been led to discover by his own surveys. This unit was the so-called "Druid cubit", a measure he supposed to equal 20.8 English inches. This is in fact very close to the length of the Egyptian royal cubit of 20·67 English inches, or 525 millimetres. Finding the cubit measure he believed clinched the cultural diffusion idea of a people migrating to Britain from the East.

There can be little doubt that it was Stukeley's claim for the "Druid cubit" which stimulated Piazzi Smyth and others of the Great-Pyramid cult to find their "Pyramid-inch" unit. Likely too it was Stukeley's "cubit" which led Flinders Petrie on his aberrant course to discover the so-called "Etruscan foot" in British hill figures and Alexander Thom to search out his "Megalithic yard".

Stukeley also speculated that the Druid builders of Stonehenge may have known about the properties of magnetism and used a magnetic compass to set the geometry of the monument. Judging from its "orientation", he deduced that Stonehenge had been erected at about 460 B.C. Stukeley's reference to early uses of the magnetic compass was a hare that has sent many a later investigator on a futile search for the construction dates of other monuments including several British churches. It was Stukeley who gave the name *Cursus* to the large earthwork monuments—sometimes also referred to as "hippodromes" in older antiquarian literature —one of which lies close to Stonehenge (Fig. 6).

Undoubtedly, to present-day astro-archaeologists, one of the primary interests of Stukeley's work at Stonehenge was his observation that the axis of the monument appears to point north-east *towards the Midsummer-Day rising of the Sun*. This is the first astronomical reference on record that can be checked with any certainty. The inferences of such a significant orientation were to lead to the most contentious debates of all about the purpose of Stonehenge and other Megalithic monuments.

Several authors soon followed Stukeley into print, supporting his colourful Druid ideas. One was the Druid convert Dr. John Smith, who in 1771 published a pamphlet entitled *Choir Gaur the Grand Orrery of the Ancient Druids called Stonehenge, Astronomically Explained, and proved to be a Temple for Observing the Motions of the Heavenly Bodies.*

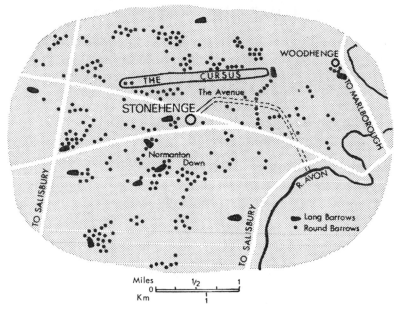

Figure 6   Region round Stonehenge.

Smith held some ingenious ideas. He wrote:

From many and repeated visits [to Stonehenge], I conceived it to be an astronomical temple; and from what I have recollect to have read of it, no author has yet investigated its uses. Without an instrument or any assistance whatsoever, but White's "Ephemeris", I began my survey. I suspected the stone called *The Friar's Heel* [Fig. 7 see page 47] to be the index that would disclose the uses of this structure; nor was I deceived. This stone stands in a right line with the centre of the temple, pointing to the north-east. I first drew a circle round the vallum of the ditch and divided it into 360 equal parts; and then a right line through the body of the temple to the Friar's Heel; at the intersection of these lines I reckoned the Sun's greatest amplitude at the summer solstice, in this latitude, to be about 60 degrees, and fixed the eastern points accordingly. Pursuing this plan, I soon discovered the uses of all the detached stones, as well as those that formed the body of the temple.

Smith's astronomical speculations are of great interest and original. He believed that Stonehenge functioned as an orrery, but instead of a mechanism to show planetary motions it was nothing less than a calendar of stones. Very plausibly he supposed that thirty stones in one of the circles (the Sarsen Ring) multiplied by the significant figure of twelve—because there were twelve signs in the Greek Zodiac—gave a total of 360, the "round" number of days known in the ancient solar year.

Smith was very convincing, but was he right?

Another Druid convert who held plausible astronomical ideas was Godfrey Higgins. In 1829, in his book *Celtic Druids,* he wrote:

> The most extraordinary peculiarity which the Druidical circles possess is that of their agreement with the number of the stones of which they consist with ancient Astronomical Cycles. The outer circle of Stonehenge consists of 60 stones [the outer sarsen circle], the basic number of the most famous of all the cycles of antiquity. The next circle consists of 40 stones [sic—this probably held 59-61 stones], but one on each side of the entrance is advanced out of the line, so as to leave 19 stones, a Metonic cycle, on each side, and the inner of one Metonic cycle of 19 stones.

Higgins's reference to the Metonic cycle is, as far as is known, the first reference to the famous astronomical cycle being involved in the layout of the Stonehenge Megaliths. The Metonic cycle was well known in ancient Greece and Babylonia—where it was known as the "year of Meton". It alluded to the discovery by the Greek astronomer Meton in the fifth century B.C. who noted that 235 lunar months equalled nineteen solar years, so that after nineteen years the phases of the Moon (First quarter, Full Moon, etc.) repeat themselves (within a few hours) on the same calendar date.

Higgins was wrong in many of his assumptions about Stonehenge, but there in print was that broad hint of the possibility of the Moon's involvement in the monument for someone to take up in the future. The number 19 is very significant astronomically. A number of circles in South-West England consist of 19 stones which *may* indeed be significant astronomically; perhaps the most noteworthy instance is the 19 inner bluestones at Stonehenge as we shall see later.

Yet another plausible astronomical clue was provided by the Rev. E. Duke, who in 1846 discovered that the North mound (Station 94, Fig. 4) lined up with the stone numbered 93 at the last light of the setting Sun on the shortest day of the year. Conversely, a line drawn from the South mound (92) to stone 91 aligned with the rising Sun on the longest day of the year. In the 1960s the British amateur astronomer C. A. ("Peter") Newham was to follow up Duke's work and extend it.

Not so plausible among early nineteenth-century astronomical references to Stonehenge—except to untrained and ingenuous minds—was an idea attributed to a Mr Waltire, who believed

> that the Barrows and Tumuli surrounding the Temple [Stonehenge] accurately represented the situation and magnitude of the Fixed stars, forming a complete planisphere ... other barrows registered eclipses which had taken place within a certain number of years and the Trilithons are the registers of the transits of Mercury and Venus.

In facile minds, Waltire's notions were to trigger many like them —some practically carbon copies of the original. The Rev. E. Duke was among those to take up Waltire's ideas. He tried to show that Stonehenge was one of the members of a planetary system—the solar system—depicted right across the adjoining countryside "set out on a meridian 32 miles in length, pivoted on Silbury Hill [nr. Avebury, Plate 10], 16 miles distant from Stonehenge". Another of these schemes particularly worth noting is the so-called "Glastonbury Temple of Stars" thought up around 1935, which proposed that a series of great designs, mostly zodiacal, were sprawled across the hills round Glastonbury, represented by outlines of natural features such as old boundaries, woods, roads, ditches, etc. This particular hare seems to hold a fatal fascination for modern-day TV producers who, having discovered its open-air, highly photogenic possibilities, trot out programme after programme about it as if it were some brilliant new theory worthy of attention.

An interesting exercise, dated about 1869, was to use Stonehenge as an observatory to trace out an astronomical cycle known as *the precession of the equinoxes*. The cycle of precession is caused by the pull of the Moon on the equatorial bulge of the Earth. This has the effect of causing the Earth's axis to wobble in a small circle over a period of about 26,000 years. In turn this causes the apparent rising and setting positions of all stars to change in time (including, significantly, the pole stars). The author of the first precession exercise at Stonehenge believed that instead of the Sun the bright star Sirius might have been used (by the Druids) to determine its orientation. The author chose Sirius, for it was then well known that the ancient Egyptians had used this star to herald the beginning in their new year. Choosing a point in the monument which is not absolutely clear—the author of this scheme calculated that Stonehenge must be dated precisely at 977·8 B.C.

In the latter part of the nineteenth century the most influential books about Stonehenge and other British Megalithic monuments were Fergusson's *Rude Stone Monuments of all nations their purpose and usage* (1872) and Flinders Petrie's *Stonehenge: Plans. Descriptions and Theories* (1880).

Fergusson did not subscribe to the Druid theory, but he did believe that Stonehenge was built in the post-Roman period. Fergusson, like Inigo Jones, was an architect by training, and it is of interest that both, on aesthetic grounds, should plumb for an origin within the (classical) modern era rather than in the (rude) prehistoric era. Fergusson's own choice for Stonehenge's origin was the battlefield theory following Geoffrey of Monmouth's claim that the monument was erected in memory of a slaughter.

Fergusson was disparaging about a theory then widely held that the Cursuses were racecourses. He argued :

> That these alignments were once racecourses, appears to me one of the most improbable of the various conjectures which have been hazarded ... No Roman racecourse that we know of [he overlooked the idea of prehistoric ones], omitted to provide for horses returning at least once past the place they started from, and no course was ever a mile, much less than a mile and three-quarters long. . . .

But if not racecourses, what were they? In Fergusson's opinion they were battlefields—adjoining the monument erected to commemorate them.

Fergusson also gave short shrift to the various astronomical ideas —remarking:

> Till some practical astronomer will come forward and tell us in intelligible language what observations could be performed with the aid of the circles of Stonehenge, we may be at least allowed to pause. Even, however, in that case, unless his theory will apply

to Avebury, Stanton Drew, and other circles so irregular to be almost unmeasurable, it will add little to our knowledge.

This challenge put out by Fergusson was answered in part in the years that followed by A. Lewis, Norman Lockyer and Vice-Admiral Somerville. A fuller, more definitive answer had to wait until the 1960s when ideas began to flow from people like Newham, Hawkins, Hoyle and Thom especially.

Flinders Petrie surveyed Stonehenge in 1880 and in his resulting book produced the first really accurate plan of the monument. Petrie was later to become the greatest ever British Egyptologist, and all his life he was deeply involved with Megalithic monuments whether they be European or Egyptian ones.

Petrie was another who opted for a late construction date for Stonehenge, believing its present-day arrangement to date back only to Romano-British times or even later—although he did believe that the site itself was of great antiquity. He too subscribed to the idea it had been erected to the memory of Aurelius Ambrosius and other local chieftains who doubtless were buried in or round Stonehenge. His date of "perhaps as early as A.D. 400" (although elsewhere he quoted a date between A.D. 530 to A.D. 930) was based on some faulty reasoning about changes in *the obliquity of the ecliptic* (another astronomical cycle)—an error subsequently detected and corrected by Norman Lockyer a few years later.

Respecting astronomical theories, Petrie concluded: "The astronomical theory has the strong evidence of the very close pointing to midsummer sunrise, but apparently none other than that will bear scientific scrutiny."

Following Petrie, the scientific investigations of Stonehenge stood in limbo until just after the turn of the century when Sir Norman Lockyer, still relatively fresh from his believed triumphs at decoding astronomical temple alignments in Egypt, descended on Stonehenge to start to unravel its mysteries. In the interim, crank theories about the origin of Stonehenge and its true purpose multiplied.

Towards the end of the nineteenth century there was a restlessness afoot against the dogmatism of the older teachings. In many ways this restlessness was akin to the later anti-authoritarian movement triggered in the Western-World student bodies during the turbulent

D

1960s which was to direct attention to the pseudo-scientific writings of Immanuel Velikovsky whose theories had been dismissed by the establishment almost two decades earlier.

In the nineteenth century the legend of the lost continent of Atlantis, much like the long-standing Stonehenge-Druid theme before it, had excited, then beset a large public. The first time the myth of Atlantis was connected with Stonehenge was in 1883 by W. S. Blacket. Soon on its heels followed the equally bizarre ideas that Stonehenge was no less than some kind of shrine to Buddha.

Even serious writers were willing to give credence to these ideas and others in similar vein. Mythology and folklore had recently become respectable and a fad of the age. The sagas of the North recounting dwarfs, goblins, elves and cavern people could not after all be mere inventions. One notes among the weird-and-wonderful writers of the period a predilectary fondness for citing the Latin *Ex nihilo nihil fit* (nothing comes from nothing).

James Frazer's epoch-making *The Golden Bough* (subtitled *A Study in Magic and Religion*), which appeared in the 1890s, became a powerful, persuasive documentary of mistletoe and tradition. It was very influential to public opinion and finally helped make anthropology and folklore academically respectable. Serious writers about Megalithic monuments were willing to believe in some of the old peasant myths, for example, because the ceiling heights of dolmens and chambered tombs were usually low, it did seem logical to suppose they were built and inhabited by a race of brownies, pucks, "little folk" or other fairy-dwarf peoples who had been expelled by the stronger and taller Gothic races acquainted with metals. One established writer, the Rev. Hutchinson, B.A. F.G.S. (*Prehistoric Man and Beast*, 1896) went to lengths to show that Robert Browning's allusion to the legendary dwarf peoples in *The Pied Piper* might, allowing for poetic licence, provide a clue to the observant reader who might see the mountain and its fairy cavern, or palace, as a mound with underground passages—nothing less indeed than a large Megalithic chamber where lived the little folk.

4 Lockyer in Egypt

In any study involving British and Egyptian Megalithic monuments the name of Sir Norman Lockyer (1836-1920) is inescapable.

Lockyer was a brilliant self-taught astronomer, but his interests were many and wide ranging. After concentrating on telescopic studies of the surface features of Mars, he switched to astrophysical studies of the Sun; and in 1870 (via the spectroscope) he detected lines of an unknown element in the Sun he called helium.

Lockyer soon rose to prominence in the scientific world. He became a very powerful (if at times contentious) establishment figure in late nineteenth- and early twentieth-century science. Much of his influence was to do with him being appointed the first editor of *Nature*. He held the post for fifty years and guided the magazine through its shaky uncertain days until under his hand it finally blossomed as the world's most influential scientific organ for announcing new discoveries.

Lockyer first became interested in ancient Sun and star worship about 1869, but it was not until over twenty years later he took up the study of the orientation of Megalithic monuments in any serious way. In his now classic seminal astro-archaeological work, *The Dawn of Astronomy* (1894), he recalled how he first became interested in the idea that ancient temples may have been purpose orientated by their builders to the Sun and the stars. He wrote:

> ... It chanced that in March 1890, during a brief holiday I went to the Levant. I went with a good friend, who, one day when we were visiting the ruins of the Parthenon, and again when we found ourselves at the temple of Eleusis, lent me his pocket compass. The curious direction in which the Parthenon was built, and the many changes of direction in the foundations at Eleusis re-

vealed by the French excavations, were so very striking and suggestive that I thought it worthwhile to note the bearings so as to see whether there was any possible astronomical origin for the direction of the temple. . . .

Lockyer, when looking at these Greek Megalithic monuments, also had at the back of his mind the familiar statement that in England the eastern windows of churches—if they were properly constructed—generally face the place of sunrising on the festival of the patron saint. As Lockyer remarked: "This is why, for instance, the churches of St John the Baptist face very nearly north-east. . . ."

Lockyer noted that this was the origin of the word "orientation" (to face or turn east). As a church-building practice, it is believed to stem from the fifth century, probably for several reasons, but principally because Jesus, on the Cross, supposedly had his face turned westwards—hence Christians during prayer should turn eastward to see it.

Although Lockyer's interest in the subject had been stimulated by his holiday in Greece, he was also long familiar with the work of his amateur-astronomer friend, the archaeologist F. C. Penrose, who had made a special study of Greek temples to determine whether they incorporated any significant astronomical orientations.

Lockyer too was quite aware that earlier French and German archaeologists had studied the "orientation" of Egyptian pyramids and temples. It was well known that many had been purpose orientated by their constructors—perhaps towards the Nile or some other significant topographic feature. The question Lockyer now reconsidered was: were these orientations significant *astronomically?*

Unknown to Lockyer, when he began his study in 1890, was that a German professor by the name of Nissen had looked into the very same question and had published his results in the *Rheinisches Museum für Philologie* in 1885. Lockyer soon discovered this, and in due course, when he published his own results, he acknowledged his debt to Nissen's earlier work—although Lockyer's own researches into the subject went much further.

When Lockyer travelled to Egypt in November 1890, he stayed over in Paris, *en route,* to consult with the great French Egyptologist Gaston Maspero. The Frenchman proved a great help to Lockyer in general questions relating to Egyptology, and he later gave a modicum of support—albeit a very cautious one—to Lockyer's celestial alignment theories.

On arrival in Egypt, Lockyer made many friendly contacts with the authorities; his stature as scientist and a public man in Europe opened doors that would have remained closed to lesser notaries. He met Brugsch Bey, who in turn became intrigued and infected by Lockyer's enthusiasm and ideas, as a result of which he then began to search old inscriptions for any clue as to how the old temples had been set out by their builders. After reading an inscription on the foundation of the temple of Edfû, Brugsch Bey was sufficiently persuaded that Lockyer might well be on the track of an entirely new line of investigation in Egyptology. . . .

Lockyer was concerned with two problems. First to check what importance (if any) the Sun might have in relation to general orientation ideas; and secondly to check if the fixed stars held any importance in determining temple alignments to a specific bright star. Lockyer was well aware, of course, that the Egyptian religion was almost wholly preoccupied with the Sun in the form of the mighty Re in his many guises. He also knew that the rising of the star Sirius had earlier been involved with the start of the Egyptian New Year.

To tackle these two problems, Lockyer's main method of attack —other than direct information gleaned from old inscriptions— was to fall back on two well-known astronomical cycles and use them as his work tools. One of these cycles is involved with the changes in the Earth's axial tilt over a period of about 40,000 years, and this alters the *obliquity of the ecliptic*. It has the direct effect of making the Sun appear to rise at a slightly different position at a specific date (e.g. 21 June) from one millennium to the next. Lockyer's second tool, *the precession of the equinoxes,* is an astronomical cycle which alters the positions of "fixed" stars in relation to their rising (or setting) positions over a period of about 26,000 years.

Using these cycles, one for the Sun and the other for the stars, he hoped to be able to show two things : a) that a particular temple had been orientated to the Sun or a specific star, and b) the exact chronological date when the Sun or the star had been used to determine this. The star-precession method had been tried before at Stonehenge, using the star Sirius, in attempts to date the monument's alignment, so the idea was not entirely new.

In theory it is a simple matter to compute backwards or forwards in time to predict the exact rising and setting point of the Sun or a specific "fixed" star for any place on Earth. Thus if a temple had been aligned to the rising or setting point of the Sun or a star in prehistoric times, it should be easy to calculate the past date when the Sun or the star aligned true with the axis—for it follows that it would not then align in A.D. 1890 when Lockyer measured the contemporary axis line of the temple.

All this is fine in theory, but in practice it is not so straightforward. In the case of the obliquity changes in the Earth's axis occuring over 40,000 years—which causes the Sun to drift back and forth on the horizon—the actual amount of the shift is very small. We now know this ranges within the tilt limits of $21°39'$ and $24°36'$. In Lockyer's day it was not known to the present-day degree of accuracy. It's value at the moment is about $23°27'$.

Another major difficulty in using the Sun is in deciding what part of the Sun the ancients used to indicate their alignment. The choice is three-fold: first gleam, estimated centre, and bottom limb —for the Sun subtends an angle of about $\frac{1}{2}°$ to an observer. This knotty problem is again encountered with solar alignments at Stonehenge. A choice among the three alternatives can lead to differences in dates of at least 2,000 years (Fig. 7)—thus giving plenty of scope for some arbitrary juggling of dates to suit a particular researcher's pet theory.

There is also the problem of the surrounding topography. If, for example, an observer sees the Sun rise or set over a hill, then it will rise later or set earlier than it would if it were observed over a flat sea-like horizon. Likewise, if there is a depression on the horizon, the Sun will appear to rise earlier than it should and set later. In addition one also needs to take into account other factors like atmospheric refraction, which is very significant at horizon level— plus several other niggling but necessary adjustments.

In the case of stars the problem is not quite the same, but there are still difficulties. There is certainly no problem about what part of a star the observer would have chosen, for all stars subtend point sources. Shifts of a star along the horizon due to precessional changes are much larger than horizon shifts of the Sun due to

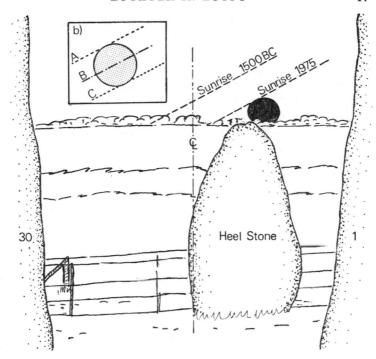

Figure 7 Stonehenge: the view north-east over the Heel Stone as seen from the centre of the sarsen circle about four minutes after the first gleam on 20 June at two different epochs. Note (inset b) how the choice of different parts of the Sun, i.e. first gleam (A); half risen (B); and fully risen (C) may make a difference of about 2000 years to a significant point on the horizon. The point at which midsummer sunrise occurs at present shifts eastwards at the rate of approx. 1° per 4000 years (or about twice the dia. subtended by the Sun or Moon).

obliquity, and they show up over a much shorter time-span. But it attempts to trace back the date of an alignment, the real difficulty now manifests itself in deciding *what star* and *at which date?* Precessional horizon shifts are reflected in the declination of a star (declination is to the celestial sphere what latitude is to the Earth's surface). For example, the bright stars Spica and Betelgeuse are well separated in declination values in the year 2000 B.C., but coming forward to 650 B.C., their declinations are practically the same value, hence they would appear to rise at the same point on the horizon, but, of course, at different times of the night. This indeed illustrates one of the great weaknesses of the star method in determining a dedication date for a temple orientation, for the implication is that one really needs to know the approximate date of a monument *first*. If this is in error, so will the assumptions be about what star was used.

Lockyer visited Egypt over several seasons in the early 1890s, developing his ideas and accumulating evidence, and this culminated in 1894 with the publication of his now classic book *The Dawn of Astronomy* in which he set out his results.

The Dawn was the first popular book in the English language to provide the general reader with a summary of the astronomical background of the great Egyptian civilization. It also touched on Babylonian astronomy and drew attention to Penrose's earlier work on Greek temple orientation. Lockyer believed his original idea had been justified in the light of his subsequent fieldwork. He claimed that Egyptian temple orientation had distinct astronomical significances. But what immediately surprised those with some knowledge of the subject was that in view of the known Egyptian preoccupation with the Sun and the fact that the Egyptian year was based on the summer solstice, involving too the morning rising of the star Sirius (and the inundation of the Nile), Lockyer had found only six (solar) solstitial temples. Nevertheless, it was considered that since the summer solstice was also heralded by Sirius, the seven temples Lockyer claimed he found orientated (dedicated) to this star should also be counted among the solstice category.

It was Lockyer's claim that the greatest of all Egyptian temples was a solstitial one. This is the temple of Amen-Re at Karnak (Plate 11). Not even dissenting Egyptologists to Lockyer's theories —and they were a formidable body—could deny that the temple was dedicated to the Sun-god Re, but they believed, as most still do, that this is *not* implied by its axis directed westward to the setting Sun—as Lockyer claimed. Egyptologists believe the temple axis is directed westwards to point towards the Nile *only*.

Lockyer had claimed that the temple axis was aligned to the setting sun at Midsummer's Day in the year 3700 B.C. But many Egyptologists protested that the date was too early. Lockyer's reply was: "Never mind,"—for it was his belief that the orientation must refer to an earlier building rather than to the ruins that then stood there. To bolster his case, Lockyer cited that Penrose had found much the same kind of thing with some of the Greek temples, and that in all probability many temples extant had been rebuilt upon older foundations. Lockyer's assertions had some substance, for there was evidence of this brought out by excavation. Nevertheless, it provides yet another example of some arbitrary justification to fit an idea.

But the solstice alignment at Amen-Re *had* troubled Lockyer. One can sense that Lockyer from the start believed he needed to find such an alignment at what was after all the greatest of all Egyptian Sun temples if his ideas were going to be at all persuasive to doubting Egyptologists.

Lockyer had opted for the western-*setting* Sun orientation rather than the more logical eastern-*rising* Sun—simply because the view eastwards of the central altar is blocked by the building known as the Hall of Festivals. One can be sure, instinctively, that Lockyer would have much preferred to have been able to cite the rising Sun. It was all a matter of dates, but Lockyer himself was never to know it. . . .

Even his claim for the setting alignment was a shaky one. Lockyer did not actually measure the alignment himself. Back in England after his first season in Egypt, he wrote to Sir Colin Scott-Moncrieff, the Under-Secretary of State of the Public Works Department in Egypt, to detail one of his officers for the job. The man sent to take the measures on 21 June 1891 was P. J. G. Wakefield, who in due course carried out the work.

In his subsequent report Wakefield wrote:

> . . . From an inspection made on June 20th it appeared to me that the setting sun would not be visible from any of the points indicated by Professor Norman Lockyer, I therefore placed the theodolite at A [Plate 11]. I regret to say that my above supposition was correct, as even from A, I was only able to see a portion of the setting sun, the remainder being hidden behind the south wall of the Great Pylon. I obtained, however, one reading the right limb at, as nearly as I could judge, the moment of impact of the sun's diameter with the hill.

Lockyer had appreciated that the Theban Hills opposite, which subtend an angle of $2\frac{1}{2}°$ above the *true* horizon, made *direct* measurement impossible, but making allowances for this difficulty, he still believed it indicated a *foundation* date of 3700 B.C. Nevertheless, he was honest enough to comment "there is still an element of doubt". And about that particular date there still is. . . .

Gerald Hawkins, whose revolutionary thesis about Stonehenge set the academic world alight in 1963, also later retraced Lockyer's steps in Egypt and visited the Great Temple of Amen-Re to check out his mentor's claim. Using the services of a computer, as he had done earlier with his Stonehenge work, and armed with more realistic data provided by modern Egyptology, he concluded that the axis alignment of Amen-Re did not point westwards to the setting Sun as Lockyer believed but *eastwards* to the rising Sun as Lockyer no doubt had always hoped it would. It was simply the problem of dates. The computer indicated that the rising Sun would have been seen along the temple axis at the summer solstice date in the period of 2000 to 1000 B.C., but that any further view of it would have been cut off in *c.* 1480 B.C. when the Hall of Festivals was erected in the way of the sight line by Pharaoh Thutmosis III. Lockyer's seminal idea, if not his modus operandi and results, seemed to be vindicated.

In his day Lockyer's findings in Egypt were quite persuasive to many people, and he even won support among Egyptologists of the stature of Wallis Budge and Flinders Petrie. But Gaston Maspero, from whom Lockyer had first sought advice, and who earlier had been receptive to these ideas, began to have second thoughts. Maspero was only too aware of the old contentions among French savants whose disputitious theories relating to ancient astronomy and Egyptology had begun soon after Napoleon's great expedition there (Chapter 14). Maspero, after reading Lockyer's book, remarked: "... if we were to attempt a refutation of all Mr Lockyer's arguments that seem to us unsound, and all the statements which are demonstrably incorrect, it would be necessary for us to write a book nearly as long as his own."

But no Egyptologist—not even Maspero—could deny that both the Sun and the stars had been used by the ancient Egyptians to set out the axis lines of temples. The evidence—via the translated inscriptions—was there for all to read. What the dissenting Egyptologists did deny was that temples were dedicated to the Sun or stars as implied by *precise* alignment at a *significant* set date. Unfortunately the inscriptions themselves do not settle this question.

Inscriptions from Karnak, Dendera and Edfû refer to laying the axis of a temple as "the stretching of the cord". This was part of the foundation ceremony and formed part of a traditional high ceremonial. Involved in these ceremonies with the ruling Pharaoh was the mythical Sesheta, goddess of "measurement". Each was armed with a stake, the two being connected by a (surveyor's) cord. The cord was aligned towards the Sun, or a star, and when the alignment was considered true, the two stakes either end were driven home with a mallet. Time of alignment took place at Sun or star rising—or possibly at Sun or star setting when the Sun,or at least the star, was just above the horizon. A star would certainly need to be a few degrees above the horizon, because near the horizon, due to atmospheric absorption, a star would be rendered invisible.

No doubt when the ritual part of the foundation ceremony was over, it would be custom for the astronomer-priests to take over and recheck the line for accuracy and extend it along the axis during the following days.

At Dendera, the temple inscription actually names the star group used by the Pharaoh while stretching the cord. This was the constellation the ancient Egyptians knew as the "Thigh" (or Ox Leg), familiar to present-day stargazers as the Great Bear, or Ursa Major (Plate 21),

The various translations for temple inscriptions vary slightly from scholar to scholar. At Dendera the inscription can be rendered as follows:

... The living God, the magnificent Sun of Asti (Thoth), nourished by the sublime goddess in the temple, the sovereign of the country, stretch the rope in joy. With his glance towards the *ak* [one of the middle stars of the Bear, or perhaps the star Dubhe] of the Bull's thigh he established the temple-house of the mistress of Dendera, as took place there before.

Lockyer also concerned himself with the ancient use of stars as timekeepers for telling the hours of the night. These were called clock-stars. Here he was on firmer ground, for it had already been established that from the time of the Middle Kingdom the ancient Egyptians had evolved some interesting devices so that the priests could gauge the hour of the night by the rising and setting of stars or group of stars (known as the Decans). This tradition of using stars as timekeepers was widely practised in the ancient world. There is an interesting direct reference to it in Greek times in Euripides (480-407 B.C.) when he writes in a chorus of one of his tragedies: "What is the star now passing?" To which the reply given was : "The Pleiades show themselves in the east, the Eagle [Aquila] soars in the summit of the heavens."

It was Lockyer's belief that the brighter clock-stars would also be used by the temple astronomer-priests as heralders to keep track of festival dates. For example, a particular star rising might indicate a festival would occur in so many days ahead; in this way they could plan. It was an idea that Lockyer was to extend when he began to investigate British Megalithic sites a decade later.

From his studies in Egypt, Lockyer compiled comprehensive lists of temples he believed were built and aligned to stars. Northern stars included Alpha Ursa Majoris, Gamma Draconis, Capella, and Spica; and among the southern stars Phat, Alpha Centauri, Canopus and Sirius. These lists included calculated foundation dates and in one instance, for Edfû, went back to 6400 B.C., while another for Dendera to 4800 B.C., which nowadays would seem to be far too early. Lockyer was convinced that his lists showed well-marked epochs for temple-building. He also briefly involved himself with the orientation of some of the pyramids and believed those at Giza to be orientated east and west. Yet in acknowledging his belief in these ideas, he was ever careful to keep well clear of the academic scandal of the Great-Pyramid controversy that had involved Piazzi Smyth, Astronomer Royal for Scotland, and his so-called "pyramid inch" (Chapter 14).

Most archaeologists and Egyptologists—no matter what others believe—remain unconvinced about Lockyer's particular brand of temple-alignment theory. Today one needs to search very carefully to find *The Dawn of Astronomy* cited in the bibliography of any definitive work on Egyptology.

5 Lockyer and Stonehenge

After another visit to Egypt in 1895, Lockyer's Megalithic studies had to take a back seat among his diverse polymathic interests. The year 1895 was a memorable one for him. It was the year when Sir William Ramsay detected the mysterious solar helium line in a terrestrial source. For more than twenty-six years many had doubted the very existence of the mysterious Sun substance, and in some quarters Lockyer's claim had been subject to ridicule. Now, with confirmation of helium, Lockyer's status as a scientific giant of the age was re-endorsed.

It shows the nature of Lockyer's wide interests when in that busy year he found time to co-author a small handbook on a subject as far removed as one could get from the Sun and his Megalithic studies. This was a work entitled *The Rules of Golf*. Although he kept up his interests in astro-archaeology, it was not until 1901, the year before he retired from his professorship at the Royal College of Science, that he found opportunity to tackle the subject which he had brooded over for some years: *was* Stonehenge aligned in the same way as he believed the Egyptian temples to be aligned?

In his Egyptian book, Lockyer had briefly touched on the subject of Stonehenge, citing its orientation to midsummer sunrise to support his ideas about Egyptian temples. Around this time Lockyer was much influenced by the colourful mythology contained in J. G. Frazer's recently published *The Golden Bough*—which contained much about Druids, mistletoe and fire festivals. Lockyer wrote:

> . . . Just as surely as the temple of Karnak once pointed to the Sun setting at the summer solstice, the temple of Stonehenge

pointed nearly to the Sun rising at the summer solstice. Stonehenge, there is no doubt, was so constructed that at sunrise at the same solstice the shadows of one stone fell exactly on the stone in the centre; that observation indicated to the priests that the New Year had begun, and possibly also fires were lighted to flash the news through the country. And in this way it is possible that we have the ultimate origin of the midsummer fires, which have been referred to by so many authors.

No doubt when Frazer read Lockyer's confirmation of his ideas for midsummer and Beltaine fires, he was delighted that a scientist of Lockyer's stature should lend support to his own scholarship which had not gone without some criticism. Lockyer, unfortunately, was often later to overstep the boundary of what should be considered legitimate scientific evidence and what is not.

Lockyer in *The Dawn of Astronomy* impressed many of his readers, but he nevertheless disappointed some of them by not including a fuller account of Stonehenge and other British "temple" monuments. He was now prepared to set right this omission.

Lockyer, perhaps, if truth be known, was never himself more than partially convinced about the correctness of his alignments in Egypt. He knew that in Egypt he was on the right track *astronomically*, but his views and ideas were tentative ones—notwithstanding what he uttered to the contrary in print and in public. But his sorties into Egypt over several seasons had given him opportunity to realize first hand what an important day-to-day role the Sun, Moon and stars played in the lives of ancient men whether they be pharaohs, priests or simple Neolithic farmers.

From the time of his first sorties into Egypt, Lockyer had realized that changes in the obliquity of the ecliptic would show up more readily in temperate latitudes. Even with faultlessly measured alignments in the latitude in Egypt, the differences in horizon-shift at the time of solstices are small, but in Britain—at Stonehenge—the differences are potentially larger. . . .

The results of his investigations into Stonehenge and other British sites were first published in 1906 and later greatly expanded to a second edition in 1909. The book, entitled *Stonehenge and Other British Monuments*, soon became a classic in Megalithic literature. This book is still very influential in the present-day Megalithic controversies while his Egyptian work is largely passed over.

When he began at Stonehenge, Lockyer joined forces with F.

C. Penrose—although Penrose himself took only a minor role. Lockyer was then sixty-five, while Penrose was twenty years his senior. But youth has no perogative when it comes to Megalithic investigations. C. A. ('Peter') Newham was later himself to confirm this at Stonehenge. While many academics of distinguished record would be ready at retirement age to seek the haven of more tranquil waters, Lockyer was still eager to run the stormy passage of academic contention which had dogged his career.

The first line of attack was a re-examination of the midsummer solstice alignment—first noted by Stukeley in 1740. This was remeasured and in turn led Lockyer into detecting an error in Flinders Petrie's earlier calculations from which Petrie had concluded that the stone circles at least were post-Roman, although the site itself was probably very ancient.

Lockyer's and Penrose's date surprised everyone. It took the origins of Stonehenge far back into prehistoric times to an indicated construction date of 1680 (give or take 200 years) B.C. Later, because of the uncertainty of several factors, Lockyer was to revise this exact figure to a more realistic estimate ranging between 1900 and 1500 B.C.

When the astronomer Edmond Halley—now remembered for the great comet named after him—saw the monument on a brief visit in 1720, he made an inspired guess that from the appearance of the stones it must be at least three thousand years old. Godfrey Higgins, in his *Celtic Druids* (1827) suggested that on astronomical grounds the monument may date back to 4000 B.C., but no one until Lockyer and Penrose came along truly believed that Stonehenge could be much older than Celtic-Roman times.

When Lockyer pondered over dating Stonehenge, he straightway came up against the problem of what features of the monument he should choose from which to make his measurements: the mid-line of the Avenue leading away from Stonehenge to the north-east; the axis determined by the complex of stone circles; or the Heel Stone (the so-called Sun index), which is *not* actually aligned to the axis of the avenue. In addition, Lockyer was set wondering whether there were other features that might provide clues to a date *and* to the real purpose the builders had in mind. . . .

The visitor to Stonehenge is usually first struck by two things: the drab-grey sarsen stones and the apparent smallness of the monument as it is approached along the road. Even official guide-books of Stonehenge have come round to warning the tourist that Stonehenge is one of those historic monuments possessed with the disadvantages of a reputation, and the first impression from afar may often be one of disappointment.

Scattered about Stonehenge on Salisbury Plain are hundreds of barrows in various groupings and of differing ages—which gave rise to Waltire's (and others') fanciful ideas that they were placed so to depict the exact position of celestial bodies. Indeed the barrows are so common on Salisbury Plain that someone nicknamed it the cemetery of ancient Britain.

Salisbury Plain forms only part of the larger evocative Wessex landscape, in itself a regional monument to ancient Britain. The Plain has captured the imagination of many a traveller. Wordsworth, as a disturbed young man of twenty-three, walked its length and recorded his lasting impressions of it in part of his great nature-poem *The Prelude*. Earlier both the famous diarists, Samuel Pepys and John Evelyn, left fleeting impressions of it. Pepys wrote he encountered "great hills, even to fright us"; while Evelyn considered its "evenness, extent, verdure, and innumerable flocks, to be one of the most delightful prospects in nature". Thomas Hardy captured its brooding atmosphere in his novels and poems, and it was at Stonehenge his tragic heroine Tess took refuge when she fled after killing her seducer. And to those with a musical bent the mystical rolling plain echoes the Englishness of Vaughan Williams's Pastoral Symphony.

Visitors now descend on Stonehenge in their thousands, and it ranks as a high priority among tourist itineraries as one place in England that must not be missed. On approach most casual visitors to this great architectural wonder of prehistoric Europe see little more than a drab-grey ruin dwarfed by the vast open skyline surrounding it. Not until the visitor is standing within the shadow of the sarsens can the massive quality of the man-made arrangements be fully appreciated. And only then is he likely to pause and, as thousands before him, speculate why ancient man chose this spot to erect a monument in grey sarsen and bluestone in the fashion he did.

The name sarsen, according to one account, is a corruption of Saracen "foreigner". Another version prefers to find the origin in the Anglo-Saxon words *sar* (troublesome) and *stan* (a stone). Another popular name is Grey Wether (or greywether)— a local Wiltshire name for the blocks of tertiary sandstone of the Eocene age which lie scattered over the Downs. When recumbent, at a distance, these grey sandstones are indeed very suggestive of a flock of grazing sheep—particularly in an area to the east of the Avebury circle, north of Stonehenge. One of the earliest references to greywethers is found in the Civil War diary of Colonel Richard Symonds. In November 1644 the King's army was camped near Marlborough at Fyfield, and Symonds remarks that it was "a place so full of grey pibble stones of great bigness as is not usually seen . . . the inhabitants calling them Saracen's stones; you may goe upon them all the way. They call that place the Grey-wethers, because a far off they looke like a flock of sheepe".

Inside Stonehenge, the visitor is greeted by a spectacle of large stones in considerable disarray. It was like this when Stukeley first set eyes on it and described its condition as one of "rude havock". But in spite of the monument's broken condition, excavations over the years have provided sufficient information to allow reconstruction of it so we can see it in its final form and even more intriguingly in the forms conceived by its earliest designers when they began to erect it.

It is the outer circle of grey stones that first suggests some semblance of order to the visitor (Plate 8). This circle once consisted of thirty upright sarsens, each worked to a rectangular section. On each pair of stones rested a matching horizontal block of which only six now survive in their original positions. These lintels probably formed a continuous architrave shaped by the prehistoric masons to fit part of the circle curve and all held in place by a system of double jointing consisting of mortise-and-tenon and tenon-and-groove joints. Examination of these joints shows them to have been carefully executed, and they reveal that the Megalithic artizans who laboured at Stonehenge included skilled craftsmen well-versed in traditional carpentry techniques which the master-designer, whoever he was, had no hesitation in adapting to the less familiar stone-jointing problems.

Taken between the inner 'worked' faces of the stones, the diameter of the outer sarsen circle measures 29·25 metres (97·5 feet). It seems that the outer faces of these circle stones were left 'rough' purposely. Each of the uprights has an average weight of approx-

E

imately 26 tons and an average height of 4 meters (13 feet). The longest stones measure up to 5·4 metres (18 feet) of which about 1·2 to 1·5 metres (4 to 5 feet) is buried.

Within the outer sarsen circle stood a circle of bluestones 22·8 metres (76 feet) in diameter. Opinion has differed about the actual number of stones that once formed the complete circle, but estimates range from fifty-nine to sixty-one. Only nine stones remain in an upright position, and many are missing. These tougher bluestones, unlike the sarsen blocks, are foreign to the Wessex landscape—but not everyone agrees how they came to arrive at Stonehenge.

Farther towards the centre of the monument once stood intact five massive trilithons ranging in height from 6 to 7·5 metres (20 to 25 feet) above ground level and arranged in the form of a horseshoe with its open side orientated north-east (Fig. 8). Each trilithon —as the name implies—consists of three stones, two forming the uprights and the third laid lintel-fashion across the top and fixed by the same methods as used on the outer sarsen ring. Between each trilithon the opening width is 30 to 33 centimetres (12 to 13 inches), but the opening of the central trilithon (55-56)—no longer standing—may have been slightly wider. This central trilithon collapsed before 1574; the fourth trilithon (57-58), now repaired, fell on 3 January 1797, probably the result of the rapid thaw of frozen ground. The fifth trilithon (59-60) was partly ruined before 1574.

Early seventeenth-century excavations may have contributed to the general disorder, for John Aubrey wrote:

George Duke of Buckingham, when King *James* the first was at *Wilton,* did cause the middle of Stonehenge to be digged; and there remains a kind of pitt or cavity still; it is about the bignesse of two sawe-pitts. and this under-digging was the cause of the falling downe or recumbency of the great stone there, twenty one foote long.

Nevertheless, there is some doubt about the correctness of this statement. What may have happened is that some digging speeded a collapse that had begun earlier.

Within the area confined by the great trilithon horseshoe of sarsens are the remains of an inner, lesser horseshoe of more

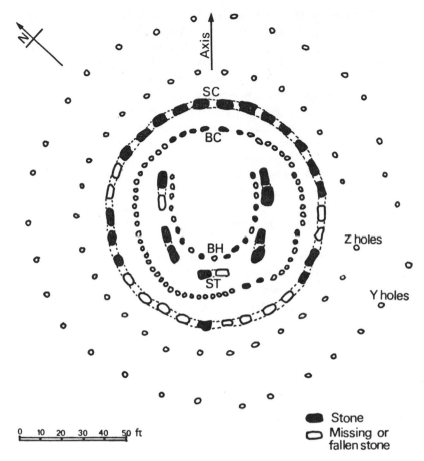

Figure 8   Stonehenge III—depicting the lintelled sarsen circle (SC); the five sarsen trilithons (ST) forming a horseshoe; the bluestone circle (BC); the bluestone horseshoe (BH); and the Y- and Z-hole arrays. The key indicates the condition of the various stones c. 1977.

"foreign" bluestones. This arrangement was once believed to consist of nineteen slender stones set to stand in height between 1·8 to 2·4 metres (6 to 8 feet). Only twelve of these stones now remain on site.

The origins of all the "foreign" bluestones long provided one of the key Stonehenge mysteries. How they got there, and from where, spawned many theories. The mystery of their origins was solved in the 1920s, but how they found their way to Stonehenge is still open to doubt as we shall see (Chapter 7).

Within the horseshoe, and lying close to the geometric centre, lies the recumbent Altar Stone, so named by Inigo Jones. This 6-ton stone, although not a bluestone, is also a foreigner to the Wessex landscape. Disturbances round the Altar Stone provide evidence of the activities of past treasure-hunters seeking the supposed gold and silver hoard belonging to a long-dead British chieftain once believed interred near the centre of Stonehenge.

Moving out from the stone circles to near the boundary of the monument—defined by a large surrounding earthen rampart and outer ditch (the vallum)—there are four very significant features of the monument usually overlooked by the casual visitor. These are the four Stations which have considerable bearing on the astronomical theories about Stonehenge. Only one of the four Stations (93, Plate 12) retains a stump of stone defining its original position; the exact position of stone 94 is uncertain; stone 91 has fallen; and 92 is known only by the surviving stonehole. Two of the Stations (92 and 94) are located on mounds (sometimes alluded to as tumuli, or barrows, in the older literature) and two (91 and 93) are at ground level.

Among other significant features of the monument are three circles of holes: the 56 Aubrey holes lying just inside the surrounding earth rampart, some of which are visible at ground level; and the Y and Z holes radiating spoke-like from the larger sarsen circle, but not easily recognizable at ground level. According to Atkinson, the intriguing choice of the names Y and Z holes stems from the 1923-4 excavation period when they were located. When the Aubrey holes had been rediscovered a little before, they were given the designation X to signify appropriately their nature as an unknown quantity. Thus the use of Y and Z for the slightly later discoveries followed logically.

Towards the north-east the earth rampart is bridged to form a feature known as the Causeway Entrance. Across it, straddling the first and last holes of the Aubrey circle, lies a large recumbent sarsen, measuring lengthwise 6·3 metres (21 feet). Although this is known as the Slaughter Stone, there appears to be no evidence to justify such a colourful, evocative name.

Outside the large sarsen circle and beyond the bank-and-ditch feature sits the Heel Stone, or Friar's Heel, the most conspicuous and (perhaps) the most important of all the single stones (Plate 13). It consists of a leaning monolith of unworked stone now standing 4·8 metres (16 feet) high in a position 76.8 metres (256 feet) from the so-called geometric centre of Stonehenge. It is *near* the apex of the Heel Stone, as viewed from the centre of Stonehenge, that the Sun appears to rise at the time of the summer solstice on or about 21 June. The alternative name, Friar's Heel, is associated with another piece of Stonehenge mythology involving a legend about a friar and the Devil.

An earlier name for the Heel Stone is "Hele" stone, a dubious name that supposedly takes its origin from the Anglo-Saxon verb *helan* "to conceal"—allegedly applied because the stone concealed the Sun at its rising on the day of the summer solstice.

Other notable features of Stonehenge, which may also escape the immediate notice of the visitor, are the Avenue and Causeway features. The Avenue is an earthwork (Fig. 6) extending approximately north-eastwards for a distance of over 120 metres (400 feet) and was first noticed and named by William Stukeley. Although this feature has no stones, he named it after the great avenue of standing stones at nearby Avebury. Because the Avenue at Stonehenge has no stones, it has been suggested that the name "Processional Way" might be more apt. As a feature it certainly seems to have been intended as some kind of roadway leading to the monument from the river Avon near by (Fig. 6), and it was perhaps the very route by which the stones arrived at the site.

The Causeway (Fig. 4) leads from the earth rampart to the start of the Avenue and contains the remains of many postholes whose presence in this part of the monument has considerable importance on the astronomical speculations about Stonehenge.

All the features which have been described are approximately those of the final development of Stonehenge. They were there (although not all known) when Lockyer and Penrose took up their study of the monument just after the turn of the century. Some minor restoration of stones and tidying up had taken place during Lockyer's time, and some more recently. A few major stones that had fallen or threatened complete collapse were reraised—hopefully to their original positions. How the monument appeared in its different construction phases in the earlier millenniums B.C. will be outlined later in relation to modern interpretations and theories.

Stonehenge was to be the only Megalithic monument to which Lockyer gave a date derived from the changes in the Sun's obliquity. Although his early date of *c.* 1680 B.C. had first surprised everyone, it was a date that agreed in order of magnitude with one derived later that same year (October 1901) by (Professor) William Gowland based on archaeological data.

Gowland himself was an archaeologist much enamoured by ancient Sun-worship ideas. He had written about the ancient Sun worship in Japan—respecting the Shinto cult where the Sun-goddess was the chief deity. He had drawn particular attention—with Stonehenge in mind—to a structure at the temple of Fûta-mi-ga-ura where the sunrise on a certain day is marked between two gigantic rocks and by a structure in the form of a wooden trilithon placed immediately behind the altar.

At Stonehenge, Gowland had been appointed to supervise the re-erection of stone 56 which—it was believed—had subsided before the middle of the sixteenth century. During the work of re-bedding it, crude stone tools were uncovered that had obviously been used to dress the sarsen stones in place and therefore pointed to a date of erection back in the Neolithic period—thought near its termination. Gowland found instances where heavily worn and discarded hammerstones had been used by the erectors to act as wedges to support the massive sarsens in their foundation sockets. In a later paper he wrote: "The occurrence of stone tools does not alone prove with absolute certainty that Stonehenge belongs to the Neolithic age, although it affords a strong presumption in favour of that view." At the time Gowland's findings greatly enhanced Lockyer's prestige.

Nevertheless, Lockyer's *modus operandi* for dating Stonehenge was suspect. While Gowland's date was convincing because he provided evidence in the form of recognizable artefacts, Lockyer's was based on plain supposition—faulty supposition many supposed.

Lockyer had surprisingly adopted as his alignment the mid-line of the Avenue feature rather than the mid-line passing exactly between stones 55-56 of the central trilithon and the midway point between stones 30-31 and 15-16 in the outer sarsen circle—considered by everyone as defining the monument's centre-line.

Lockyer's final axis line defined the mean axis of Stonehenge through the Ordnance Survey bench mark situated at Sidbury Hill 13 kilometres (8 miles) to the north-east which on the same line passes through Grovely Castle 10 kilometres (6 miles) to the south-west. Although the difference between this line and the line passing through the true centre-line of the monument is small, Lockyer's choice in relating Stonehenge to landscape features which have nothing to do with Stonehenge in the context of its period incurred much subsequent criticism and is nowadays generally not accepted.

Lockyer, like others who had measured the axis, ignored the Heel Stone whose estimated centre-line lies 1·8 metres (6 feet) east of the Avenue mid-line. Although, as seen from the centre point of the axis line inside the stone circle, the Sun now appears to rise (approximately) over the Heel Stone, in more ancient times, because of changes in obliquity, it rose north of it (Fig. 7). Yet, whatever the doubtful merits for the Heel Stone as a precise ancient solar marker-point *in its present-day slumped position*, it would seem beyond all doubt that it was used as *some* kind of celestial marker-point at an earlier age.

Passing on from examination of the general orientation of Stonehenge, Lockyer believed that there was much else hidden in the stones of the monument that needed searching out. He wondered, for example—in the vein of his Egyptian temple researches—whether there had been an earlier circle on site. Lockyer, who had a declared fondness for the mystics, may also have had in mind those lines of antiquarian inspiration written by Sir Thomas Browne in his *Religio Medici*: "Large are the treasures of oblivion . . . more is buried than recorded."

Lockyer now examined the tumuli and Station stones and reassessed the Rev. Duke's ideas about Stations 94 and 93 lining up with the last light of the setting Sun on the longest day. Lockyer saw that a line drawn from 91-93 marked sunset on about 6 May and 8 August and in reverse direction marked sunrise about 7 February and 8 November. These alignments he believed must have marked the ancient mid-quarter days of the year or dates about forty-five days before and after the solstices. The line 91-93 almost passes through the monument's centre defined by the large sarsen circle which is about 1 metre (3 feet) north of the monument's centre defined by the Aubrey circle.

What Lockyer had in mind, looking at these stones, was that

they were ancient indicators of important solar-calendar dates. In Celtic and earlier times there were probably only two main recognized seasons—cold and warm. The year began on 1 November, and this date indicated the turning point in the pastoral/agrarian cycle of the farming communities when surplus cattle not to be carried through the winter were killed off. The second festival was 1 May when cattle were probably turned out for grazing. The two lesser Quarter Days were marked by 1 February when the lactation of ewes began, and 1 August when crops were ripe for harvesting, which in later times became Lammas Day—the consecration day of loaves made from the first ripe grain.

Lockyer, in pondering over the alignment of these stones, became preoccupied by the May and August festival dates. Had he not become so preoccupied and instead been fully alert to explore several alternatives, including a possible connection with the movement of the Moon, he might have stumbled on the lunar-swing hypothesis that others who followed him over half a century later discovered.

When pondering the question of an earlier circle, Lockyer began thinking about the problem of the origins of the "foreign" bluestones. If the apocryphal tale of Geoffrey of Monmouth was to be discounted, their presence on Salisbury Plain needed an explanation. One of his professional colleagues at the Royal College of Science, the geologist J. W. Judd, had looked into this question several times. Judd had considered that the bluestones had been transported from an earlier circle in some district local to Stonehenge, and that they had been moved either as trophies of war or as the sacred treasure of a wandering tribe. As for the origin of the stones, Judd favoured the glacial ice. He summed up the problem:

> I would therefore suggest as probable that when the early inhabitants of this island [Britain] commenced the erection of Stonehenge, Salisbury Plain was sprinkled over thickly with the great white masses of Sarsen stones ('grey wethers'), and much more sparingly with darker coloured boulders (the so-called 'blue stones'), the last relics of the glacial drift, which have been nearly denuded away. From these two kinds of materials the stones suitable for the contemplated temple were selected . . .

Judd added as a rider:

It is even possible that the abundance and association of these two kinds of materials so strikingly contrasted in colour and appearance, at a particular spot, may not only have decided the site but to some extent have suggested the architectural features of the noble structure of Stonehenge.

Judd's summation was indeed a highly plausible one. By the late nineteenth century, the idea of the universal Ice Age, fashioned chiefly by Louis Agassiz, had firmly taken root in scientific thinking. Everyone could appreciate that ice could pluck great masses of stone from a native mountain bedrock and subsequently deposit it hundreds of miles away. . . . If the glaciers could carry those curiously spotted, dull-red stones of rhomb-porphyry (once believed to be discarded ballast from Viking ships) across the North Sea from Norway and dump them far and wide inland along the eastern coasts of England, then equally plausibly ice could bring "foreign" stones to Salisbury Plain, and one could dismiss once and for all that colourful story of Geoffrey of Monmouth. But, was Judd's glacial theory too glib—too plausible? The archaeologists—ignoring Judd's thesis—were later to conjure up an entirely different idea.

6 Megaliths and May Worship

When at Stonehenge, Lockyer re-examined the Rev. Duke's earlier ideas about Station alignments made by the Station stones and discovered that 91-93 marked the sunset lines for 6 May and 8 August, this was to direct most of his subsequent energies into an investigation into the ancient cult of the May year and May worship, which on occasions was to totally obsess him. Not long after beginning his researches of Stonehenge, Lockyer was firmly treading the path that was finally to lead him on to the Druids. . . .

It was soon Lockyer's contention that Stonehenge was involved with the ancient year measured from May (and its Quarter Days) as well with the June solstitial year. In addition to the evidence he believed contained in the Station alignments, he cited supposed confirmation from legendary-cum-mythological sources. For example, he believed corroborative evidence for the May year at Stonehenge was provided by a clue in Geoffrey of Monmouth's account of the slaughter of the Britains by the Saxons—"the Treachery of the Long Knives" as it is sometimes referred to. Lockyer, in dragging up this story again, posed the question: "Now what time of year did this take place? Was it at the summer solstice on 21 June?" Then delving into Davies's *Mythology of the British Druids* and Guest's *Mabinogion*, he was delighted to find that the banquet took place on May eve "Meinvethydd". Lockyer asked: "Is it likely that this date would have been chosen in a solar temple dedicated exclusively to the solstice?" He now maintained that the worked sarsen stones and the magnificent trilithons were a reconstruction of a much older temple which was originally used for worship in connection with the May year. In hindsight we know he was right about the fact that the present-day Stonehenge is a reconstruction of an older temple, but his ideas about its involvement in worship of the May year is still without a firm base.

To support his thesis that the May year and May worship had preceded the solstitial use of Stonehenge, Lockyer readily drew comparisons between Stonehenge and the Megalithic structures round Carnac in Brittany. Like Stonehenge many of the Carnac menhir alignments had been claimed to be solstitial. Lockyer drew upon the ideas of Felix Gaillard, author of *L'Astronomie Préhistorique*, who was one of the French pioneers in developing what was then known as "The Orientation Theory of Carnac". But Lockyer was not overimpressed by Gaillard's methodology; for although Lockyer credits him with providing the correct azimuth for solstitial points, he remarked that his observations were not sufficiently precise to enable a final conclusion to be drawn.

Gaillard had in turn been persuaded that not only were the great avenues at Carnac orientated, but so too were the dolmens. Gaillard had suffered severe criticism from French archaeologists about his ideas. Like Lockyer, Gaillard was annoyed because archaeologists often confused numbers and principles. One French archaeologist, in trying to demolish Gaillard's theory, had confused the precessional shift of stars with the equinoctial shift of the Sun. Needless to say he did not escape lightly. But French archaeologists were just as unhappy about using numbers as their British counterparts. Gaston Maspero had written to Lockyer after reading his Egyptian book: "... I am still not sure what is my final opinion: the application of mathematics to archaeology gives an appearance of rigour and certainty which always makes me mistrustful...."

Lockyer, ignoring much of Gaillard's work, was more impressed by the work of another Frenchman, a Lieutenant Devoir of the French Navy, who had also made an intensive study of French Megalithic sites, looking specifically for astronomical orientations. Lockyer believed Devoir's work had firmly established midsummer (solstitial) orientations for French Megalithic sites "beyond question". In addition the Frenchman had made important observations "which prove that the May and August sunrises were also provided for in systems of alignments".

Many French sites came under Devoir's scrutiny. He noted that on some sites there were alignments inclined $12°$ to the solstitial line "always towards the east". Lockyer seized on this significant piece of information remarking: "... for it gives us the ... direc-

tion of sunrise at the beginning of the May and August years."
In a summing up, Lockyer concluded: ". . . the appeal to Brittany is entirely in favour of the May-November year worship
having preceded the solstitial one . . . I may justly claim the
Brittany evidence as entirely in favour of the suggestion put forward with regard to Stonehenge."

Some of the most interesting parts of Lockyer's Stonehenge book
are his sections devoted to "Astronomical Hints For Archaeologists" and his hints for would-be investigators of the numerous
stone circles in Aberdeenshire, Scotland. In the section devoted to
"Astronomical Hints . . ." he sets out model principles he thought
should be followed in investigating Megalithic sites. Subsequently
he published these under a separate cover in a book entitled *Surveying for Archaeologists,* now quite rare.

It is in his "Hints" we can read his views on possible stellar
orientations for North-West European sites—comparable to the
star alignments he believed he had proven in Egypt and what his
co-worker Penrose had proven in Greece.

Lockyer writes:

> We both discovered that stars, far out of the Sun's course, especi-
> ally in Egypt, were observed in the dawn as heralds of sunrise—
> 'warning-stars'—so that priests might have time to prepare the
> sunrise sacrifice. To do this properly the star should rise while the
> Sun is still about 10° below the horizon. There is also reason to
> believe that stars rising not far from the north point were also used
> as clock-stars to enable the time to be estimated during the night
> in the same way as the time during the day could be estimated by
> the position of the Sun.

But Lockyer is soon back on his May-day theme when he cites
the star Spica as the warning star that heralded the Sun on May-
day 3200 B.C. in the temple of Menu at Thebes—about the time
he believed the star Sirius was associated with the summer solstice.

May-day connections and associations now became Lockyer's
Megalithic *leitmotif.* He was persuaded that May-day worship
came to an end at Stonehenge when the monument was redesigned
in 1680 B.C. He relates how he says he obtained clear evidence in
different parts of Britain of Megalithic sites used for night work
and (of course) sites constructed in relation to the May year. At
one point Lockyer proceeds to demonstrate the methods he thought

might have been employed by ancient British 'astronomer-priests'. Here he gives free rein to his imagination. In the 1960s, Alexander Thom, as one of Lockyer's heirs-apparent, was to carry Lockyer's ideas further, and in his book *Megalithic Lunar Observatories* he provides passages of an imaginary dialogue between an older, experienced astronomer-priest and a pupil.

Lockyer concluded that the easiest way for the astronomer-priests to carry out star observation in a stone circle would be to erect a stone or barrow that indicated the direction of the place on the horizon at which the star to be used would rise as seen from the centre of the circle. If the stars to be observed at dawn were to herald summer, the stone or barrow might be placed at a distance. There was good reason, he supposed, why the sighting device should not be too close, for "in a solemn ceremonial the less seen of the machinery the better".

The indicator stones and barrows would need to be illuminated in the dark by a light placed strategically near by (again Thom was later to echo this same idea). Lockyer noted that cups (in so-called cup stones) which hold grease are known in connection with such stones. But he realized these would be suitable only in good weather when there was no wind. In windy weather, Lockyer supposed, a cromlech (chambered grave) or some other structure must have been provided for a priest's shelter. We now come to the nub of Lockyer's beliefs, for he tells us that in his opinion the astronomer-priests lived in cromlechs—these being a later stage than the caves where the priests lived in earlier times. A cromlech, Lockyer thought, was a structure specially erected by the Megalithic peoples to protect priests from the elements and wild animals. Lockyer was right back to the ideas that had held sway earlier.

In some detail Lockyer describes the problem of the priests' living accommodation—of keeping out damp. Lockyer, as a man of 65, knew only too well about damp—clambering round Megalithic monuments on British moors in thick mists in the middle of winter! Then, to justify a set belief, he makes three wild assertions: "There were no carpenters in those days. They could not cut down trees. They could not make a door. . . ." These assertions were to justify his belief that the entrance of a cromlech would be closed by a stone "capable of being handled by one or two men, the only way of sealing it".

It is in making credulous assertions of this kind that Lockyer unfortunately gave astro-archaeology a bad name. The archaeological record shows unambiguously that carpentry was a skilled craft in Neolithic times. The mortice-and-tenon and the tenon-and-groove joints at Stonehenge are evidence enough that the stone masons borrowed their techniques from skilled carpenters. The great postholes found round countless British sites, which once held massive man-shaped timbers, give lie to Lockyer's ridiculous claim that the ancients could not cut down trees. As for doors, it seems beyond doubt that a carpenter of c. 4000-2000 B.C. could have fashioned such a device had social custom required it.

In a section devoted to Cornwall—a county rich in Megalithic remains—he expressed opinion that certain basic knowledge for setting out alignments would not be knowledge held by the "local Druid" but by

> peripatetic astronomer-priests who went from place to place establishing and orientating the circle and the priests' house (a cromlech), and then leaving subordinate priest-Druids—curates-in-charge—who could not go far wrong when the alignment of both circle and cromlech fixed the May, August, November and February festivals; the solstices they could easily fix for themselves because then the Sun rose in the same place on three successive days.

Thom, again, was later to echo Lockyer's theme of a wandering mastermind-priest with his ideas of how his Megalithic-yard unit was carried from site to site throughout Britain.

Lockyer believed quite plausibly that "... the ancient priest need not have been a profound astronomer to build his monuments, which were simply calendars". He remarks:

> I do not mean to say that they were calendars and nothing more, but they were from an astronomical point of view, simply calendars, enabling people to know and recognize from past experience the different parts of the year by the place of sunrise or sunset; and they were also night-dials, enabling them to differentiate between the early and the late hours of the night.

Many today would certainly not disagree with these ideas.
Lockyer was particularly attracted to the Megalithic avenues

and to those on Dartmoor in particular. These very strange avenues may be marked out by single, double or multiple rows of stones, some straight and some crooked which follow any number of directions of the compass and sometimes several within the same monument. Earlier French work on the Brittany alignments persuaded Lockyer that these were monuments erected for worship of the Sun in relation to the May year. They were in fact, concluded Lockyer, the earliest attempts of ancient man to measure the calendar by the Sun after he discovered the Moon to be unsatisfactory as a long measure of time.

After looking carefully at the problem, Lockyer dismissed as non-astronomical those stone rows and avenues which are very long and crooked and follow several directions. In some cases he supposed they may have provided useful guides at night, in mist, or in difficult country with streams to cross.

One of the best known avenue structures that Lockyer examined is at Merrivale (nr Walkhampton in Devonshire). At Merrivale there are two double avenues of upright stones, 180 metres (600 feet) and 265 metres (870 feet) long and blocked by a triangular stone to the east. Working from his hypothesis that a long avenue directed to the rising point of a star would not necessarily be *exactly* straight over undulating ground, *and* if two avenues were directed to the rising place of the same celestial body at different epochs, they could not be parallel for reasons of precessional shift.

It was these two factors that Lockyer marshalled as "evidence" to counter what he referred to as the "curious arguments of critics of the astronomical theory". The point made by these critics was that the *absence* of parallelism was a strong argument which could be used *against* the avenues having had an astronomical use.

At Merrivale the two avenues are most certainly not parallel, and Lockyer fancied that their alignments were sometime involved with the Pleiades (the Seven Sisters), and that they were used as warning stars to herald the rise of the May Sun. Juggling the azimuths and assuming that the Pleiades *were* the warning stars in question (which announced the May sunrise), Lockyer derived results showing dates when the alignments were in use. Those for the northern alignment lay between 1710 to 1580 B.C. while those for the southern alignment between 1420 to 1400 B.C. By discovering what he considered hard evidence for the Pleiades as warning stars, it concurred with some of Penrose's results for

Greek temples citing the same stars. For example, at Hecatomp-
edon at Athens, Penrose had cited an alignment date to the
Pleiades in 1495 B.C.

The Pleiades were indeed a group of stars well known to the
Greeks, but whether their temple foundations had been aligned
to them is another matter. In Hesiod's day, around the eighth
century B.C., the Greek farmers reaped their corn when the
Pleiades rose at sunrise in May and ploughed their fields when
they set at sunrise in November. The Pleiades were possibly one of
the most observed and discussed groups of stars in the ancient
world. The Sumerians knew them as the Seven Gods; the Egyptians as the Seven Hathors and the "Thousands"; and to the
Florida Indians they were known as the Company of Maidens.
One tribe of Australian Aborigines believed them more important
than the Sun and attributed the cause of summer heat directly to
them. In the Bible, Job refers to them in the passage: "Cans't thou
bind the sweet influence of the Pleiades or loose the bands of
Orion?" Every civilization has recorded their presence in the sky,
and in their season there is little reason to doubt that they were
very familiar objects to the Neolithic farmers of Europe.

At the Merrivale Avenue, Lockyer noted rather astutely that
the alignments ran approximately parallel to the Cursus feature
near Stonehenge. Consequently it was his opinion that, like the
Merrivale Avenue, the Stonehenge Cursus had been intended as a
processional road to watch the rising of the Pleiades. The blocking
stone to the east was, thought Lockyer, likely a sighting stone. He
noted that the end stones of the avenues are longer than the rest,
and this perhaps provides a clue to the true direction to which
other avenues were aligned.

Lockyer was fascinated by the wealth of examples he found in
the Cornish and Dartmoor stone monuments. But he had insuffi-
cient time to examine them all himself. He hoped that at some
future period they would be carefully scrutinized by students of
the orientation theory. Whetting the appetite of future field-
investigators, and unfortunately, in hindsight, sending off many
to chase some very illusive hares, he wondered, for example,
whether the avenues consisting of two rows of stones were a reflection of the Sphinx Avenue in Egypt. Was there double worship
going on in the avenues and circles at the same time . . .? Did all
the cairns and cists (or kists—stone boxes to house remains of the

1 The Trethevy Quoit, Cornwall. Funerary chambers of this kind are usually referred to as dolmens, but earlier they were often referred to as cromlechs or quoits. Sir Norman Lockyer believed that this monument was orientated by its builders towards November sunrise, or in the opposite direction to the May sunset.

2 Woodhenge, near Stonehenge: an aerial view, looking southeast. Concrete marker blocks now denote the old postholes. Note the ghost barrow circles in adjacent fields.

3 Stone avenue alignments at Carnac in Brittany.

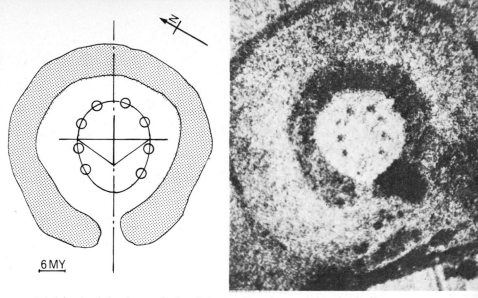

4 (*right*) Aerial view of the Megaxylic site at Arminghall, nr Norwich, showing the location of the eight (1-metre dia.) postholes which once formed its inner structure. The inset (*left*) is a reconstruction of the monument's supposed geometry (outer ditch omitted) according to the ideas of Lyle Borst (*see* Chapter 12).

5 Group of tall menhirs in Brittany.

6 Avebury, oblique aerial view, looking east. The monument is now straddled by the modern village (*see* also Fig. 5).

7 Stonehenge, looking from the south-west.

8 Stonehenge, looking south-west from near the Slaughter Stone. Centre (between stones 1 and 30) is a tall upright with an exposed tenon (stone 56) marking the ruined central trilithon. (For key to stones *see* Fig. 4).

9 Stonehenge restored – showing six trilithons – according to the ideas of Inigo Jones *c.* 1621.

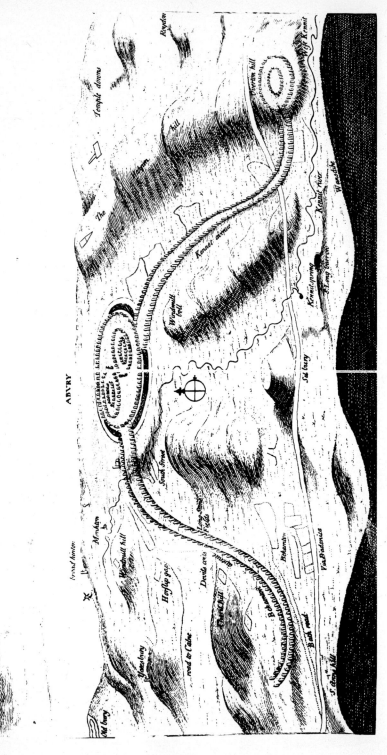

10 Region round Avebury and Silbury Hill depicting the West Kennet and Beckhampton Avenues restored according to Stukeley's ideas.

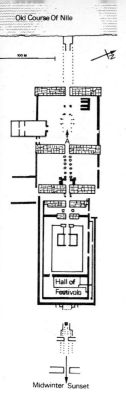

Old Course Of Nile

100 M

Hall of
Festivals

Midwinter Sunset

11 The temple of Amen-Re at Karnak, looking west along the axis which Lockyer claimed was aligned to the setting Sun on midsummer's day in the year 3700 B.C. Insert shows a schematic plan of the temple denoting various features (*see* page 49).

12 (*below left*) Station Stone 93 at Stonehenge. This is the only Station whose exact original position is known.

13 (*below right*) The Heel Stone, Stonehenge.

14 (*above*) Dagger, axe and assorted graffiti engraved on trilithon 53 at Stonehenge.

15 (*right*) Axe engravings on stone 4 at Stonehenge.

dead) in the avenues represent later additions? Running against the tide of informed opinion, Lockyer remarks with the heresy:

> I have always held that these ancient temples, and even their attendant long and chambered barrows, were for the living and not for the dead ... There was good reason for burials after the sacred nature of the spot had been established, and they may have taken place at any time since; the most probable time being after 1000 B.C. up to a date as recent as archaeologists may consider probable.

Not surprisingly, Lockyer's avenue theories suffered much criticism at the hands of archaeologists. Lockyer, however, hinted broadly there were those critics who were either unwilling or incompetent to test out his theories by actual observation and observed:

> It is no doubt difficult for the average Englishman of the present day, unless he happens to be a sailor, to picture to himself a townless world without artificial light and any useful purpose served by looking at the Sun by day or the stars by night. Calendars, almanacs, clocks, and watches have done away with the necessity of using his eye in this direction, and the modern priest, like the modern layman, though he prates about the heavens declaring the glory of God and the firmament showing His handiwork, too often does not know that the Sun rises to the eastward, and, if he does, he imagines that it rises in the same place all the year round. . . .

After publication of the first edition of his Stonehenge book in 1906, Lockyer had persuaded the Royal Society of London to set up a committee to carry out an astronomical survey of ancient monuments in Britain. Although he was now seventy years of age and professed himself too old to undertake the new work, it was around this time that his fancies turned towards the Welsh stone circles and he began to immerse himself deeply in Celtic mythology. Traditional Druid-lovers everywhere now saw Lockyer as their champion.

In 1907 he attended the Eisteddfod—the national bardic congress—held that year in Swansea. Earlier that year his attention had been drawn to the traditional Welsh assembly, the Gorsedd.

F

The Gorsedds were traditionally held both in Wales and in Cornwall and are ceremonials almost identical with the Eisteddfods and involve a ceremony that takes place inside a specially built circle of twelve stones 30° apart—including stones arranged to indicate the solstices and equinoxes.

Lockyer was greatly intrigued to learn that in Gorsedd history the May year had come first, later to be replaced by the solstitial one. He was also intrigued to discover that the total count of stones in the circle arrangement was nineteen—this was the same number of stones he had frequently encountered in Cornish circles—where a common name for such circles is "Nine Maidens" ("nine" being short for nineteen).

Lockyer's new enthusiasm for Welsh bardic lore attracted several Welsh correspondents who supplied him with much colourful background material which he unhesitantly wove into his May theories.

When Lockyer attended the 1907 Eisteddfod, he was conferred the title of "Gwyddon Prydain", meaning literally Britain's "Man of Science". In his speech to the grand bards at the assembly he said that he was sure such meetings had been held at stone circles for at least four millenniums. In 1909, when the Eisteddfod was held in London, the Committee of Bards secured Lockyer's expert advice, for they were anxious that the new Gorsedd circle should properly indicate the point of the solstices and the equinoxes.

Perhaps Lockyer's attraction and absorbing interest in Celtic-cum-Druid matters were in no little way fostered by what French archaeologists had told him about the origin of the Lockyers—who, they supposed, descended from the Ligures, an early Celtic swarm who had settled near the Ouse. The temptation by Lockyer to attribute astronomical knowledge and great learning to his immediate forebears was perhaps subconscious, but it does nevertheless appear to have coloured his ideas about the shadowy Celts.

In his Stonehenge book, Lockyer devoted a great deal of space to a rambling discussion showing how folklore and tradition provided "dim references to ancient uses of stars". There were also sections devoted to sacred fires and trees, holy wells and streams which no self-respecting student of astro-archaeology would now believe relevant to the subject. In this vein Lockyer's book still provides a valuable mine of mish-mash information for the lunatic-fringe groups like the "ley-hunters" (Chapter 12).

Today in the field of scientific research, Lockyer's naive *modus operandi* would be rare. Lockyer, as undisputed editor of *Nature* for fifty years, was never plagued with the problem of having to justify his speculative arguments to anonymous scientific referees appointed by scientific magazines to vet contributions. Consequently he became self-indulgent and often allowed a good idea to run unchecked and degenerate into hyperspeculative fancy. At the same time it may be argued plausibly that he was only showing his true mettle as a polymath and researcher after wider truths in the tradition set by the great nineteenth-century master-polymath Alexander Humboldt.

The problem with Lockyer, common to all polymaths, was that he had too many fingers in the scientific pic for his own good. He did not spare sufficient time to chew over some of his rather naive half-digested ideas and often rushed into print prematurely. Then, when the manuscript was sent to the printers' and forgotten, he was galloping towards the next fence in quite another race. Lockyer's astro-archaeological interests from the 1890s onwards formed only a small part of his wide interests in the cosmos. For example, in 1903—one of the busiest years of his life and at the peak of his scientific fame—his overriding passion centred round meteorology.

As a man of science his fertile imagination was fired by diverse influences. He was much inspired by Tennyson and was greatly impressed by the apparent breadth of the poet's scientific knowledge—especially with astronomical detail. Together Lockyer and Tennyson seemed to have formed a mutual admiration society, for Tennyson wrote gushingly to Lockyer: "... in my anthropological spectrum you are coloured like a first-rate star of science"; while Lockyer, in collaboration with his daughter Winifred, was later to write a book (his last) entitled *Tennyson as a student and a Poet of Nature*, which set out to demonstrate to the public the extent and accuracy of the poet's scientific knowledge.

Living in a period when folklore and mythology had just become academically respectable, Lockyer drew freely from the writings of Tylor, Frazer and Max Muller.

Frazer in particular was highly influential to Lockyer's Mega-

lithic studies. Frazer himself was a true pioneer of the interdisciplinary approach. His book *The Golden Bough* rocketed him
to fame, and he was quickly labelled as the leader of the "new
humanism". Like Lockyer he invaded several scholastic domains,
ignoring the accepted demarcations, to root out facts; if the specialists did not like it, it was too bad. Like Lockyer it was Frazer's
firm belief that one should not let ignorance of a particular dis-
cipline of learning stop one from taking it by the throat to see what
it had to say for itself. *The Golden Bough* was a fertile source from
which Lockyer gleaned much. The book, however, was an exhaus-
tive piece of mainly *library-based* scholarship. Published in twelve
volumes, its impact on the academic world was tremendous. Although Frazer nowadays is in eclipse academically, the abridged
paperback version of the *Bough*—running to some 971 pages—
enjoys a remarkably healthy sale, and it is still the most widely
read book on anthropology. Indeed it remains a book that anyone
claiming any pretence of knowledge of literature is expected to
have read (or at least to have dipped into sometime). Sigmund
Freud and others were also to borrow heavily in factual material
from Frazer but placed on it quite a different interpretation.

The gist of Frazer's theme was that the Golden Bough grew on
a certain tree in the sacred grove of Diana at Arica, and the
priesthood of the grove was held by the man who succeeded in
breaking off the Bough and then slaying the priest in single com-
bat. The priest in question represented the god of the grove—
Virbius—and his slaughter was regarded as the death of the god.
It was this that raised the question about the widespread custom
of killing men and animals regarded as divine. Frazer collected
many examples of this custom and proposed that the Golden Bough
was mistletoe, and the whole legend could be connected with the
Druidical reverence for mistletoe and the human sacrifices which
accompanied their worship; it could also be connected with the
Norse legend of the death of Balder.

Frazer used his Golden Bough researches to lead on to new
explanations of the meaning of totemism, ancient mythology and
custom; he introduced subjects such as taboo exogamy and the
worship of nature. He showed the origin and source of divine
kingship and other long-standing human customs in the context of
widespread social and cultural patterns. When published, *The
Golden Bough* marked a landmark and turning-point in anthro-

pological studies. It forced the scholars of the older literary tradition to enlarge their vision and look again at classical writings.

Frazer, nevertheless, was often criticized for his emphasis on a
library-based approach to anthropology. Like Lockyer he lacked
time. He was certainly no field-worker prepared to live for years
with a band of Aborigines to root out first hand their social
customs. Because he was overtly sensitive to this particular criticism, he considered the greatest compliment ever paid him was
when a home-leave visitor from a distance shore once exclaimed
in admiration: "Why you know my blacks better than I know
them myself!"

Frazer is said to have pioneered the working method that later
earned the nickname of the "If-I-were-a-horse" method—allud-
ing to an aprocryhal story of an American farmer who when told
that a horse was missing from his paddock went there for himself
to chew some grass and ruminated about the problem of how he
would behave and where he would go in the circumstances if he
were the horse! Lockyer, it appears, subscribed to much the same
method, and it also has parallels with the method which Conan
Doyle made fashionable with Sherlock Holmes: "You know my
methods in such cases Watson. I put myself in the man's place,
and having first gauged his intelligence, I try to imagine how I
myself should have proceeded under the same circumstances."

In pursuing the origin of British Megalithic worship, Lockyer
fancied that ancient coast-following voyagers—prospectors in
search of tin—from the Eastern Mediterranean might have made
contact in Cornwall in the early millenniums B.C. Citing some
doubtful evidence, Lockyer asserts: ". . . the bulk of the population
of these islands [Britain], before the arrival of the Celts, spoke
dialects attuned to those of North Africa." And ". . . there was an
astronomer-priesthood class in Britain familiar with Egyptian
methods as early as about 3600 B.C." According to Lockyer,
British Megalithic culture then could be traced back to a diffusion
of Semitic peoples from the East who had migrated to Britain, and
the Druids themselves were their lineal descendants.

By the summer of 1909, Lockyer had amassed what he called
certain evidence in Britain of over 100 positive astronomical alignments associated with Megalithic monuments. These he summa-
rized under the headings Sun and Clock-stars. With the Sun he
claimed 15 positive alignments to the May year, 9 to November,

17 to the summer solstice, and 11 to the winter solstice.

Optimistically, Lockyer described his evidence as overwhelming and believed that blind chance had nothing to do with the setting out of various alignments.

Discussing the various monuments chronologically, it seemed to Lockyer that the avenues and cromlechs (chambered tombs) formed the earliest, primitive stage, and the stone circles came later —representing a more advanced practical astronomical knowledge. The avenue was single purpose and could only be orientated towards the rising (or setting) of a single astronomical subject, whereas the circles in combination with several outlying stones near them were multi-purpose and may have marked several different astronomical events. Undoubtedly, in Lockyer's mind, the earliest sunrise observations related to May—the vegetation year (closely associated with growth and fertilization) —which Lockyer supposed had been Paleolithic man's first solar marker-point on a distant horizon. Later the orientations were associated with the solstitial year beginning in June. Thus at Stonehenge the early circles associated with May (preceding the present-day solstitial circle) had begun as a May temple—a British Memphis—and had ended as a solstitial one like that of Amen-Re at Thebes.

Lockyer opinioned that British circles were in full operation "more than a thousand years before the Aryans or Celts came upon the scene". Yet there could be little doubt that the Druids of Romano-British times were the descendants of the astronomer-priests of more ancient times, and through the Druids one could study the achievements of the earlier more shadowy astronomer-priests.

Lockyer is still affectionately remembered by astronomers if not by archaeologists. His numerous books, now long out of date, ranged in title from *Chemistry of the Sun* to *Stargazing Past and Present*. His works dealing with astro-archaeological topics have now become expensive, hard-to-find collectors' items. Whatever his failings as a critical referee of his own work, there can be little doubt that the subject of astro-archaeology would not have developed along the lines it has without his earlier stimulus.

His close friends recognized his weaknesses. After his death one friend wrote aptly:

The Sun is our supreme historian, and the astronomer is his

prophet. Lockyer's astronomical interpretations, often tentative in suggestion, often based on defective measures, and at best but holiday work, are a legacy left by a great interpreter of the Sun himself to students of archaeology and anthropology which they cannot afford to ignore.

7 Brits and Bluestones

In the years following Lockyer's death, the astronomical theories about Megalithic monuments went largely out of fashion. Although his estimated date of Stonehenge had been vindicated by Gowland and it was vindicated again by the excavations of 1919-26, many believed that Lockyer's estimate based on the Sun's obliquity was nothing better than a fortuitous guess.

Nevertheless, the official guide-books did not continue to include brief summations of Lockyer's and Penrose's work. Frank Stevens, curator of the Salisbury Museum and editor of the official guide-book *Stonehenge: Today and Yesterday*, which hundreds of thousands of visitors must have read between the two wars, very fairly summed up the situation as it stood in the late 1920s when he wrote:

> The fact that the Sun rises over the Hele Stone on the Summer Solstice, and that it can be observed in direct alignment with the centre of the Great Trilithon can hardly be due to accident. Chance might bring two stones into such a position on the Solstice, but in this case, the earlier monument is so arranged as to place the rising Sun in a due line with its axis on this particular day ...

With due caution Stevens added:

> While it is possible that the Hele Stone was erected to mark the Solstice and to afford a definite means of determining the year, this may not justify the theory that the entire structure was an astronomical observatory and dedicated entirely to sun worship ... weighing, therefore, the archaeologist's and astronomer's evi-

dence, it is fairly safe to conclude that Stonehenge can be dated at about 1700 B.C., and that its use was religious; probably a temple, in which the Sun may have been adored in some way ...

Frank Stevens, recognizing that astro-archaeology (although he did not call it that) was an interdisciplinary activity, and a contentious one, remarked:

The astronomer, archaeologist, geologist, and anthropologist have each their share in the solution of the problem but each also has a bias due to his own special science [how right he was !]. The mineralogist solves the problem of the Foreign Stones by suggesting a "glacial drift" without reference to the geologist, who will tell him that the local gravels contain no pebbles which belong to those classes of stones known as Foreign Stones. The astronomer, in his quest for alignments, will convert barrows into observation mounds, without reference to their uses and contents, and without allowing for the ignorance of the period, while the anthropologist often allows his imagination to carry him beyond the limits of actual fact.

One notices, however, that Stevens has no immediate brickbat for the archaeologist, and continues: "Time, and constant careful investigation, will pierce some of the mists which must always shroud the origin of Stonehenge, but the true solution will be for the field-archaeologist, rather than to the weaver of theories or the student in his library."

Over the years more evidence came to light when further excavations were carried out. The site was partially excavated between 1919 and 1926 under the direction of the archaeologist Colonel William Hawley. This period of excavation has subsequently been much criticized for the lack of care which its director showed. In a forthright condemnation, R. J. C. Atkinson believed it to be "one of the more melancholy chapters in the long history of the monument".

In the early 1950s, Atkinson was himself involved in excavations along with fellow-archaeologists Stuart Piggott and J. F. Stone. It was now that a much clearer picture of the history of the monument began to emerge, and some of Frank Stevens's mists began to disperse.

It was clear that Stonehenge indeed had a long history. The post-Roman dating of Fergusson and Petrie could now be dismissed with certainty. Excavations had given up pottery shards and other artefacts that could be dated with reasonable accuracy to between 1900 to 1700 B.C. It was also realized that if only Lockyer had known a later, more accurate, value for the change in the Sun's obliquity, his astronomical date for Stonehenge would have been 1840 B.C. (give or take 200 years). Piggott and Atkinson showed that the monument had grown and developed in later Neolithic times from an earlier simple arrangement—comparable to other British henge monuments—to one of much greater complexity. What we see today of Stonehenge, therefore, is only the last of several stages of building, which followed one another over a long period of time.

In the building phase now called Stonehenge I, the monument consisted of a circular ditch and inner bank 2 metres (6 feet) high and 96 metres (320 feet) in diameter with a 10·5 metres (35 feet) entrance-gap facing north-east (Fig. 4). From this period there are also several other significant features: the Causeway postholes and other scattered groups of post and stoneholes B, D and E (Fig. 4); the 56 Aubrey holes which were dug and then refilled shortly after, three large postholes later found in the visitors' car park and possibly others of this kind yet undiscovered; the 4 A postholes; probably *timber* posts at Station 92, 94, and Heel Stone 96, with the later erection of stones at Stations 91 and 93. In this period stone D was possibly moved to C position, and stone E was dismantled and subsequently buried along its original position.

In the building phase which followed known as Stonehenge II, a structure which can no longer be seen, several additions and changes came about: the construction of the Avenue; the filling of the Heel-Stone ditch; the arrival at the site of the bluestones (at least for erection), and the beginning of their erection in the form of a double circle at the centre of the enclosure. However, the double-circle scheme was never apparently completed, and only about two-thirds of the stones were placed in position. When they were later removed, the holes were back-filled with tightly packed chalk in preparation for the erection of the later sarsens.

During the building phases of Stonehenge III, the larger sarsen stones arrived on site and were erected as: (a) the 5 trilithons in the form of a horseshoe layout, and (b) a circle of 30 upright stones capped with lintels to form a complete architrave, or connecting ring. The bluestones, dismantled from building phase II, were re-erected to form a circle of 59 to 61 (the precise number is debatable) stones arranged in a circle 2·4 to 2·7 metres (8 to 9 feet) inside the sarsen circle, and a horseshoe layout consisting of 19 stones positioned inside the 5 trilithons. The 59 Y and Z holes were dug and then later allowed to fill up again naturally.

The presence of the mysterious foreign bluestones at Stonehenge had stimulated many speculations over the years. No one could be really sure which agency to invoke: Man or Nature. One thing was certain, no bluestones except for a few tantalizing fragments—associated with remains from the so-called Wessex Culture—have been found in the districts round Stonehenge in modern times; neither do any appear to be incorporated in local buildings or other modern constructions—contrary to frequent reports that this occurs.

Fergusson, back in 1872, believed the old Irish legend for the bluestones to be substantially true and related that this idea was corroborated by geologists because similar stones were well known in Ireland. Fergusson had asked: "Why may we not suppose that these were erected in memory of the kings or others who were buried in front of them?"

Over the years suggestions for the place of origin of the bluestones had ranged from Killare (Kildare?) in Ireland to North Wales, Cornwall, Cumberland, Dartmoor, Shropshire, Brittany and even to Scotland. In 1923, H. H. Thomas of the Geological Survey of Great Britain was able to put an end to the speculations by a remarkable piece of petrological detective work which demonstrated beyond doubt that the stones recognized as foreign to Salisbury Plain had their natural *in-situ* home in a relatively confined area in South Wales. All the harder bluestones—varieties of spotted dolerite or preselite, rhyolite and volcanic ash—could be traced unambiguously to the Prescelly Mountains, while the Altar Stone and other softer foreign stumps likely came from the Cosheston (sandstone) Beds at Milford Haven immediately to the south of the Prescelly Mountains.

Several local Welsh circles composed of bluestones are still standing. Thomas, in his search for the bluestone origins, had carefully sifted the evidence provided by past authors to narrow the field. He noted especially one reference by the Rev. W. Done Bushell who had written that dolmens and remains of stone circles were extremely numerous in the eastern part of the Prescelly Mountains. Bushell had gone as far as describing the southern slopes of the mountains as a "prehistoric Westminster" and "a land of circles". These were clues Thomas could not resist. Petrological evidence in the laboratory proved the rest.

But how did the bluestones and the other foreign stones find their way to Stonehenge? The distance—even as the crow flies—is over 200 kilometres (c. 125 miles). Subsequently, the route and the *modus operandi* of how the bluestones found their way from the Prescellys and Milford Haven to Stonehenge have vexed both the archaeologists and geologists.

Back in Lockyer's time Judd, it will be recalled, opted for the idea of their transport to Salisbury Plain via the mechanism of glacial ice. Thomas claimed—and at least he convinced the archaeologists—that glacial transport could not now be considered a tenable idea. It was Thomas's assertion that subsequent to Judd, more was known about how the various ice advances had affected Southern England. Ice could be ruled out. But if ice could be ruled out, what other mechanisms could accomplish such a radical shift of the bluestones . . .? Thomas believed only Man could be held responsible, and he proposed good reasons why he favoured transport entirely overland.

But why would anyone want to transport stones to Salisbury Plain—an estimated total distance of 270 to 300 kilometres (170 to 180 miles)—when there were plenty of massive sarsens lying about the Downs in the near vicinity of the Stonehenge site? Consensus among archaeologists had it that it seemed probable the South-Wales stones were sacred stones—stones believed by their transporters to possess magical and medicinal properties. Archaeologists speculated that to the primitive minds of the ancient Brits, the bluestones and other foreign stones might indeed seem magical; and after the occasion of some tribal war in which the Salisbury Plain peoples were the victors, the stones of a captured sacred circle in the Prescellys might easily be carried off as a trophy of war to be re-erected at Stonehenge. It looked again as if the yarn spun by that "shameless and saucy liar" Geoffrey of Monmouth might at least have a grain of truth.

The majority of archaeologists, however, rejected Thomas's land route and favoured a more plausible part-water, part-land route. It was more logical that ancient man would choose the longer, but more practical, water route to transport eighty-odd stones, weighing up to four tons apiece. What also seemed certain was that the ancient Brits in the second millennium B.C. had no wheeled transport capable of carrying such loads long distances—none at least that has come down in archaeological record—and again the distance appears too great and the terraine too undulating for manhauled sledges to have been used.

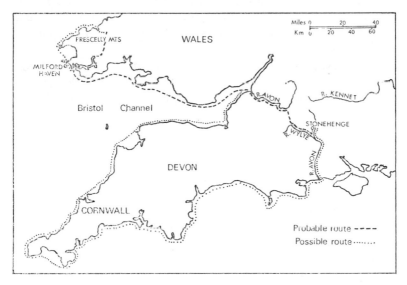

Figure 9 The possible routes by which the bluestones may have been transported (by man) to Stonehenge from the Prescelly Mountains in South Wales.

Much has been written about the possible routes (Fig. 9) and probable methods and techniques employed by ancient man to transport these stones to Salisbury Plain. Some possible modes have even been re-enacted for television audiences. The archaeologists remain unshaken that it was the hand of Man rather than that of Nature which brought them to Stonehenge. Even so, the geological mechanism has not yet been entirely discounted. Contrary to Thomas's assertion that transport by ice could be ruled out, it cannot be so lightly dismissed. If more were known about the sketchy dry-land record of the various stages of the Pleistocene —especially of the Lower and Middle periods—it would be easier to reach a firmer conclusion. In 1971, much to the apparent annoyance of archaeologists, the geologist G. F. Kellaway of the Geological Survey again reargued a very plausible case for ice.

It seems certain that the sarsens incorporated in Stonehenge came from the Marlborough Downs region. If these were in any way transported by Man, then the distance for hauling overland to Stonehenge was not great—a maximum of only 30 kilometres (20 miles). It has been estimated that by the direct overland route one 50-ton sarsen block would require a gang of 250 men to haul it up the steepest inclines (on rollers or sledges), whereas a gang of 50 would suffice on level ground.

Much has also been written about how the great sarsens were lifted in place. The older antiquarians used to marvel that such feats could be performed by primitive peoples. Now we no longer marvel, for it is appreciated that ancient peoples with plenty of available muscle power, large timbers, time, and a modicum of common sense could perform "miracles" *if the social incentive were there.*

In the light of the 1950s' field-work carried out by Piggott, Atkinson and Stone and the acceptance of the idea that the stones were transported to Stonehenge by Man, who then were the builders of Stonehenge, and who was the architect who master-planned its unique arrangements?

The Megalith builders were believed to be Neolithic colonists to Britain who had entered Western Britain from Europe. Gordon Childe—whose thinking influenced the whole school of British archaeology—had formulated a broad chronological system of prehistory which began in Egypt and Mesopotamia. From here there had been a diffusion of peoples and ideas, first through Crete (and perhaps Anatolia), then into the Aegean and Troy, followed by a movement on to Iberia, Italy and East Europe, in turn to France and Central Europe, then finally into Britain and Northern Europe.

In Britain, under this system, the first Megalithic monuments were the Severn-Cotswold tombs believed influenced by diffusion of people and ideas from Iberia. The British and Scandinavian Neolithic were gauged to have begun about 2400 B.C. Thus the Mesolithic period in North-West Europe had supposedly lasted until very recent times.

The first Neolithic farmers in Britain were the Windmill Hill peoples who, after migrating into Britain, were thought to have lived side by side with the then indigenous Britains. The indigenous Britains had arrived in Mesolithic times after the Ice Age when a North Sea landbridge still connected Britain to Europe. It was not until about 6000 B.C. that the vestige landbridge, probably the Straits of Dover, fell to the onslaughts of the sea.

The Windmill Hill peoples, like their Mesolithic predecessors, lived a semi-nomadic life. Yet they were not hunter/food-gatherers, but true pastoralist-farmers who moved from place to place with herds of cattle, raising crops sporadically. The integration of the two peoples gave rise to what Piggott called the Secondary Neolithic. But a really clear picture of what was going on in respects to cultural integration is complicated by the arrival in Britain in waves from the east of the so-called Beaker cultures— aptly named for their distinctive drinking vessels. It was the Beaker people who introduced the practice of individual burial under round barrows which was a break from the older British tradition of collective long-barrow burials (Windmill Hill people—"long headed, long barrows"; Beaker people—"round headed, round barrows"). The Beaker people opened up trade routes to Ireland; and if it were the Beaker people who had transported the Welsh bluestones to Stonehenge, it seemed they had the necessary maritime know-how to accomplish this.

The Beaker people were also attributed with the earlier Megalithic architecture of stone circles and the henge-type monuments of the kind where a stone circle lies outside an enclosing earthwork. Thus the construction of the great circles of Avebury was considered Beaker influenced as was Stonehenge from building phase Stonehenge II.

Out of this unclear, nebulous mist of primary cultures and secondary cultures, superimposed by waves of new arrivals—distinguished by archaeologists by different pottery wares and modes of burial—finally evolved the more clearly focused Wessex Culture, demarking the Early Bronze Age in Britain. It was from this time that burials are numerous in the archaeological record—

some of which have great richness in grave goods. Inside these Early Bronze-Age barrows are found heroic-age warrior chieftains of the kind that have come down to us in the semi-historical sagas in late Saxon and Viking times. Also in these barrows are gold ornaments and strong artefactual evidence of regular trade with Mediterranean cultures. Gold was probably imported from Ireland, Europe or the Mediterranean, but the strongest artefactual evidence of Mediterranean trade lay in the finding of the so-called faience beads—small blue beads with brilliant colour. These were believed to be of Egyptian manufacture, and the clear inference was that they reached Britain by an established sea-route trade.

All the evidence fitted a picture of a well-to-do British farming society with the command of labour and skilled craftsmen necessary for the construction of an Early Bronze-Age monument of the complexity of Stonehenge III.

But? the archaeologists asked. Could the essentially barbarian peoples of the Wessex Culture *alone* conceive a monument as grand as Stonehenge III?

Stonehenge is closely associated with a cluster of Wessex-period round barrows of the Early Bronze Age. They had been dated as Early Bronze Age from their apparent links with Mycenae *c.* 1550 to 1400 B.C. Gordon Childe had repeatedly stressed there was strong evidence for cultural contacts between the Wessex Culture and Mycenae, "... resemblances that may be individually fortuitous, but their cumulative effects are too remarkable to dismiss".

Could then the final stage of Stonehenge III have been inspired and master-minded by a builder in stone from Mycenaean Greece? Atkinson, in his book *Stonehenge* (1956) concluded :

It seems to me that to account for those exotic and unparalleled features of Stonehenge one *must* assume the existence of influence from the only contemporary European culture in which *architecture*, as distinct from mere construction, was already a living tradition; that is the Mycenaean and Minoan civilizations of the central Mediterranean. . . .

An unexpected and exciting discovery, which at the time appeared to clinch the very plausible theory linking Stonehenge with Mycenaean Greece, was a dagger carving found accidentally by Atkinson while photographing one of the sarsen monoliths in

July 1953. While staring at the surface of sarsen 53 through the camera view-finder, he was suddenly confronted with the shadowy outline of a dagger blade, down-pointed, and a single-bladed axe, edge uppermost, engraved in the stone (Plate 14). Quickly moving his eye from the camera, he recognized the engravings were real enough and quite unmistakable in the slanting light of the afternoon Sun.

It is related that when Atkinson called over his colleague J. F. S. Stone to see the marks for himself, Stone became so excited that he bit his pipe and broke a tooth; which, although unfortunate, does at least prove that some archaeologists are not as phlegmatic as their books would often lead us to believe.

To Atkinson and Stone the axe engraving looked very familar. Irish weapons were practically identical with it, and axes like it had been found in the Wessex barrows near by. The hilted dagger was even more intriguing. About 30 centimetres long, it was of a type found in the shaft graves of Mycenae. Could the dagger carving itself be of direct Mycenaean origin?—Perhaps the trademark signature of the well-travelled builder himself?

This unexpected discovery of carvings led to other discoveries. People began to take another close look at the sarsens. But carvings of a kind were not unknown at Stonehenge. There is hardly a stone that does not bear at least one inscription, and one could catalogue an interesting miscellany of graffiti left by visitors in recent historic times. Perhaps the best known was the one being photographed when Atkinson spotted the dagger and axe. This is a deep-cut engraving, positioned slightly above eye level, and probably one of the earliest of the modern inscriptions which reads IOH:LVD: DEFERRE (Johannes Ludovicus [or John Louis] de Ferre). When one now sees this engraving and the prominent dagger and axe engraving below it (Plate 14), one really wonders how Atkinson's discovery escaped detection so long.

But there are several other axe engravings on this stone, shown with the cutting edge upwards as most photographs reveal (Plate 14). Some of these carvings (perhaps sky-god cult symbols) have been subject to severe weathering. In addition there are traces of vague, more conjectural markings, too affected by weathering to be deciphered with any certainty.

Atkinson relates how a few days after the first discovery the ten-year-old son of one of his helpers found the first of an even larger

G

group of axe carvings on the outer face of stone 4 (Plate 15). During the following week R. S. Newall, veteran Stonehenge excavator of the 1920s, discovered a number of shallow, very weathered axe carvings on the same stone, plus another three more clearly defined axes on stone 3.

Indeed, the first discovery by Atkinson was only a beginning and served to alert everyone to the possible existence of additional carvings. Several other traces of axes, daggers and more vague rectangular designs have been noted since. Stones known to contain designs include 3, 4, 23 and 57. According to Atkinson, stone 156, which carries a carving once claimed to be prehistoric, was actually cut by an itinerant stone-worker in about 1829. Another interesting carving is one discovered by Newall on the face of stone 57; this supposedly resembles carvings that occur in Brittany chambered tombs known as "shield-escutcheons". The inscription is now very indistinct and has been almost entirely worn away by continued abrasion from visitors' footwear.

But in spite of the modern field-work of Piggott, Atkinson and Stone that threw fresh light on the construction sequences at Stonehenge, there remained many inexplicable puzzles. For example, what purpose had the Aubrey holes and the Z and Y holes served? Were there still undetected significances in the four outlying Station stones? The Heel Stone and Avenue directions were accepted as astronomically—or leastwise seasonally—important, but there was little or no evidence round the monument to provide for more than the simplistic picture of it being some kind of prehistoric ceremonial centre linked with the summer (and winter) solstice and the quarters of the year important in cultus ritual and the farming calendar.

8 Secrets of the Sarsens

Few discoveries at Stonehenge had been as exciting as the findings of the prehistoric carvings. There could be no doubt that they were absolutely genuine and not the result of some hoaxer like the nineteenth-century Swedish-American farmer who tried to fool historians and archaeologists with the infamous rune inscription on the Kensington Stone.

The prehistoric carvings at Stonehenge were especially significant to those archaeologists who firmly believed that the final Stonehenge-III construction phase owed much, perhaps all, to cultural diffusion. J. F. S. Stone, writing about Stonehenge in 1958, remarked: ". . . I feel sure that we must look to the literal civilizations of the Mediterranean for the inspiration and indeed for the actual execution under the hands and eyes of some trader or mission from that region." No one could then imagine that less than a decade later some new astronomical theories would upset the archaeolgical apple-cart.

Gerald Hawkins published his spectacular ideas appropriately in *Nature,* in the issue dated 26 October 1963. *Nature,* since Lockyer's incumbency as editor, had announced many spectacular and dramatic discoveries in the fields of science. Hawkins's ideas brought an immediate and interested response from all quarters of the globe. Stonehenge was no longer of only parochial interest. If someone had a new theory—a revolutionary theory—and that person was a respectable scientist and an astronomer to boot, this was hot scientific news, not fare to be confined to the academic journals but also grist for the popular news media.

Hawkins's first paper in *Nature* set out to show that not only were Lockyer's ideas regarding Stonehenge as an indicator of the summer solstice correct, but this was only the tip of the iceberg. Many of the alignments could be shown to indicate, quite unambiguously, rising and setting points of the Moon in its rather complicated path round the ecliptic, in addition to which there were several other highly significant Sun and Moon marker-points hidden in the monument.

Hawkins had begun his researches assuming a construction date of 1500 B.C. for Stonehenge. Then, with the aid of an IBM 7090 electronic computer, he processed all the relevant data to determine significant horizon positions for the rising and setting points of the Sun, Moon, stars and planets for epoch 1500 B.C. Following this, the various positions of stones, holes and midpoints were measured, using as a basis the then existing survey of the monument published by the British Ministry of Public Buildings and Works which has a scale of 20 feet to 1 inch.

A total of 165 recognized positions were fed into the computer. Primed with the co-ordinates of each one, the computer was commanded to perform three tasks.

1. Extend lines through 120 pairs of surveyed positions both ways (thus 120 x 2 = 240 positions).
2. Find the true azimuth of these lines (viz. the angle measured from true north).
3. Work out the declination at which these lines extending outwards would intercept the skyline.

This was, of course, only a more rigorous extension of Lockyer's basic methods. Nevertheless, since there are more than an estimated 27,000 or so possible alignments at Stonehenge, it can be seen that without resort to the modern computer the task of calculation is a Herculean one.

Hawkins recounted his methods and ideas in his subsequent book *Stonehenge Decoded* (1965). He relates that the programme for the computer took about one day to work out. The basic card information was transferred to magnetic tape, and then the computer took over. . . . In less than a minute the machine had its answer. Hawkins estimated that a human calculator would have been kept busy for about four months in performing the same task.

The results from the computer looked very interesting. It was immediately apparent that the declinations provided by the computer showed a large number of duplications. Hawkins's brain was set buzzing. Were they significant? What did the repeated (approximate) declinations $+29°$, $+24°$ and $+19°$ and their southern-sky analogues $-29°$, $-24°$ and $-19°$ imply?

First Hawkins and his assistants checked the planets. He noted that Venus was the only one which might show declinations of this kind. However, since Venus's maximum declination is $\pm 32°$, this seemed too big a discrepancy (from $\pm 29°$) to provide a convincing fit. Saturn was then tried and found equally wanting, for its maximum declinations are only $\pm 26°$. The rest of the brighter planets were also unlikely candidates.

Next to be considered were the brighter stars. . . .

Hawkins, of course, was familiar with the detail of Lockyer's work at Stonehenge and elsewhere, and it was inevitable that some of the stars frequently cited by Lockyer such as Capella, Arcturus, Sirius, Canopus, Vega and Alpha Centauri would be on the list of stars checked out. Since Hawkins had adopted 1500 B.C. as the chosen epoch for investigation, it was necessary to compute the various star declinations backwards in time (because of the effects of precession). But this done, he again drew a blank. Nowadays Arcturus has a significant declination of $+19°$ 21′, but in 1500 B.C. it was about $+42°$; Sirius now has a declination of $-16°$ 39′, but in 1500 B.C. it was $-19°$. Although at first glance Sirius's declination in 1500 B.C. looked significant and a close fit to 1500 B.C., Hawkins considered that this particular fit was pure chance. None of Lockyer's other stars gave significant declinations.

If then the planets *and* the stars could be discounted, what about the Sun? Hawkins had already suspected that some of the extreme declinations would roughly fit the Sun. This was to be anticipated in view of the long established (approximate) midsummer solstice alignment. But what about the Moon? Hawkins relates he now went back to the computer, this time to determine the extreme declinations of both the Sun and the Moon for epoch 1500 B.C. and the extreme directions (on the Stonehenge horizon) of their risings and settings at this time.

It was not known of course—except for Lockyer's ideas—how the Stonehenge observers in ancient times might have interpreted risings and settings of the Sun and Moon. Lockyer had been accused by his critics of arranging the facts in an arbitrary fashion to suit his different theories. At Stonehenge he considered that first gleam (the top edge of the Sun) had been the ancients' chosen point for measuring, while at Karnak he had defined it as the moment when the Sun's centre (half orb) reached the horizon. Hawkins believed that this problem might also be resolved by the computer.

The Sun has two extreme positions for rising, one at the winter and the other at the summer solstice. To an observer at Stonehenge these shifts show as a shift from a true azimuth 129° at the midwinter (sunrise) solstice when the Sun's declination is −23°·5 to a true azimuth 51° at midsummer solstice when the Sun's declination is +23°·5. Thus in *six months* the sunrise (and sunset) point swings along the horizon at Stonehenge by 78° (Fig. 10). Because the Moon's orbit is inclined to the ecliptic (the apparent path of the Sun) by a little over 5°, the Moon's rising and setting points show even greater extremes of swing along the horizon. These swings are further complicated by the slow regression of the lunar nodes over a period of 18·61 years (Fig. 10).

All these factors Hawkins took into account when the computer was reprogrammed. This new task was performed by the computer in a few seconds. When Hawkins and his assistants compared the figures, he relates that they were left with no doubts. The supposition that the Stonehenge alignments followed the paths of the Sun and Moon in relation to their horizon movements was "all but complete".

Hawkins confessed that he was prepared for some Stonehenge Sun correlations but not for a *total* Sun correlation; neither had *he* suspected that there might also be a total Moon correlation as a bonus. Lockyer had never once hinted at a Moon correlation for Stonehenge or any other British or French alignments—and Hawkins least expected any. There were broad hints in the apocryphal Druid literature which might have alerted someone. A post-Lockyer reference was provided by Vice-Admiral Boyle Somerville. In a paper in the *Journal of the British Astronomical Association* dated 1912 he had suggested that there was a lunar alignment in the Callanish monument in Scotland.

Unknown to Hawkins, others had been hard at work on deciphering Megalithic alignments. Over the years Alexander Thom had followed up both Lockyer's and Somerville's earlier work but

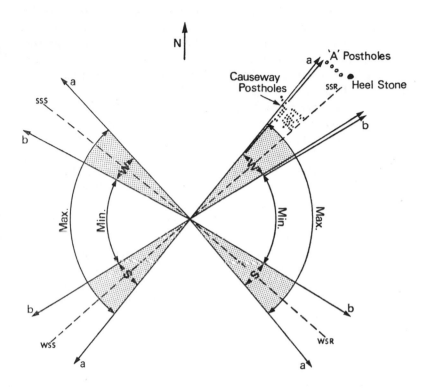

Figure 10   Maximum and minimum rising and setting points (azimuths) traced out on the Stonehenge horizons by the Sun and Moon. The pecked lines mark the Sun's horizon azimuths at summer solstice rising (SSR); summer solstice setting (SSS); winter solstice rising (WSR); winter solstice setting (WSS).

Moon risings and settings are more complex. The shaded sectors (a–b) show the maximum limits of Full Moon risings and settings in winter and summer, i.e. winter (W) Full Moon rising (north-east); winter (W) Full Moon setting (north-west); summer (S) Full Moon rising (south-east); summer (S) Full Moon setting (south-west). Because the nodes of the Moon's orbit regress in a cycle of 18.61 years, winter moonrise beginning at 'a' will, in about nine years, have shifted to 'b'; about nine years later it will be back at 'a', completing the nodal cycle. Note that the corresponding summer moonrise will trace out similar 'a' to 'b' and 'b' to 'a' movements. The double line shown in the Heel-Stone sector takes into account the difference in choice of azimuth between first gleam and fully risen (*see* Figure 7), plus minor lunar perturbations.

with little or no publicity. By the 1950s Thom had come to the firm conclusion that many stone circles and groups of stones, in addition to other astronomical and novel metrical features, showed positive lunar orientations. His coverage, however, had not included Stonehenge, and he did not examine this monument in detail until 1974.

Hawkins's immediate rival was C. A. ('Peter') Newham, a British amateur astronomer who had a year or two previous to Hawkins's work looked into both lunar and solar alignments at Stonehenge. Yet by one of those quirks of fate that frequently beset scientific discovery, his work was ignored until Hawkins's first paper appeared in *Nature* and re-stirred the long-dormant Stonehenge astro-debate.

Newham's involvement with Stonehenge began in 1957 when after a casual visit to the monument with his wife he subsequently became intrigued by Lockyer's ideas. An acquaintance advised him to read Atkinson's doubts about Lockyer's findings which Atkinson set out in his Stonehenge book. Having read these, Newham was soon set on a fresh tack about possible new approaches to the whole subject.

About the time Newham retired, he also became a widower. After forty-six years as a gas-industry engineer, he found himself at a loose end. He was now about the same age as Lockyer when he began to look at Stonehenge back in 1901. As an engineer himself, Newham decided to start some preliminary field-work at Stonehenge to recheck Lockyer's axis and various alignments. It was during his first sortie he realized that one of the main tasks would be to settle doubtful measurements and examine the differences shown up in various published plans of the monument which confused the arguments.

During the following three years, travelling on each occasion from his home in Yorkshire, he visited Stonehenge many times—always accompanied by his old transit theodolite. As time went by, his practical knowledge about Stonehenge increased. He was considered by the wardens officiating at the monument as just a friendly eccentric like the scores of others who periodically visited the place with bees in their bonnets about this or that theory.

One day Newham began to suspect that the alignment Station 92 to a point known as disturbance G was positively aligned to the extreme moonrise. It was now that one of those odd quirks entered the story. Because his ideas and his arithmetic were only tentative, he wrote to a friend—a professional astronomer at the London University Observatory—for confirmation of his own calculated positions. In the letter he requested what the true azimuth of the Moon should be for this position. In reply to his query the figure was given as 45°. Newham was disappointed, for this was several degrees different from a figure he had in mind to fit his ideas. But, as he later recalled, being only an amateur astronomer, who was he to argue with a professional? He now temporarily put aside the Moon-alignment ideas and began to look into possible Sun and star alignments.

He was now corresponding with several people over various topics to do with Stonehenge. In November 1962 he received a list of possible stellar, Sun and Moon risings from an amateur astronomer friend, F. Addey, then Director of the Solar Section of the British Astronomical Association. The list was composed of risings which might have been observable in early times over the Heel Stone. It had occurred to Newham that the Heel Stone might have been involved by night as well as the rising of the Sun at the time of the summer solstice round 21 June.

It was late evening when Newham opened the letter and casually cast his eyes over the list of risings just before retiring to bed. There was no immediate reaction, but for some inexplicable reason he found sleep impossible that night; then subconsciously his brain began mulling over those numbers. . . . They kept passing through his mind; one in particular seemed vaguely familiar, but yet so elusive. Then suddenly the mist cleared. Around midnight the problem of his previous anomalous Moon alignment had been solved; the figure quoted him by his friend at London University should have read 40°·5 and not 45°·0. Clearly a stupid unchecked typing error had misdirected the whole of his subsequent work. Now fully aroused, all ideas of sleep that night were forgotten. By 4 a.m. not only was the alignment 92-G confirmed but also two new Sun alignments.

Newham, who along the way had been much influenced by Atkinson's Stonehenge book and by Newall's role in pre-World-War-II excavations, wrote immediately to both of them to present his results. Newall had always had an eye open for possible astronomical significances at Stonehenge. Earlier he had suggested that the most significant alignment might be midwinter sunset—rather than midsummer sunset—and he was sceptical of all but New-ham's idea for an equinox alignment. Atkinson, however, was in general accord with all the ideas and advised Newham to seek publication, suggesting *Antiquity* as the appropriate journal.

By acting on Atkinson's well-meaning but misguided advice, Newham blundered. Had he, like Boyle Somerville and Alexander Thom, chosen to submit his first paper to the *Journal of the British Astronomical Association*, the paper most certainly would have been accepted by its editor as a sound, original contribution from one of the Association's well-known members.

As it was, an outline communication setting out his results was duly submitted to Glyn Daniel, Editor of *Antiquity*, along with a query whether Daniel would be willing to accept a more extended treatment. Daniel himself was keenly interested in the whole Megalithic problem and then had a standard book in print. New-ham sat back to await reaction. But for two months Newham's communication apparently languished on the Editor's desk before, at long last, Newham received a letter rejecting it. In reply Daniel wrote that since he was no astronomer, he did not properly under-stand it—but in any case he did not believe it suitable material for his journal. . . . Little did Daniel realize that material of this kind would soon be *forcing* its way onto the pages of *his* journal. What is still unclear is whether or not Daniel, while fearlessly and honestly admitting—as an archaeologist—his inability to judge its astronomical merits, had ever submitted it to a referee who could assess it. Ironically, he had only to walk next door to the premises of the Royal Astronomical Society and the British Astronomical Association, or across the yard of Burlington House to the Royal Society to locate any one of a score of men who could have refereed it in a couple of days.

Newham himself always felt that his communication was re-jected simply because he was an amateur astronomer rather than a man of recognized academic standing. It is likely, however, it was because he was an astronomer of *any* kind. For although now dead for almost half a century, the nightmare *bête noire* spectre of Lockyer and his Druids still haunted the chambers of the Society of Antiquaries at Burlington House, W 1.

In his disappointment Newham still overlooked the obvious of sending the material to the very Association that would have welcomed it. Back in Leeds, where Newham was active in the University Astronomical Society and had served in the office of President, he now openly discussed his ideas with astronomical friends. One of them, the Science Correspondent of the *Yorkshire Post*, was sufficiently impressed that Newham was on to something original and as a result wrote up a popular version of Newham's work as a three-column article which appeared in the pages of this influential but provincial North-Country daily on 16 March 1963, a full seven months before Hawkins's own original paper in *Nature*.

To satisfy journalistic taste, Newham's work was written up under the eye-catching title : "The Mystery of Hole G" (page 100). The subject title is still relevant because archaeologists, particularly Newall, have good reason to doubt that this hole (among several others) was man-made. But hole G was not the fundamental issue raised by the article. What it set out to show was that the Station stones could be used to indicate several alignments—particularly lunar ones.

Newham had discovered an equinox alignment 94 to stonehole C, but he had also noted that a line extended from mound 94 to 91 appeared to coincide with the point on the horizon where the Moon rises at its most southerly point during the 18·61-year nodal cycle. Conversely, the line from 92 to 93 marked the moonset at its most northerly setting point. It was Newham's belief that these two lunar alignments were significant because of the curious fact that the main sarsen circle is about 1 metre (3 feet) out of true centre with the Aubrey holes. Had their centres been concentric, the 92-93 sight line would have been obscured. This off-centre puzzle had long been a contentious discussion point among archaeologists.

Newham believed that the controversial G hole (possibly a natural hole or a hole left by the rotted stump or a shrub or tree) *should* be taken as significant, for a 94 to G alignment marks the rising Sun on the shortest day of the year. Also mound 92 to G marks the moonrise at its most northerly point.

Thus it was Newham's contention that six of the eight major solar/lunar events of the year could be accounted for within the theory. But speculating further (and speculation is a genuine and necessary scientific tool if handled in a disciplined way), Newham introduced a hypothetical marker hole in the unexcavated part of

The Mystery of Hole G

BY DOUGLAS EMMOTT

Attention this week has once again been focused on Stonehenge, where one of the uprights was blown down in a gale. In this article, The Yorkshire Post Science Correspondent discusses an amateur astronomer's intriguing theories which may add a new chapter to the story of Stonehenge.

Mr. Peter Newham: A new theory about Stonehenge.

STONEHENGE, that mysterious monument which rises above Salisbury Plain, may be a little less inscrutable than had been supposed. An amateur astronomer, Mr. Peter Newham, 63, of Tadcaster, has formulated an intriguing hypothesis which, if proven, might open up whole new fields of inquiry in a subject which has yielded very little significant new information since the last major excavation nearly 40 years ago.

If Mr. Newham's line of reasoning is sound, the positions of certain hitherto inexplicable features of Stonehenge would be explained For the purposes of this inquiry the plan of Stonehenge given here is reduced to the elements bearing upon the new theory.

In 1846, the Rev. E. Duke discovered that the North mound 94 lined up with a stone numbered 93 at the last light of the setting sun on the shortest day of the year. Conversely, a line drawn from the South mound (92) to stone 91 aligned with the rising sun on the longest day of the year.

It was discovered, too, that the axis of the Sarsen stone circle was similarly aligned. In fact, the positions of sunrise and sunset are slightly different today owing to the progressive shift of the earth's axis.

So much, then, is established. What follows is speculation. On several occasions in the past few years Mr. Newham has visited the site and made careful observations of his own.

The first remarkable discovery he made was that a line drawn from mound 94 to 91 would appear to coincide with the point on the horizon where the moon rises at its most southerly point during its 19-year cycle.

Conversely, the line from 92 to 93 marks the moonset at its most Northerly setting point. The suggestion that these two alignments are of significance is bolstered by the curious fact that the main Sarsen circle of stones is about a yard off-centre with the outer Aubrey circle of burial holes.

Had it been quite concentric, the 92-93 sighting would have been obscured. Is this the reason for the off-centredness which has puzzled generations of archæologists?

It must be remembered that the layout of Stonehenge has been drawn up generally with remarkable precision. The ancient architects were evidently knowledgeable geometricians: indeed, the feat of measurement would tax a modern surveyor with the most up-to-date instruments and techniques.

Unusual feature

From this point, attention is turned to another unusual feature. This is catalogued as "hole" G, the middle of three equally spaced "holes" lying to the East and just beyond the Aubrey circle, and for which there is no convincing explanation.

Most Stonehenge authorities

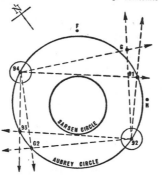

have dismissed disturbances as natural or "shrub-holes." Their disconcerting symmetry and the absence of similar features within the whole of the area that has been uncovered have prompted doubts in more cautious minds.

Mr Newham has noted that a line drawn from 94 to G appears to mark the rising sun on the shortest day of the year. Mound 92 to G marks the moonrise at its most Northerly point.

Thus, six of the eight major solar/lunar events of the year are apparently accounted for within the theory. To complete the octet, Mr. Newham has postulated the existence of a further marker hole in the unexcavated part of the site, about 16 yards South of 93. This he has provisionally designated G2.

Now, a line drawn from 92 to G2 would mark the setting sun on the longest day, while 94 to G2 would mark the moon set on its most Southerly point. Thus, the hypothesis has the added merit of inviting confirmation. If the hypothetical G2 should, in fact, be discovered the possibility of coincidence could be virtually eliminated. The key which now seems to fit the lock would surely turn.

Advanced culture

It would seem, therefore, that Stonehenge was a far more comprehensive calendar in stone than has been supposed. This, in turn, would suggest that the builders of the later portions of the monument were of a more advanced culture than the native inhabitants of Britain at that time says Mr. Newham. There is supporting archæological evidence for this view.

A few years ago, there would have been no difficulty in obtaining permission to search for positive confirmation of the existence of G2. One would simply have dug about the point indicated and sought the necessary proof.

Today, however, archæologists tread with infinite care. In the past, crude pickaxe excavating has destroyed a wealth of detailed information which modern science would have been capable of deciphering. Such brutal methods have wrought such havoc with the "shrub-holes," for example, that it is now almost impossible to determine their real significance even with advanced techniques.

Reluctant to dig

Conscious of this fact and realising that future generations of investigators will read much greater meaning into undisturbed evidence than we might hope to do, the custodians of Stonehenge are reluctant to dig. Nearly one half of the site remains virtually unexplored below ground and only in exceptional circumstances will the Ministry of Works sanction further excavation.

It is conceivable, however, that archæological advisers will recommend a search for Mr. Newham's ghost-hole, G2 by preliminary above-ground detection methods. Encouraging soundings would indicate a call for spade and trowel—and, perhaps, the opening of a new chapter in the story of Stonehenge.

the site about 10·5 metres (35 feet) south of 93 which he provisionally designated G2 (page 100). From this the hypothetical alignment 92 to G2 would mark the setting Sun on the longest day,
while the assumed alignment of 94 to G2 would mark the moonset
on its southerly point. By raising the possibility of a significant point
hidden at G2, Newham believed that if such an alignment position
were later discovered by excavation, the chance of sheer coincidence having influenced the arrangement of Stonehenge alignments could be very nearly eliminated.

Atkinson, following discussions with Newham about this idea,
searched for G2 using a primitive, but effective, surface-bumping
technique (known as bosing). A hidden cavity below the ground
(an old stonehole or posthole) readily shows by a change in sound
pitch when a heavy hammer or similar tool is bumped above it
and across it. Later Atkinson tried probing and a resistivity survey,
but nothing was found in Newham's designated position. Newham,
however, was correct in his intuition about looking for a southerly
moonset point. . . . Although it still appears he was wrong about
the particular hypothetical 92 to G2, such a true azimuth exists
elsewhere in the monument which later finds confirmed.

The G2 ghost hole drew attention to the point that only half
the site had been excavated. The remaining half—except for
bosing—was *terra incognita* below surface level. It was known
that only in very exceptional circumstances would the Ministry of
Works, who administered the monument, wave the embargo on
further excavation. Field-archaeologists of post-World War II
were still embarrassed by the crudity of the methods of their nineteenth-century and pre-war colleagues whose excavation and recording techniques often left a lot to be desired. In the future,
some believe traditional field-excavation may be superseded;
newer sub-surface exploration techniques might resolve problems
without disturbing the valuable—and irreplaceable—four millenniums of debris buried underfoot.

In the same week that Newham's findings appeared in the *Yorkshire Post*, Stonehenge had been in the news following the collapse
of one of the sarsen uprights in a gale. The collapse of the sarsen
attracted wide comment in the media, but Newham's work created
not a ripple of response. The seminal message that the sarsens of

Stonehenge perhaps formed part of a complex of stones of an advanced prehistoric culture, perhaps unique to Britain, had fallen on very deaf provincial ears.

The lack of interest was surprising. What was even more surprising was that Fred Hoyle, himself a Yorkshireman and a regular reader of the *Yorkshire Post* (and soon to become deeply involved with the new theories), admitted later that somehow he too had overlooked Newham's intriguing article.

Newham was again bitterly disappointed at the lack of response. But convinced that his ideas were sound, he did what no professional literary adviser would have recommended—he decided, at his own expense, to print and publish his findings in full.

Yet even now the Fates were still against him. A local printer promised delivery of the booklets ready for sale by June 1963. Three days after receipt of Newham's manuscript, the print shop was razed to the ground by fire. Although new premises were promptly found, it was not until late October (three days before Hawkins's paper "Stonehenge Decoded" appeared in *Nature*) that Newham received the first galley pulls for correction. Newham's booklet, *The Enigma of Stonehenge and its Astronomical and Geometrical Significance*, finally saw light early in 1964.

On the same day that Hawkins's paper appeared in *Nature*, the whole world knew about the new Stonehenge theories, and his ideas were given the widest publicity by the press, radio and television. Atkinson, recognized as the chief authority on Stonehenge theories, was asked by the media for his comments, but surprisingly failed to mention Newham's work. It was not Atkinson's fault, however. He did later apologize to Newham in a letter, giving the reason that the TV interviewer had failed to ask a previously agreed leading question. Such indeed is the spontaneous method by which fact and truth reaches a wider public in the modern age!

Nevertheless, Hawkins's own work was highly original, and although following up the same basic ideas as Newham, he had taken them much further which he was able to do mainly because of his superior technological resources. He had gone much further than Newham by citing additional alignments defined by midpoint gaps in the sarsen trilithons—a doubtful addition that was later to engage him in much contention with dissenting archaeologists.

With the help of the computer, Hawkins and his team had verified several puzzling Stonehenge alignments. The ±24° declination of the Sun was there, but more frequently were the very significant ±29° and the ±19° extreme declinations traced out by the moon during its 18·61-year swing round the ecliptic. Hawkins and his team found much beyond their earliest expectations: to a mean accuracy of 1° they claimed they had found twelve Sun correlations; and to a mean accuracy of 1°·5 twelve Moon correlations. Hawkins related that following up the initial idea which had occurred to him during a visit to Stonehenge as an ordinary tourist with his wife (echoing Newham's own visit), the research was done over the course of a single year : ten hours were spent on measuring charts; twenty hours preparing the computer programme; and one minute of computer time with the IBM 7090. Statistically, Hawkins believed that there was less than one chance in a hundred million that the alignments were the result of chance.

Hawkins assumed that the Station stones belonged to the Stonehenge-I building phase. But this included in the Stonehenge-I chronology did not meet with wide acceptance among archaeologists. In reckoning his alignments, he had rather surprisingly missed 94-stonehole C, detected by Newham, which is most certainly a Sun equinoctial line (due east about 21 March, 21 September). A fundamental difference between Hawkins's alignments and those of Newham's was over the old question of what part of the orb of the Sun and Moon does a Stonehenge alignment refer to (Fig. 7b)? Hawkins believed his computer studies showed that the critical point of sighting was when the full orb of the Sun and Moon was tangent to an artificial horizon, while Newham based his alignments (more plausibly) on the first and last gleams as seen on the actual horizon at the time of rising or setting. Acceptance of one idea in preference to another has the effect of suggesting some alignments in a reverse direction.

It was Hawkins's involvement with the sarsen architecture of Stonehenge which archaeologist critics found most difficult to accept. Hawkins had been persuaded early on that the five trilithons forming the central horseshoe were most likely intended to frame the rising or setting of the Sun and Moon at the winter and/or summer solstice. Indeed, he recalled that when he first visited the monument as a tourist in June 1961, he was struck by the fact that it was impossible to see through all three of the narrow openings of the surviving trilithons from any single point. Since he believed this violated what he supposed to be traditional architectural design, it immediately suggested that the trilithons were intended primarily to fix viewing lines. Thus it was this particular facet of Stonehenge which had been the very root of Hawkins's own motivation in trying to unlock the monument's hidden secrets.

9 Megaliths and Masterminds

Although the whole of Stonehenge had now been given an astronomical basis, influential British archaeologists like Atkinson and Jacquetta Hawkes were not the least bit convinced by the evidence put forward by Hawkins. They believed that the whole idea advanced by him seemed much too fanciful and totally beyond the intellectual capabilities of the so-called barbarian races who had inhabited the British Isles during the prehistoric period. The conflict of ideas between archaeologists and astronomers—the unfinished argument which had been smouldering dormantly like some quiescent volcano since Lockyer's day—suddenly boiled over in print.

Hawkins's article in *Nature* kindled response from all quarters. The archaeologists who were familiar with Stonehenge were largely hostile, but some were sympathetic. Newall, although not totally convinced about many of the ideas, nevertheless felt that both Hawkins and Newham were on the right track. Hawkins seemed to have missed several important references in the older writings which *might* refer to Stonehenge, in particular the long-familiar Greek legend about the mysterious island of Hyperborea. Lockyer had referred briefly to the legend, but since his time it had become a much hackneyed theme in Stonehenge literature.

The legend surrounds a so-called lost *History of the Hyperboreans* and is quoted by Diodorus Siculus in his own *History (V)*. But in many respects Diodorus is an unreliable source of ancient history, and his "factual" tales are occasionally on a par with those of Geoffrey of Monmouth.

Diodurus quotes Hecataeus of relating that

in the north opposite the land of the Celts, there exists in the Ocean an island not smaller than Sicily situated under the constellation of The Bear and inhabited by a race known as the Hyperboreans [viz. 'a race beyond the north wind'] who worshipped the Sun-god Apollo.

In brief, Diodorus tells us that the country was fertile and produced two harvests each year. This certainly does not pin down any particular country, for even as far north as Norway two harvests a year of certain crops are feasible.

It is related that Leto, Apollo's mother, was born on this mysterious island, and for this reason Apollo was honoured above all other gods. On their island the Hyperboreans erected a sacred precinct to Apollo and a temple, spherical in shape (Stonehenge?). From an astronomical point of view Diodorus's remarks are more interesting, for they refer to the appearance of the Moon, as viewed from the island where it seemed to be only a short distance from the Earth. The most significant gleaning from Diodorus is that the god visited the island every nineteen years. This was likely an oblique reference by Diodorus to the Metonic cycle (the "year of Meton")—well known to Greeks and Babylonians since the fifth century (*see page 38*)

When the god appeared, he supposedly played on an instrument known as a cithara (a kind of lyre) and danced continuously through the vernal equinox until the rising of the Pleiades. The supervisors (astronomer-priests) of the sacred precinct were known as Boreales, and succession was maintained by clan nepotism.

For many years the significance of "the god dancing continuously" has been recognized by astro-mythologists as an allusion to some celestial event acknowledged by the ancients. But no one is yet really sure what was implied. George C. Lewis discussed the dances of the stars in his *Astronomy of the Ancients* (1862), and he believed it alluded to the circular "dance" of the circumpolar stars.

Newham trotted out the Hyperborean story at some length in his booklet *The Enigma of Stonehenge*. Newall had discussed the story with Newham. Newall called attention (as others had done before him) to the intriguing possibility that the nineteen bluestones may be associated with the nineteen years of the Metonic cycle. In addition it was suggested that it might be fruitful for someone to work out the position of the Pleiades for the years 2000 to 1000 B.C. so that a check against the Diodorus reference might be made.

F. Addey, who earlier had supplied rising lists to Newham and put him back on course, followed up this suggestion but found that neither the Pleiades nor any number of alternative suggestions—except the Moon—coincided with any stone alignment when seen from the centre of the monument. But the Full Moon *would* appear once every nineteen years over the Heel Stone at the winter solstice about eight minutes after sunset when viewed through the Great Trilithon (55-56).

When Hawkins was made aware of the equinox alignment and he had opportunity to think about the Metonic cycle, he soon saw them as additional vehicles with which to probe further into the mysteries of Stonehenge. He already had a feeling that the title of his first contribution to *Nature* might have been "presumptuous and premature". Newham and Newall had provided more clues; Newall, in particular, when he later posed the highly intriguing question: "Could the Full Moon do something spectacular once every nineteen years at Stonehenge?"

Hawkins returned to his study of the alignments and now included those represented by stoneholes B, C and E (Fig. 4)—taking his cue from Newham's significant equinoctial alignment 94 to C. Stoneholes B, C and E had been omitted from Hawkins's first calculations because he assumed them to be non-unique. As these stoneholes were positioned very close to the Heel Stone centre-line, he had dismissed them on first consideration as only clumsy marker-points to midsummer sunrise.

It was in January 1964, two years after his first calculation, that Hawkins relates he went back to the computer. The machine was fed with new data, and again the answers forthcoming were truly astonishing. The stoneholes B, C, E and F, when aligned with 93 and 94, showed four almost zero errors of declination close to two of the Moon's four recognized midway points (Fig. 11). All the new alignments fell within the same accuracy as the first alignments.

Hawkins was able to confirm some of Lockyer's earlier midway points—located between the solstices and the equinoxes—which Lockyer had interpreted as solar calendar divisions of the year;

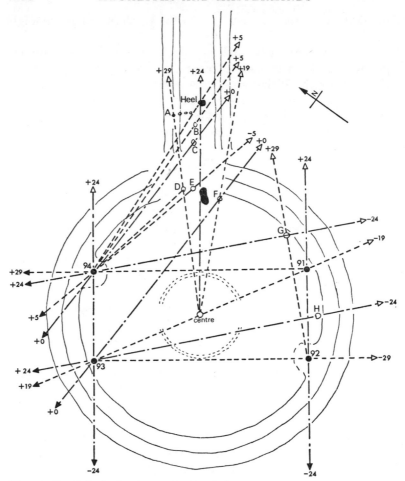

Figure 11 Principal solar and lunar alignments for Stonehenge (after Newham and Hawkins).

but Hawkins himself now believed they indicated the Moon at declination ±19°.

It was now time for Hawkins to cast his thoughts back to the Metonic cycle and the haunting question of a possible spectacular event performed by "something" at Stonehenge once every nineteen years. In the early literature of Stonehenge a Wiltshire clothier, Henry Wansey, writing in 1796, remarked:

> Stonehenge stands in the best position possible for observing heavenly bodies, as there is an horizon nearly three miles distant on

all sides. But till we know the methods by which the ancient Druids calculated eclipses with so much accuracy, as Caesar mentions, we cannot explain the theoretical use of Stonehenge ...

One hundred and sixty-eight years later Hawkins was on the verge of it.

In his first contribution to *Nature*, Hawkins himself had already commented that the monument might prove to be a reliable calendar and might have functioned to signal the danger periods for eclipses of the Sun and Moon. Now Hawkins posed the question : might not the big event at Stonehenge be an eclipse of the Moon over the Heel Stone—or alternatively in the gap of the Great Trilithon? Hawkins, falling back on the "If-I-were-a-horse" comparative method practised earlier by J. G. Frazer, tried to put himself back in the minds of the Megalithic priests whose status in the community might depend on accurate eclipse predictions. . . .

Among celestial phenomena widely observed by the ancients, eclipses, comets and falls of meteorites were the most impressionable. But probably only eclipses were predictable (this disregards some extremely doubtful evidence via Diodorus Siculus that the Chaldeans could predict the returns of comets). It is generally believed that the Chaldeans were the first to discover the art of eclipse-prediction using the so-called Saros method, but they did not succeed in doing so before *c.* 750 B.C. The Saros method is often cited in serious astronomical literature as the method used to predict one of the most famous eclipses in history—the eclipse of Thales now dated 28 May 585 B.C. But the whole episode was a hoax or deliberate fraud. Certainly the eclipse took place, but Thales certainly did not predict it, and the event was only known to him after it had occurred. Indeed—based on known evidence—if the Stonehenge astronomer-priests did succeed in predicting eclipses, they preceded the rest of mankind in doing so by nearly two millenniums.

But several ancient races noted that eclipses of the Sun and Moon are linked together in a certain chain, or sequence, which takes rather longer than eighteen years to run out when the sequence repeats itself *ad infinitum*. The eighteen-year period is known (wrongly) by the name Saros. It is widely—but mistakenly—believed that this was the name given it long ago by the

Chaldean Babylonians. In truth, the word *Saros* in Old Babylonian has a highly ambiguous interpretation and probably is
best described as meaning "a measure". As a number we know
it also equalled 3,600. It was Edmond Halley, the English
astronomer, who made a gaffe about its meaning and assumed
that it was a Babylonian word associated with eclipse cycles.
In spite of repeated protests, the usage has unfortunately per-
sisted into modern times.

There are two kinds of eclipses : solar and lunar. Solar eclipses
occur at the time of New Moon; lunar eclipses at the time of
Full Moon. At these times the Sun, Moon and Earth are aligned
in the same plane.

Because the Moon moves in an orbit round the Earth which
is inclined a little over 5° to the ecliptic (the path of the Sun),
eclipses can only occur when the Moon's path intersects the
ecliptic at the nodes (Fig. 12 upper)

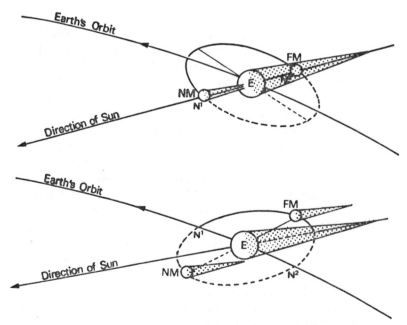

Figure 12   Eclipse occurrences. Owing to the Moon's orbit being inclined
a little over 5° to the ecliptic, eclipses can only occur at New Moon (NM)
and Full Moon (FM) when the line of nodes (N¹–N²) of the Moon's orbit
coincides with the direction of the Sun. (Upper fig.)

A complication in the occurrences of eclipses is introduced because the nodes of the Moon's orbit do not occupy a fixed position but regress (revolve) in a period of 18 years $218\frac{7}{8}$ days (=18·61 years).

To bring about an eclipse of the Sun, two things must combine : (a) the Moon must be at or near one of its nodes, (b) this must be a time when the Moon is also in conjuction with the Sun, twelve or thirteen times a year (the time of New Moon). The Sun only passes through the nodes of the Moon's orbit twice a year (at intervals of 173·31 days)—hence an eclipse of the Sun does not and cannot occur at every New Moon.

The Moon in its monthly course round the Earth completes a revolution in respect to its nodes in 27·5 days, but to get back to conjuction with the Sun it takes 29·5 days. The first period is known as the draconic month (or nodical month), an excellent descriptive name given for reasons we shall come back to. The second period is called the synodical month (or conjunction month).

Those ancient nations who discovered the art of eclipse prediction found that 242 draconic months, 223 complete lunations of the Moon, and 19 returns of the Sun to the same node of the Moon's orbit (known as 19 eclipse years) all occur in the *same time* to within about 11 hours. Thus if the Sun and Moon start together from a node point, it will not be until a lapse of 6,585 days and part of a day they will be found together again very near the same node. Thus eclipses recur in about, *but not quite*, the same regular order every $6,585\frac{1}{3}$ days.

But yet more complications. . . .

Because of the slight time difference amounting to about 11 hours, eclipses will not occur at exactly the same spot on the Earth's surface when the cycle begins to repeat itself after 6,585 plus days, but they will start again at 8 hours longitude (120°) west of the original spot. Because of this and other factors, it is not easy to predict eclipses of the Sun, and it seems extremely unlikely that the ancient races could ever have done so. Eclipses of the Moon, however, are much easier to predict, and unlike total eclipses of the Sun, which are only visible across a very narrow track at any one time, total eclipses of the Moon can be observed anywhere on Earth where the Moon is above the horizon.

The Metonic cycle, cited by Diodorus, refers to another very interesting cycle connected with the Moon. In the fifth century B.C., Meton found that after a lapse of 19 years, the phases of the Moon recurred on the same days of the same months (within about 2 hours). The number 19 is the smallest number of years that is a multiple of the synodical month which equals one complete lunation period, and there are very nearly 235 synodical months in 19 Julian years (one Julian year equals 364·25 mean solar days). The 19-year cycle is quite an accurate one; it is only after 310 Julian years that the computed mean New Moons fall one day earlier than they should. It was this simple Metonic cycle which formed the basis of the calendar of the Seleucid Babylonian empire in antiquity and also the later Jewish and Christian religious calendars, particularly in the computation of Easter. The same cycle also found its way into India where it masqueraded in a different guise. In Europe, during the Middle Ages, this cycle solved all the problems of establishing the dates of the New Moon. It was of great significance to all calendar makers, and the lunar phases shown in the famous *Book of Hours*, made by the brothers Limbourg for the Duc de Berry (*c.* 1400) to help while away his time in church, were all obtained by reference to the Metonic cycle.

The Metonic number 19 became known in the Middle Ages as the Golden Number, for its significant dates were inscribed in gold on public monuments. The Golden Number is simply the number denoting the position of any year in the Metonic 19-year cycle. It is found by adding 1 to a given year and then dividing by 19; the remainder then equals the Golden Number unless the remainder is equal to zero, in which case the Golden Number is 19 (e.g. the Golden Number of 1979 is 4).

We must be clear that the Metonic cycle of 19 years is *not* in itself an eclipse cycle, neither is the 18·61-year nodal period of the Moon. Unfortunately Hawkins (and others), in developing their arguments, confuse the issue by implying that both *are* eclipse cycles. But, of course, we can see that *the number 19* itself is important in eclipses in the Eclipse year, which equals 346·62 days, which equals the interval between successive passages of the Sun through the nodes of the Moon's orbit; and approx-

imately 242 draconic months, which equals 223 lunations, which
equals 19 eclipse years.

Hawkins utilized the cycle of 18·61 years of the lunar nodal
period because he felt that this was very close to the 19-year
Metonic cycle. At Stonehenge, Hawkins noted that during the
lunar nodal period of 18·61 years, the midwinter Full Moon
moved from north maximum declination of +29° at stone D
across the Heel Stone to a north minimum declination of +19°
at stone F, and then back again (Fig. 11). In a similar fashion
the midsummer Full Moon switched back and forth across the
viewing line reckoned through the archway of the Great Central
Trilithon.

Hawkins now fell back on the standard reference work for
eclipses that had occurred between 2000 to 1000 B.C. in order
to find the months in which eclipses of the Sun and Moon had
actually resulted. Using the computer again, he noted that an
eclipse of the Moon or the Sun always occurred when the winter
Full Moon nearest the time of the winter solstice rose above the
Heel Stone. But not more than about half of these eclipses were
actually visible from Stonehenge. Nevertheless, Hawkins believed
that the fact that an eclipse might be visible would be incentive
enough for the astronomer-priests to mark the occasion of the
winter moonrise above the Heel Stone as an eclipse-warning
danger signal. Hawkins read into this idea the possibility that the
astronomer-priests would claim for themselves that their skilled
intervention had averted disaster. This was a plausible suggestion,
for there is solid documentary evidence that both in the ancient
and medieval worlds eclipses of both kinds were frequently cited
as the prime cause of disasters.

Following his intuition, Hawkins showed that when the swing
of the winter Moon carried it over D or F, the Harvest Moon
was eclipsed that year. He reckoned that one of the key numbers
to the solution was the interval between the nights of the winter
moonrise over D which was 18·61 years. The other key number
he reckoned was the Metonic cycle number of 19 years. The
interval he sought was *almost* 19 but not quite. If he chose 18·61,
this clearly would not fit with a Metonic-cycle series of 19 years.
An extended series, without any system, would mean there was

a jumble of 19s and 18s, with an average of two 19s to one 18. Hawkins recognized that a simple 19-year interval looked all right for two successive intervals, but a third interval would be in error by a full year. Soon after, any extended series based on a whole number 19-year cycle would lead to considerable and unacceptable errors. The best fit was provided by a triple-time measure of alternate whole numbers, viz. $19 + 19 + 18 = 56$ years. From his graphs Hawkins supposed that the Stonehenge Moon phenomenon was repeated every 56 years, and that the triple interval giving a sum of 56 years accurately reflected winter moonrise over Stone D for centuries. Thus, to Hawkins, the number 56 seemed positively connected with the Stonehenge Moon-rising cycle; but 56 was a strange astronomical number and did not immediately call to Hawkins's mind any known astronomical cycle.

But as a Stonehenge number, the number 56 sounded familiar enough. And indeed it was : the 56 Aubrey holes. It was the cry of "eureka !" two thousand years on.

There had never been put forward a satisfactory account to explain the presence of the strange Aubrey holes—except as receptacles for human cremation, but why the deliberate number 56? The archaeologists had noted they were carefully spaced. Only about half had been excavated, and the rest were found by probing and bosing the surface. Those that had been excavated contained the remains of cremated bones and other prehistoric objects. It was Atkinson's belief that the holes had been dug about 200 years after the construction of the Bank feature; apparently they were filled again shortly after this. Most of the holes showed signs of disturbance or re-excavation at a later date—some of them several times probably for interment. It was Atkinson's belief that the holes had never been intended to hold any kind of upright, neither wooden post, sarsen nor bluestone. If any worthwhile theory might be forwarded, they perhaps reflected some kind of ritual significance for cremated remains or incinerated human sacrifices.

Hawkins published his second paper in *Nature* in the issue of 27 June 1964 under the intriguing title : "A Neolithic Computer". In this he explained how in his opinion the 56 Aubrey holes

served as an eclipse computer—a built-in feature of the monument by which the Stonehenge astronomer-priests kept track of
the Moon and perhaps other celestial events.

But how could such a crude computer work? Easy: if one
tally (maybe a pebble or stone) was shifted round the circle, one
Aubrey hole each year, the extreme positions of the Moon and
eclipses of the Sun and Moon might readily be foreseen. But the
best *modus operandi* was using 6 stones. By using 6 stones, of
which 3 were white and 3 black, "astonishing" powers of prediction could be achieved, and every important Moon event was
within reach of the operators for hundreds of years.

But if archaeologists had strong doubts about the implications
of Hawkins's first ideas, the new ideas that Neolithic man could
conceive and then operate such a computer-like device left them
astonished and open-mouthed. To design and then operate such
a device implied the Stonehengers were Megalithic masterminds
—veritable Einsteins of the first order. It was now that Hawkins
became the prime target for all dissidents of astro-archaeological
theory.

Yet some archaeologists were not entirely negative to the
ideas of accepting astronomical alignments built into Stonehenge—especially in the way cited in the exemplary cautious
ideas of Newham's. This approach—with reservations—was
acceptable. Newham's ideas were acceptable as a working
hypothesis from which—with the co-operation of archaeologists
—the astronomers might take the next cautious step. But Hawkins had initially not sought any aid from expert archaeologists,
and he was now in the academic dog-house as far as they
were concerned. The idea that the Aubrey holes were some
kind of prehistoric eclipse predictor was totally unacceptable
to all but a tiny minority of archaeologists no matter how fav-
ourably swayed towards the idea some astronomers appeared to
be.

There can be little doubt that eclipses held a remarkable fascination for peoples of the ancient world, and they played an
influential role in all affairs. We have, of course, no way of
knowing what the Stonehenge builders thought about eclipses
or whether they guessed their true cause, and we have no clue
to what they believed were the consequences which followed the

occurrence of an eclipse. But there is nothing to make one doubt that they held similar views to later ancient peoples who left written accounts. The very term *draconic month* (of 27·5 days) owes its origin to the eclipse cycle, and to Eastern peoples it alluded directly to the battle of the dragon and the Moon which supposedly occurred at the time of a lunar eclipse. On Oriental zodiacs the dragon's head was depicted as the ascending node of the Moon's orbit, and the dragon's tail as the descending node. It is in ancient Chinese records we can read that when a lunar eclipse took place, the Emperor and his Mandarins devotedly prayed to the gods that the Moon might not be eaten up by the great dragon which hovered about her. After the event, when the Moon was seen to have escaped the dragon's influence, a great pantomime was staged when sometimes 200 or 300 priests, bearing lanterns, would dance and caper about during a reinactment of the event.

In Mesoamerica, Maya chronicles tell much the same story. A description of a solar eclipse relates that "... the face of the Sun was eaten" and "a monster plunged head down towards the earth during darkness".

Babylonian astronomical "diaries" tell stories of general and widespread belief of fatal and unfavourable consequences following eclipses. In the *Anglo-Saxon Chronicle* we read that "The Moon [during a lunar eclipse] was as if it had been sprinkled with blood and Archbishop Tatwine and Bede the Venerable died ...". Nearer our own time there is the story of the smart trick Columbus played on American primitives when they refused him provisions. Columbus, forewarned by his almanac of the arrival of the lunar eclipse for 1 March 1504, threatened to deprive the natives of the light of the Moon—and, of course, he kept his word! When the eclipse began, the terrified natives flung themselves at his mercy and subsequently brought to him all he required.

These examples serve to underline the point that Hawkins was well justified in believing that lunar eclipses might be truly significant events in Neolithic times which the Stonehenge masterminds wished to register. But this is not sufficient evidence in itself to support a contention that the 56 Aubrey holes were actually utilized as a Neolithic computer. Nevertheless, Hawkins was not the only one enamoured by the 56 Aubrey holes. Soon one of the real giants of astronomy tossed his hat in the ring ... and again astounded archaeologists with some equally novel, breathtaking ideas.

10 'The Rules According to Hoyle'

One principle objection raised by critics to Hawkins's theory about the use of the Aubrey-hole complex was that as a computer it could be operated several ways and anyone could make up his own set of rules for working it. Hawkins himself was keenly aware of this, but tended not to overemphasize the point lest it provide ammunition for the more numerate dissenters.

On 30 July 1966 the scientific world was again startled when *Nature* published a paper by Fred Hoyle, one of the world's foremost astronomers and originator of the Steady-State theory of the Universe. Hoyle's paper was entitled "Stonehenge—A Neolithic Observatory"; indeed, according to Hoyle, no matter what the archaeologists felt about the matter, there could be no doubts that the 56 Aubrey holes could operate as an ingenious eclipse-cycle computer.

In arriving at his conclusion, Hoyle had reworked Hawkins's alignments, and in his opinion (an opinion which carried great weight in the scientific world because of Hoyle's high academic standing) the arrangements were not random as some archaeologists claimed. Nevertheless, he believed Hawkins's assumption that the Aubrey holes served simply to count cycles of 56 years to be a weak idea. According to Hoyle there was no necessity to set out 56 holes at regular intervals on the circumference of a circle of such a great radius in order to count cycles of 56. Also he found it difficult to imagine how the astronomer-priests would have calibrated the counting system proposed by Hawkins and noted that Hawkins himself had used tables of known eclipses in order to discover this. But the most telling criticism made by

Hoyle was the inescapable fast that the Aubrey-hole predictor provided only a small proportion of all eclipses that had occurred. Hoyle wondered what merit could have accrued to the builders in predictions that may have intervals as far apart as ten years? And what about the eclipses that were observed but the astronomer-priests had failed to predict?

With Hoyle's paper we can study at first hand the workings of an original scientific mind improving on an earlier idea in a very pragmatic way. . . . In place of Hawkins's ideas, he now suggested that the Aubrey circle actually represented the ecliptic itself (the imaginary circle round the heavens along which the Sun and the planets appear to move, and at the angle to which [at $5\frac{1}{4}°$] the Moon circles the Earth). This was indeed a novel idea that was vaguely reminiscent of some of the pre-twentieth-century ideas on the subject—*vis-à-vis* Stonehenge as a kind of planetarium. But how would such a model operate in practice? Some readers may prefer to accept on trust the following section and pass on to Hoyle's conclusions (below).

Beginning with Fig. 13—which depicts schematically the circle of Aubrey holes—Hoyle's scheme assumed a start when the Moon is Full. The first point in Aries (Υ) is at Aubrey hole 14; S represents the position of the Sun; the angle $\odot$ is the solar longitude; M denotes the position of the Moon projected on the ecliptic; N^1 the descending node of the Moon (N is the ascending node); C, at centre, is the position of the observer.

As time proceeds, the points S, M, N and N^1 move in the direction indicated (by Fig. 13). It follows that S (the Sun) makes one circuit per year, but M (the Moon) moves in one circuit per lunar month. Now, according to established eclipse rules, when the Moon is at N (ascending node), a solar eclipse occurs when the Sun is within roughly $\pm15°$ of N, and a lunar eclipse of the Sun is within $\pm10°$ of N. Conversely, if the Moon is at N^1, a solar eclipse will occur if the Sun is within $\pm15°$ of coincidence with the Moon, and a lunar eclipse if it is within roughly $\pm10°$ of the opposite end of the line of lunar nodes.

Hoyle's idea was to represent S, M, N and N^1 by markers, and if the operator knows how to move the markers so as to represent the actual observed motions of the Sun and Moon, with reason-

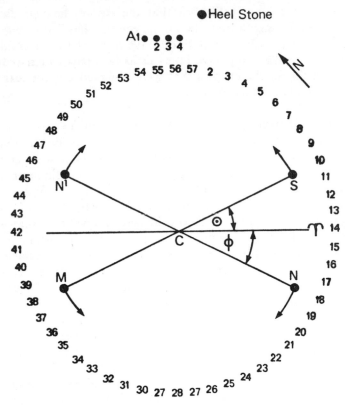

Figure 13   Fred Hoyle's Aubrey-hole eclipse-predictor.

able accuracy, he can predict almost every eclipse; this he can do in spite of the fact that only half of them will be visible from the position of the observer.

Hoyle believed that this achieved a great improvement on the widely scattered eclipses predictable under the system advocated by Hawkins.

Hoyle's *modus operandi* for moving the markers was as follows:

1. Move S counterclockwise two Aubrey holes every thirteen days.
2. Move M counterclockwise two Aubrey holes each day.
3. Move N and N[1] clockwise three holes each year.

Hoyle believed it to be a reasonable assumption that the Stonehenge builders possessed knowledge of a) the number of days in the year, b) the number of days in the month, and c) the period of regression of the nodes (18·61 years). The last could be found by observing the azimuth at which the Moon rose above the horizon (i.e. the Moon swings).

Hoyle noted that with the periods of S, M and N known with reasonable accuracy, these would provide an approximate prescription to enable the observer, via the Stonehenge alignments, to predict ahead what the positions of M, N and S are going to be and therefore to foresee any coming event. Nevertheless, this would only work for a limited period because inaccuracies in the prescription cause the markers to differ increasingly more from the true positions (in the ecliptic) of the actual Moon, Sun and the ascending node.

First to deviate is the lunar marker, for the prescription provides for an orbital period of 28 days (instead of 27·32 days). However, a correcting adjustment to the lunar marker (M) is made twice every month by resort to the simple expedient of the observer aligning M opposite S at the time of Full Moon, and by placing it coincidental with S at New Moon. The prescription for S gives an orbital period of 364 days, which Hoyle considered was near enough to the actual true period, because it is possible to correct the position of S on four occasions every year. This could be done by practical observation checks along the actual midsummer, midwinter and equinoctial alignments at Stonehenge.

Hoyle pointed out that Stonehenge is also constructed to determine the instance when the ascending node (N) sets at ♈. By placing N at ♈ when the Moon rises at the farthest northern point of its swing (Fig. 13), the N marker can be calibrated once every 18·61 years. Since the error in one revolution is small, the N marker, if started correctly, would only be 1°+ out of true position at the end of the first cycle. Now, since the tolerance for eclipse prediction is about 5°, an adjustment to N, every cycle, would enable the predictor to continue to operate indefinitely without appreciable inaccuracy.

In practice, however, Hoyle recognized that the minimum azimuth of moonrise is difficult to determine and found it could not be determined in the method he first described. Now Hoyle

I

introduced an interesting idea about the arrangement of the Stonehenge postholes A1, 2, 3, 4 (Fig. 4) which he considered to have a regular and apparently exact and appropriate placing. What Hawkins in his scheme had supposed should be reckoned as errors in alignment of azimuth markers, Hoyle believed were deliberate efforts by observers to obtain more accurate northern and southern extremes at the azimuths where the Sun and Moon appear to "stand still" (the solstitial standstills). In ten out of the twelve values Hawkins cited as errors (because Hawkins assumed that the Stonehenge builders intended to sight *exactly* to the extremes of azimuth), Hoyle believed he could demonstrate that such apparent errors could be cancelled out because the builders had *not* intended to mark azimuth exactly for reason of the practical difficulties in doing so. One of the outstanding cases was the alignment marked by the centre of the monument to the Heel Stone where the azimuth error was zero; this suggested to Hoyle a special case, an exception to the general rule and it may, according to Hoyle, have been done by the builders for aesthetic or ritualistic reasons—to keep the true direction of midsummer sunrise. The other outstanding example was alignment 91-94 which Hoyle again (but somewhat arbitrarily and glibly) felt constituted another case where true alignment was all important.

Not content with one solution, Hoyle also explored other methods by which the N marker might be periodically calibrated. One method that suggested itself was the special situation at the time when Full Moon coincides exactly at an equinox (i.e. 21 March, 21 September). The evidence that this method may have been tried by the astronomer-priests is contained in several alignments. But even so Hoyle noted that the method is really unworkable because of the unavoidable errors in judging by practical observation the exact moment of Full Moon which can introduce large errors in the positioning of N, and because of the low (5°) inclination of the lunar orbit to the ecliptic. Hoyle speculated that if ever attempted at Stonehenge, this method might well have caused a furore in its day due to the significant emphasis it places on the Full Moon *and* the equinox, and this indeed might well have been responsible for the traditional Easter dating later used by the Christian Church.

Hoyle made out a case that eclipse calibration can be operated successfully *almost* by complete numerology. In operation, S and

N move in opposite directions. The Sun moves through N in 346·6 days; 19 such revolutions equals 6585·8 days, whereas 223 lunations is equal to 6585·3 days. Therefore after 223 lunations the N marker must bear almost the same relationship to S as it did previously. Now, if the correct relation of N to S is known by the operator at any one time, N can be reset every 223 lunations (or once every 18 years 11 days). This near-miss commensurability is sufficiently accurate to provide satisfactory predictions for 500 years or more. But S needs to be set as before, but an advantage is that in the case of N it needs no practical observation to control it, although *without* observation the correction initial configuration cannot be determined unless the problem is turned round. Hoyle felt that the calibration might be set by practical trial and error—citing that this was probably the method later developed by the Chaldeans.

To conclude his ideas Hoyle had some philosophical speculations to provide humanistic overtones to the absract numerical arguments. Again this is very typical of Hoyle's distinctive style as the complete natural philosopher. He believed that from his own studies of the Stonehenge problem, several cultural features presented themselves. Assuming that Stonehenge gave the Sun (S) and Moon (M) god-like qualities, he asked : what about N? At the time of eclipse S and M are eliminated, and perhaps N must then be a still more powerful god. But N is unseen. Hoyle asked; could this be the origin of the concept of an invisible all-powerful god, the god of Isaiah? Hoyle then wondered if M, N and S might be the origin of the doctrine of the Trinity (shades of Stukeley); three-in-one and one-in-three? He believed it would be ironic if the very roots of our contemporary culture were determined by the god-like quality exercised by the lunar node. . . .Indeed, in restating this idea, Hoyle had himself been very forgetful of his astronomical history, for had not the ancient Chinese thought along these lines with their concept of the draconic month?

Fred Hoyle's paper in *Nature* made almost as much scientific impact as did Hawkins's original contribution. In the same Issue, the magazine's own editorial described Hoyle's new ideas as "breathtaking" not only for their ingenuity but for their sheer practicality.

To those interested in the subject, Hoyle's ideas were indeed stimulating, pragmatic stuff. He had demonstrated in a very convincing manner that Stonehenge *could* have functioned as a Neolithic observatory. This was strongly reinforced by C. A. Newham's paper "Stonehenge : A Neolithic Observatory" that followed Hoyle's in the very same issue of *Nature*. Hoyle's and Newham's ideas might even be construed as a sophisticated development of the earlier simplistic lunar notations on scratched bones cited by Marshack. These had perhaps over a long period given Upper Paleolithic and then Mesolithic man insights into lunar motion and then in Neolithic times had enabled the Megalith builders to finally crack the secrets of the solar/lunar eclipse cycle. Thus Stonehenge may have represented a synthesis of some thousands of years of accumulated astronomical knowledge in the same symbolic way that the 200-inch glass giant at Palomar does today. . . .

Hoyle's theories, although they modified Hawkins's earlier theories, seemed to clinch the basic eclipse-prediction claims for Stonehenge. With Hoyle's more pragmatic approach, contemporary astronomers could themselves play the "If-I-were-a-horse" game and enact the methods of the astronomer-priests, and in doing so—unlike the archaeologists—appreciate the simplistic beauty of the numerical methods involved.

Yet not everyone agreed that the ideas were truly pragmatic ones, for the concept of node-stones has the implication of abstraction from practical observational theory and credits the Stonehenge astronomer-priests with intellectual abilities much on a par with their twentieth-century interpreters. And yet, why not?

Neither would the "primitive" Stonehenge astronomer-priests be alone in their concept about the node-stones, for, although still not fully understood, it appears that the "primitive" Maya astronomer-priests had the same ideas in pre-Columbian times.

But Hawkins's and Hoyle's methods of eclipse prediction are not conclusive that these *were* the actual methods used at Stonehenge. Both had shown it could be done, but both had admitted to several alternative *modi operandi*. Hawkins, following Hoyle's contribution, later published an account of a simplified method whereby 1 stone is moved 3 Aubrey holes each year. In this *modus operandi* the Aubrey-hole complex performs as an analogue computer and follows exactly the regression of the nodes.

Newham's contribution on the subject had been somewhat overshadowed by the more breathtaking ideas encompassed by Hoyle. Nevertheless, Newham had several ideas in common with Hoyle : Both were concerned to show how the postholes grouped at the north end of the monument—not included in Hawkins's earlier ideas—were somehow significantly connected with the Megalith builders' experiments to obtain refined measurements at Stonehenge. Newham had studied the posthole layout in great detail. From his survey, the postholes grouped round the Causeway Entrance seemed to radiate from the centre of the Aubrey circle and lie within a 10° arc north of the alignment to the Heel Stone solstice line. They were arranged roughly into six ranks. If one compared them with the computed times for winter moonrises spanning the period 2000 to 1000 B.C., there appeared to be a close relationship between moonrise sequences and hole patterns. The pattern of postholes including the stones near by could then be interpreted plausibly as the experiments of the astronomer-priests to find the 18·61-years nodal cycle, the 19-Julian-year eclipse cycle and even perhaps the 19-year lunar-phase Metonic cycle.

Newham had several ingenious suggestions to make. He believed : (a) That the small stone 11 (Fig. 4) in the large sarsen circle was intentional to the builders' scheme by representing a half-day count—thus the large sarsen circle represented the 29·5 days of the lunar month (this is an ingenious suggestion). (b) That the double circle or spiral of Y and Z holes were the 59 days of 2 lunar months (the double lunation that Marshack claimed was frequently depicted on his scratched bones); there was also the strong possibility of the 59-stone complex of bluestones inside the sarsen circle providing another (more suitable) means of representing the same idea. (c) The 19-year phase (Metonic) cycle was indicated by the 19 bluestones located inside the trilithon horseshoe. All things considered, emphasized Newham, the evidence pointed directly to a "Soluna" site where observations of the Sun and Moon were carried out by Megalithic peoples.

Indeed, Newham's and Hawkins's ideas together provide the interested student with several opportunities for playing astro-archaeological numbers games at Stonehenge. Admittedly they are rather arbitrary, but take the following examples :

Arbitrary Game (1): First remember the Metonic cycle, i.e.

Meton noted that 235 lunar months equal 19 solar years, so that after one cycle of 19 years the Full Moon occurs again on the same calendar date. Let us suppose for a minute that—as Hawkins believed—the Metonic cycle may be a previously unrecognized cycle to aid eclipse prediction.

Now keep in mind the significant number 235. At Stonehenge the inner bluestone horseshoe has 19 stones, each one can be reckoned as representing a solar year (i.e. 19 bluestones = the Golden Year numbers). The trilithons have 10 uprights; the outer bluestone circle is attributed with 60 stones (but also remember opinion ranges 59-61); the sarsen circle numbers 30 stones, while the Z- and Y-hole counts are 29 and 30 respectively; finally we have the 56 Aubrey ("computer") holes.

Now add up all the holes and upright stones beginning from the outer circle; 56 Aubrey holes, 30 Y holes; 29 Z holes; 30 sarsen stones; 60 bluestones; 10 upright trilithon stones and 19 horseshoe bluestones. Total holes and stones = 234.

Hole position number 8 in the Z circle (not included in the above count) was never dug. This is significant (and intentional), for it provides, by its conspicuous absence, a natural starting *and* finishing point for the cycle count. By recognizing the position as significant, we can add it to the total which is now 235.

Or alternatively, supposing there were only 59 *bluestones*, this gives a total of holes and stones numbering 234. Because hole position number 8 in the Z circle was never dug, it seems that the builders intended it as the starting point for the count and *also* the finishing point and should therefore be counted *twice*, thus we have a total which now reads 235.

Again, alternatively, supposing there were 61 *bluestones*, since this provided a total of holes and stones numbering 235, it indicates that the omission of hole position number 8 in the Z circle was intentional to the astronomer-priests' purpose of providing the correct significant number 235.

Thus in addition to the presently accepted 29- or 30-day lunar-month counts, the 59-60 double lunar-month count and the 19-year solar-year count supposedly hidden in the Stonehenge circles, the astronomer-priests possessed a built-in means of keeping tabs on the entire 235 lunar-month count of the Metonic cycle.

Arbitrary game (2): 19 synodic revolutions of the node of the

Moon = 6585·78 days (important in the so-called Saros eclipse cycle); 223 lunations = 6585·32 days.

Problem: find a Stonehenge count to follow 223 lunations (6585·32 days) = to 19 synodic node revolutions (6585·78 days).

Keep in mind the significant number 223. Add up all the holes and stones (beginning from the outer circle) but not the horseshoe trilithon upright stones which in this game are *not* significant: 56 Aubrey holes; 30 Y holes; 29 Z holes; 30 sarsen stones; 59 bluestones and 19 horseshoe bluestones. Total holes and stones = 223. Thus the Stonehenge astronomer-priests had a built-in method of keeping count of both the 223 lunations *and* the 19 synodic (node) revolutions connected with eclipse cycles.

How convinced is the reader?

But perhaps the most convincing evidence for Stonehenge having been a Megalithic observatory is the key factor that Newham very astutely noted. Unknown to Newham, the same thing had been noted by the French architect G. Charrière, who had also made a study of Megalithic monuments in North-West Europe. What both realized was that the "rectangle" formed by the four Stations (91, 92, 93 and 94) corresponds *almost* to the latitude (within a few kilometres) required for azimuths (angles) of the Sun and Moon to be separated by 90° at their extreme declinations. On this piece of very significant evidence alone it therefore seems beyond doubt that the Stonehenge latitude (51°·2) was the result of a deliberate choice by the builders. Thus just to confuse the archaeologists and the geologists even more, it seems that the monument's location on Salisbury Plain had been dictated by the astronomical requirements rather than by the availability of large stones or other factors which might have led its builders to favour Salisbury Plain. This evidence together with that of the individual alignments, shows very convincingly that Stonehenge, whatever else it was, was indeed a very unique ancient astronomical structure.

11 Moonstones or Moonshine?

In September 1966 the archaeologists launched their full-scale counter-attack on the astronomical theories in *Antiquity*—choosing as their target Hawkins's book *Stonehenge Decoded*. Atkinson, in the guise of chief executioner—and chief authority on Stonehenge, had earlier criticized Hawkins's work in *Nature* in a review entitled "Decoder Misled". Now firmly on homeground in *Antiquity* he followed this up with the equally provocative review entitled "Moonshine on Stonehenge".

Glyn Daniel, as editor of *Antiquity*, and a finger deep in the Megalithic pie himself, also had a score to settle with the astronomers—particularly with Hawkins. In his editorial (as a preamble to Atkinson's review) Daniel wrote: ". . . The *double entendre* of the title will be lost on no one, least of all Professor Hawkins . . . We all feel disinclined to listen to a man who has not bothered to listen carefully to archaeologists and learn what they have to say." Indeed Daniel himself had but a short memory, quite forgetting that *he* himself had not been prepared to listen to Newham only three short years before. . . .

Atkinson, except for being a little pedantic, was fortunately a fair reviewer in his 2,000-odd-word broadside. Indeed, the title of the review carried more sting than its content. His chief criticism was that the alignments Hawkins had chosen were not sufficiently accurate to warrant his general conclusions about the monument as a whole. He did admit, reluctantly, that some of Hawkins's ideas were excellent. Nevertheless, he believed that Hawkins, because of "his undoubted enthusiasm for the subject", had overreached himself.

Following this review, *Antiquity* opened its pages to a general debate on the Stonehenge problem. First Fred Hoyle was invited to comment on Hawkins's theories. In turn *Antiquity* then invited comments on Hoyle's article and subsequently printed replies from Hawkins, Atkinson, Thom, Newham, D. H. Sadler (an astronomer who had drawn attention to some inaccuracies in Hawkins's and Hoyle's eclipse-cycle reasoning) and Newall, whose first article on Stonehenge, in *Antiquity,* had been written some thirty-eight years previous. These comments were mostly a reiteration of the old pros and cons of the on-running Megalith debate. Hoyle's article, "Speculations on Stonehenge", was the most interesting—choosing as a theme how *we* might go about constructing a "Stonehenge" if landed on a strange planet and arrived only with crude ropes, stone boulders and wooden posts. . . . In respect to general conclusions about Stonehenge, the upshot of it all, Hoyle conjectured, was far reaching, for it not only required Stonehenge to be designed and built to operate as an astronomical device, but the consequences of the idea demanded a level of intellectual attainment for its builders above that believed standard among a community of primitive farmers. Hoyle concluded : "A veritable Newton or Einstein must have been at work—but then why not ?" Finally, at Daniel's invitation, the debate was topped off by a curious summing up by a very partial Jacquetta Hawkes—wife of the English man-of-letters J. B. Priestley. It was obvious from her content and tone that she had no sympathy with the astronomical theories and, if truth be known, could not really understand them. She frankly admitted, in her summing up for the archaeologists, that after reading Hoyle's contribution, "few of us were confident that we were capable of following his reasoning".

When Atkinson criticized Hawkins's work in *Antiquity,* he felt nevertheless that one should be grateful to him for guiding the interests of prehistory into the early development of observational science and metrology. In this review he cited—in contrast to Hawkins's work—Thom's work in the same field and referred to it as "the meticulous work of Professor Thom". This official blessing of Thom's work was no accident, for it reflected the widespread acceptance by Atkinson and other archaeologists of Thom's own thesis regarding Megalithic structures—surprising since some astronomers held (and still hold) serious doubts whether

Thom had not fallen into the same obsessional metrical trap as had Stukeley, Piazzi Smyth and Flinders Petrie before him (*see below*).

Long before the Stonehenge investigations of the 1960s got under way, Alexander Thom had for years been quietly surveying Megalithic sites up and down the length of the British Isles, and he had already reached several far-reaching conclusions. In formulating his theories he had utilized clues left by Lockyer, Somerville and several other earlier investigators.

Although Thom's work was known to interested parties, it raised little comment except that it was thought a bit eccentric for a professor of civil engineering at Oxford to busy himself with surveying obscure stone circles during the vacations—particularly those in the remoter parts of Scotland.

Some astronomers—if not archaeologists—knew about Thom's work after he published a paper entitled: "The Solar Observatories of Megalithic Man", which appeared in the *Journal of the British Astronomical Association* in 1954. In the next few years this was followed by contributions to other journals with papers entitled: "A Statistical Examination of the Megalithic Sites in Britain" and "The Geometry of Megalithic Man". It was Thom's work that led to the development of what later became known as "Megalithic astronomy", and many still prefer to use this terminology in reference to British and French sites rather than the term astro-archaeology, which now has a more cosmopolitan inference and extends its scope across a much broader chronology.

By the early 1960s, Thom had drawn attention to many of the obscure, less impressive-looking Megalithic remains, some of which were undoubtedly of great importance. He was now convinced that Megalithic man in Britain knew a great deal more about geometrical construction than prehistorians had given him credit for—including the properties of ellipses and the means of designing compound circles. From the evidence that Thom had accumulated it also seemed to him that ancient man in Britain had a standard unit of length which had influenced the geometrical constructions and the dimensions and shapes of stone "circles". Although many circles are indeed round, others are curiously egg-shaped, elliptical or distorted in some way.

Thom's ideas became better known to the public after the wide publicity afforded Hawkins's discoveries at Stonehenge which kindled a world-wide interest in Megalithic monuments. It was now soon recognized that Thom had gone beyond the ideas of his predecessors and even his contemporary fellow astro-archaeologists.

The outcome of Thom's perserving Megalithic surveys, up to the late 1960s, is contained in two slim hard-cover volumes, *Megalithic Sites in Britain* (1967) and *Megalithic Lunar Observatories* (1971). While neither volume sets out to be overtly technical, neither is a popular rendering of the subject. Many an eager reader or archaeologist, unfamiliar with astronomical jargon but keen to digest Thom's ideas, come away from these books apparently baffled by the complexity of the subject—for Thom makes few concessions.

Thom's method was to visit Megalithic sites and, with theodolite and tape, measure the positions of the remaining stones as accurately as possible; fallen and buried stones were sometimes located by prodding with a bayonet. Since many of the British Megalithic sites are situated in remote spots amid boggy moorland away from roads and even rough cart tracks, Thom's journeyings to the 450 sites he claimed to have visited often involved long solitary walks with the awkward theodolite and its tripod slung over his back. His earliest surveys began in the 1930s, and by the late 1960s he had made what he claimed was over 300 accurate plots, in addition to which he claimed to have studied detailed stone arrangements at many other sites.

The crux of Thom's theories concerns his concept of the so-called Megalithic yard of 2·72 Imperial feet, and the double yard or Megalithic fathom (5·44 feet). Much of Thom's reasoning hinges on the *a priori* assumption that such a standard unit of measurement was in usage in North-West Europe *c*. 2000 B.C. Thom claimed he discovered this unit by an analysis of his own surveys. He claimed that only by supposing that such a unit existed was it possible for him to make geometric sense of the schemes of the Megalith-builders.

Thom argued that this measure is very close to the old Spanish *vara* (meaning 'rod', 'stick' or 'yard measure'). As a measure it was taken to the New World by the Conquistadors where its usage can be traced through the old Spanish territories of Middle and South America.

Thom speculated that the *vara* probably came to Britain via the migrations of Megalithic peoples from Iberia. But whether any such large-scale migrations ever took place to Britain now appears unlikely when judged in the framework of the New Archaeology which, post-Thom, upset the traditionally held time-scale of Megalith-building in Europe (Chapter 13). Much more convincing evidence of the antiquity of the measure (if it existed) is that the Megalithic yard is very close to the human pace and the Megalithic fathom to the double pace. The double pace, at least, can be traced back to Roman times in the *passus* (= 5 Roman feet; 1 Roman foot = 11·6 inches [296 milli-metres]), and the *passus* is likely to have had long antecedents before being adopted by the Romans.

Thom's investigations into supposed prehistoric and ancient measures were by no means the first. Some of the great con-troversies of the past, which would now fall into the province of astro-archaeology, were involved in so-called standard unit lengths. Stukeley will always be remembered for his apocryphal ill-fated "Druid cubit", and Piazzi Smyth (Chapter 14) for his infatuation with Pyramid inchology and his "Bible-in-Stone" ideas that still have loud echoes in contemporary pseudo-scientific journalism.

Measures used in the ancient world are widely recognized to have been based on simple, easily remembered units such as the finger "digit", palm or span, foot, arm-length, pace and arm-stretch. There is the well-documented Roman digitus, or width of thumb nail, the Roman foot and the related pace; earlier there was the Egyptian cubit—a measure of the length from elbow to fingertip; later there was the standard foot of Charlemagne, the standard arm-length yard of Henry I and the archaic barley-corn measure still retained in modern shoe lengths. One of the best known documented linear units of the Middle Eastern civil-izations is the Babylonian cubit. An example of this is found inscribed as a standard measure on a basalt statue of Gudea of Lagash now one of the prize exhibits in the Paris Louvre. This cubit is dated *c.* 2130 B.C. and depicts a measure of 19·5 inches (495 millimetres) and an ancient "foot" measure of $\frac{2}{3}$ cubit equal to 13 inches (330 millimetres). But some old measures nevertheless seem unrelated to natural sizes such as the old English ell—a unit derived from elbow measurement, but later it came to represent a much longer measure.

In Egypt measurements were complicated by the use of two different cubits. There was the everyday short cubit of 17·72 inches (0·454 metres) and the royal cubit of 20·62 inches (0·528 metres). The royal cubit was used in the setting out and in the construction of the pyramids; some even believe that this cubit measure of 7 palms (1 palm = 4 digits [jeba] = 28 digits) may be related to an early twenty-eight-day lunar cycle. The royal cubit was also used in Egyptian land measurement, and the basic unit, the "double remen" was the diagonal of a square having sides of one cubit length. In practical measurement, the Egyptians round about (or before) 3000 B.C. recognized that in a triangle with sides in the ratio 3 : 4 : 5, the angle opposite the longest side was always a right angle. But this knowledge was the result of experience rather than any ability to work out a formal mathematical proof in a manner known later to have been accomplished by Pythagoras. But it is certain that the Pythagorean theorem was known thousands of years before Pythagoras; this is confirmed by Babylonian texts and can, without a shadow of doubt, be acknowledged as genuine widespread geo-mathematical knowledge possessed by several prehistoric peoples.

But was it known to the ancient Brits in North-West Europe c. 2500-2000 B.C. ? Thom firmly believed it was.

Thom, after concluding that an ancient quantum measure was involved in the design and layout of Megalithic circles, arrived at a figure of 2·72 feet for his standard "Megalithic yard" (MY). Then after applying the unit to constructions and sizes of the various shaped "circles" he had surveyed, he was sure that such a basic unit existed. He believed that a rigorous analysis of his results showed three things : (a) The precision of the measurements did not increase with the length of a measurement; (b) the results were the same whether the unit was later derived from English or Scottish circles; (c) the builders of the circles appeared to have measured to the centres (or centre-lines) of the stones in a ring.

Thom supposed that the key to the problem of apparently distorted or oval circles was that Megalithic man was not prepared to accept the incommensurability of *pi* ($3\frac{1}{7}$) and searched for a whole round number to set out the geometry of his circles. By accepting that Megalithic man abhorred the acceptance of "something more than 3" and had decided that an integral number "about 3" would suit him better, the apparently distorted and irregular-figured circles which had long perplexed archaeologists, and astronomers, suddenly gained a new meaning. Thom's contention was that for large circles and longer distances it seemed likely that Megalithic man had used a measuring rod of $2\frac{1}{2}$ MY (6·80 feet) and of 10 MY (27·2 feet). Analysis of differing categories of circles revealed to him that the ratio of circumference to diameter (*pi*) was always about 3—proof he believed that the long puzzled-over irregular circles were not the result of crude or sloppy setting out as some supposed but was indicative of a premeditated choice by the circle designers.

Boyle Somerville (a disciple of Lockyer's) writing in 1927 about some large-scale plans he had drawn up of twenty-seven stone circles, remarked:

> In not one case are the stones composing the ring placed in a true circle; that is to say, it is not possible to draw a line which joins all the stones and is mathematically circular. The best that can be done is to draw two consecutive circles, forming a band, wide or narrow within which the stones forming the ring may fall...

It is likely that Thom—as a direct heir to Lockyer, A. Lewis and Boyle Somerville—had been strongly motivated by all their writings, and Boyle Somerville's latter remarks may likely have been the very stimulus for Thom to try to solve the mystery of the irregular circles.

As a result of his work carried out over several decades, Thom believed he was able to classify stone rings into different categories: flattened circles, types A, B and D; egg-shaped, types I and II; ellipses (Fig. 14); and compound and concentric circles. The egg-shaped rings in particular, Thom supposed, provided him with the insight that, in addition to using a standard quantum, the builders in the process had discovered the principle of Pythagorean triangles. In construction he considered that circle dimensions were often adjusted slightly by the ancient "engineers" to conform to integral numbers, thus making the circumference as near as possible to a multiple of the larger unit.

Thom did not publish any data on Stonehenge until 1974, but his earlier work had included a very comprehensive study of the great circle at neighbouring Avebury 25 kilometres (16 miles) to the north.

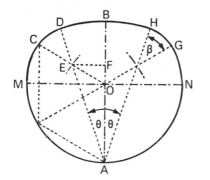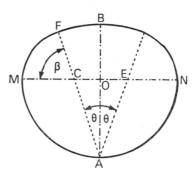

Figure 14   Alexander Thom's alleged geometry relating to flattened and egg-shaped circles.

      Type A   Flattened circle.   Type B   Flattened circle.

      Type I   Egg-shaped circle.   Type II   Egg-shaped circle.

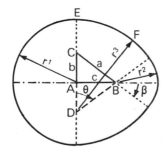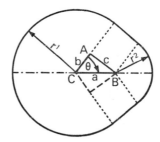

Avebury is the greatest and most remarkable (compound) circle in Britain, if not in the whole world. Thom suggested it was not only its size that contributed to its greatness. Avebury, he believed, is remarkable because of the exceedingly high precision in the setting out and the distinctive manner in which its arcs were built up from a basic Pythagorean triangle so that each triangle of the construction retains integral units.

But Thom says the clues that led him to unravel the geometry of Avebury did not spark from Stonehenge or any other
large circles but rather from some small unimpressive circles
on remote Scottish moors and among the hills of Wales. . . .
When he had finished his study of Avebury, he considered it
the most conclusive and "the final proof" of the exact size of the
Megalithic yard—demonstrating to him the use of the even larger
linear units of $2\frac{1}{2}$ and 10 MYs.

Avebury, like Stonehenge, greatly attracted the attentions of
the seventeenth- and eighteenth-century antiquarians. John
Aubrey remarked that Avebury far surpassed Stonehenge "as
a cathedral doth a parish church". Its sheer size, 11·5 hectares
($28\frac{1}{2}$ acres)—five times as great an area as that of St. Peter's
in Rome—once gave rise to an estimate that upwards of a
quarter of a million people could stand within the boundaries
defined by its inner ditch (Plate 6).

Unlike Stonehenge, which at first glance tends to disappoint
the visitor because its stones are dwarfed in the open Wessex
landscape, Avebury rarely fails to impress. Sir R. Colt Hoare
in his *Ancient Wiltshire* (1812) writes : "With awe and diffidence
I enter the sacred precincts of this once hallowed sanctuary, the
supposed parent of Stonehenge, the wonder of Britain and the
most ancient, as well as the most interesting relict which our
island can produce." Earlier, Stukeley in his book *Abury* also
waxes forth—writing that it showed "a notorious grandeur of
taste, a justness of plan, an apparent symmetry, and a sufficient
niceness in the execution : in compass very extensive, in effect
magnificent and agreeable. The boldness of the imagination we
cannot sufficiently admire".

It was from Stukeley's researches at Avebury that we now
know a great deal about the monument. He became much more
enamoured with Avebury than with Stonehenge, for it was at
Avebury he could trace out on the ground the great snake of
the serpent temple "Dracontia". Overton Hill (the Hakpen)
was assumed to be the head of the snake (Plate 10) and the sin-
uous West Kennet Avenue the neck; the sarsen circles represented coils in the snake's body, and the rest of the serpent was
made up of other Megaliths and avenues—including the lost
Beckhampton Avenue.

In ground plan Avebury consists of a great rampart of earth roughly circular in form, and whose outline has a diameter of *c*. 360 metres (1,200 feet). Inside this rampart and situated close to the inner foot of it is a ditch, and close again to the inner side of the ditch is the Great "circle" that once consisted of about a hundred upright stones.

Within the large outer circle lie the remains of two smaller circles, both measuring, in accordance with Thom's survey, 340 feet (125 MY) (Fig. 5). It was once believed there were three inner circles, but this now seems very unlikely. At the centre of the northernmost circle (known as the central circle) are the remains of a stone Cove (purpose unknown); in the centre of the southern circle is a single upright stone. All the stones incorporated in the monument are of local sarsen and typical of those that can still be seen strewn about the district.

Nowadays the monument lies straddled by the village of Avebury (Plate 6), which has obscured many of the ancient features of the monument. Rivalling the remains of the Great Stone Circle is the West Kennet Avenue (Plate 16). If the visitor approaches from the south, this will be the first part of the monument he sees. Originally it consisted of about 200 upright sarsens, sometimes set in curiously shaped (sexed?) pairs, spaced 24 metres (80 feet) apart in the direction of the Avenue. The Avenue was the connecting link between the Great Stone Circle and a feature a mile away on Overton Hill (Plate 10) known as the Sanctuary (Stukeley's Hakpen or Snake's Head Temple); this began as a circular Megaxylic structure of timber uprights and was later rebuilt in stone.

In Aubrey's day most of the Avenue stones were either standing in their original holes or fallen near by. Round this time or shortly after, a deliberate destruction began when stones were buried or broken by heat. Stukeley left to posterity a now famous print depicting how in his day the local farmers attacked the sarsens in order to clear their fields—cracking them into smaller more manageable fragments by the expedience of the age-old fire-and-water method (Plate 17).

Stukeley in his day had counted 72 remaining sarsens in the Avenue, but by the 1920s only 19 were in position. Between 1925 and 1939, stones found buried beneath the overburden of soil were restored to their former positions wherever possible;

K

positions of missing stones are now marked by concrete marker stubs.

A second Avenue known as the Beckhampton Avenue (Plate 10) was claimed by Stukeley to have extended to the sarsen circles from the south-west. Two stones (marking part of it, or perhaps part of another "lost" circle) known as Adam and Eve can still be seen in the fields a short walk west of Avebury Church.

The result of Thom's work at Avebury was to persuade him that the geometry of the circles had been set out to an accuracy approaching 1 in 1,000. This, on the face of it, appeared to be an ambitious claim for Megalithic man who had no resort to modern tapes or theodolites. Yet in the context of history this claim for accuracy *c.* 3000 to 2000 B.C. is not extravagant. Flinders Petrie's survey of the Great Pyramid built by Khufu (Cheops) *c.* 2500 B.C. showed it set out to about the same degree of accuracy that Thom claimed for the builders of Avebury at about the same period. No one at present can be quite certain about the precise method used by the Egyptian surveyors in the period of the Old Kingdom, but it is likely they used northern stars in a similar manner to that which Lockyer had noted on ceremonial inscriptions of this period.

It will be recalled Thom claimed that it was clues derived from lesser-known stone circles which enabled him to unravel the more complex geometrical structures of Avebury. He also claimed that without *first* knowing the exact length of the Megalithic yard, he would have been unable to decipher Avebury. By adopting the module yard as 2·720 feet he was able to redraw a construction based on his field-survey measures. Had he adopted a value of 2·730 feet, the large ring would have been too large by some 1·5 metres (5 feet) and would have passed outside the stones remaining on site. This he believed was "a striking proof" that the MY was a real quantity and the very unit adopted by the Avebury builders to set the size of the ring.

As a result of his geometrical reseaches round British sites, Thom compiled a list of over 250 observed astronomical sight lines later published in his book *Megalithic Sites in Britain* (pp. 97-101). Most of the stars cited are the same as Lockyer's stars: Capella, Rigel, Castor and Pollux, Antares, Bellatrix, Spica, Altair, Arcturus and Procyon. All these stars were reduced to

azimuth for dates between 2000 to 1500 B.C., for the archaeological evidence *then* indicated this to be the peak period when
the circles and associated Megalithic structures were built. With
the advent of more accurate radiocarbon dating (cross-calibrated
with tree-ring dating) it seems probable that most of these dates
are now too *recent* (Chapter 13). The list contains many
supposed Sun alignments, but where it differs most radically
from Lockyer's work is in the inclusion of numerous Moon
alignments.

But for a monument that is patently a complex one, celestial
alignments at Avebury are disappointingly few. Lockyer claimed
that the Beckhampton Avenue and the feature known as the
Cove, inside the central inner circle, were both orientated to
the May sunrise and May ceremonials; while he believed the
West Kennet Avenue was once used to observe the rise of Alpha
Centauri (Rigel Kent) as a morning star. Thom offers Deneb
(Alpha Cygni) as a star which might have been used as a time-
keeping star—its setting line indicated by the extended line join-
ing the two large inner circles.

Nevertheless, some of the Scottish sites were much more
promising.

At Megalithic sites, Thom cites astronomical azimuths being
provided by :

1. a slab;
2. two or more stones not separated too far away;
3. a circle and a closer outlier;
4. two circles.

But for the Sun and Moon the minimum requirements are :

1. an extended alignment;
2. two well-separated stones;
3. a circle which has an outlier some hundreds of feet distant; or
4. a natural foresight identified by some simpler indicator.

Thom, like Lockyer, considered that the stars were used as
timekeepers. They could be used at times of rising, at culmination on the meridan (the observer's north–south line) or at

setting. Thom particularly noted that many of his stellar align-ments seemed to indicate the use of Capella. In northern Europe this star always seems to have been important in agriculture and husbandry, and in the Middle Ages it was known more famili-arly as the "Shepherd's star". Lockyer in his Egyptian studies claimed he had found at least five temples orientated to Capella, and Penrose in similar fashion cited several Greek temples—in-cluding one to the goddess Diana Propyla at Eleusis.

A surprise omission from Thom's star list was Sirius, the brightest star in the sky and known to the Egyptians as Sothis (and related to the Sothic year). This star, according to Thom, had no indicators on British Megalithic sites. However, he be-lieved that no such indicators were necessary for the Megalithic observers—for the three stars forming Orion's Sword Belt pro-vided a sure enough guide to the point where Sirius would rise above the horizon. According to Lockyer's ideas the rising of Sirius was indicated by at least seven temples; he also suggested it was indicated at several sites in Britain, including the mon-ument known as the Hurlers near Liskeard in Cornwall.

In addition to his metrical and alignment theories, Thom forwarded some ideas about the ancient calendar. Lockyer and others claimed evidence for the division of the ancient year into at least eight parts which regulated the ceremonial or the farmers' year. From his study of British (and later French) alignments, Thom claimed that at least *sixteen* equal divisions of the year were discernible with each of the sixteen "months" made up of periods of 22/23 days. There was also a hint, he believed, that a thirty-two "month" calendar may have been used.

In his second book *Megalithic Lunar Observatories* (1971) Thom set out to show that it was possible to date Megalithic monu-ments using the Sun and Moon via the obliquity method tried earlier by Lockyer for the Sun. This could be done if one had sight lines long enough to derive azimuths accurate to 1' of arc or less.

It will be remembered that Lockyer, using the obliquity method, dated Stonehenge using the so-called mid-Avenue line. Since Lockyer's time a more accurate value of the change in the Sun's obliquity had become available. Thom's *modus oper-*

andi, however, was a much more rigorous one than that adopted by his predecessor, and on the way he made claims for an accuracy and understanding (particularly about the Moon's movements) among Megalithic observers that Lockyer would not have believed possible. Thom's second book made difficult reading even for some academics. When D. Kendall, Professor of statistics at Cambridge, was asked to review the book in *Antiquity,* he described it as "a remarkable book by a remarkable man" and commented it was exceedingly difficult reading even for a mathematician.

What then was the nub of Thom's thesis?

It hinged on his belief that the Megalithic astronomer-priests *c.* 2000 B.C. had already detected a minor fluctuation in the Moon's orbit only appreciated in more modern times, and in addition the astronomer-priests had sometimes used very long sight lines to gain high accuracy.

To appreciate his work it is necessary to first look again at the factors controlling the apparent movement of the Moon. It will be remembered that in relation to lunar alignments marked out at Stonehenge it was essential to take into account the 5° inclination of the Moon's orbit to the ecliptic. It will also be remembered that the crossing points of the Moon's orbit— the nodes—appear to regress round the ecliptic in 18·61 years. The 5° inclination of the path described by the Moon causes its rising and setting points (azimuths) to swing back and forth along the horizon with a much greater amplitude and rate of change than that of the Sun. Lastly it will be remembered that an eclipse can only occur when both the Sun and Moon lie approximately in the line of the nodes (Fig. 12 upper).

Now the accurate value of the Moon's orbital inclination is 5° 8' 43"—but this is only a *mean* accurate value. It was Tycho Brahe (1546-1601), the famous Danish nobleman-astronomer and the last great pre-telescopic observer, who noted (in the Western World) that the inclination of the Moon's orbit to the ecliptic was not a constant value as the Greeks had earlier supposed. Tycho found that it ranged through a minor swing of about 9' on either side of the approximate mean value of 5° 8'. This results in a mean inclination of 4° 58½' and a maximum of 5° 17' (at times of quadrature and syzygy respectively). Although this discovery is attributed to Tycho Brahe, it appears to have been known to the Arabs in the tenth century and then forgotten. Thom, however, believed that from his study of this 9′ swing, it was a factor well familiar to Megalithic man when he built his monuments round the beginning of the second millennium B.C.

The 9′ variation is now known to be due to a perturbation effect. This causes the pole of the lunar orbit to move uniformly on a small circle of a radius of about 9′ over a period of 173 days. The 9′ variation is a sufficiently large enough quantity to be eclipse important. It was Thom's contention that if the Megalithic observers were able to detect this highly significant perturbation effect via circle and stone alignments, and could gauge its period, they would then be armed with sufficient data to predict eclipses.

Thom's reasoning and methods of showing how he worked his various examples are beyond the scope of this general treatment but can be studied in his book *Megalithic Lunar Observatories*. Thom's ideas, if proved correct, have far-reaching implications for the intellectual capacity of Megalithic man—much on a par with those cited by Hawkins and by Hoyle for the design and operation of their eclipse-predictors at Stonehenge. If we accept uncritically all that Thom had claimed was hidden in the various Megalithic monuments he has studied, it indicates quite clearly that prehistoric man had a knowledge of the Moon's movements only rediscovered by Europeans in more modern times.

One of the most remarkable Scottish sites studied by Thom is at Kintraw in Argyll. According to Thom there is a natural foresight notch formed by two hill peaks (the Paps) on the island of Jura some 45 kilometres (28 miles) to the south-west. Working from the solar-obliquity principle, Thom believed the natural notch provided a midwinter sunset position as seen *from* the monument *c.* 1700 B.C. Kintraw is a remarkable site for several reasons. It provides some of the longest sight lines yet claimed for Megalithic observatories, but it is the configuration of the various elements involved in the stone complex which has attracted most comment and speculation. The site itself is situated on a small plateau on a steep hillside. From ground level the mountain target area is obscured by a nearby (*c.* 1·6 kilometres [1 mile] distant) foreground ridge. To enable the observer to see the col notch, Thom reasoned that it had been necessary to establish an observation platform on a steep hillside to the north of the plateau across a deep gorge. This in turn would lead to a cairn being erected on the observation site, in line and at a height, so that the notch could be seen. A "platform" was actually located in the steep hillside where two boulders provided a notch suitable for viewing the col.

This supposed observation platform has been subject to fairly rigid scrutiny to determine whether it was indeed a partly man-fashioned feature of the landscape or whether it had been formed fortuitously by the accumulation of scree debris and other natural factors. So far (c. 1977) no signs of human occupation have been found, but the absence of material such as charcoal and other material suitable to allow radiocarbon-dating calibrations has not deterred Thom and his co-workers from claiming that the platform provides strong evidence for its use as an observation point in Megalithic times.

Another of the remarkable aspects of Thom's Megalithic studies at Scottish sites was his interpretation of the curious fan-shaped stone arrays in remote Caithness. In several of these arrays the slabs are positioned with their long axes laid parallel to the direction of the row. These stone rows were first surveyed in 1871, but their curious layout, with the individual stones seldom more than 45 centimetres (18 inches) high, had long provided an even bigger puzzle as to their intended purpose than had Megalithic circles.

According to Thom, however, these stone rows perhaps represent primitive stone computers used by the astronomer-priests to solve complex problems involving extrapolation which arises as a consequence of the Moon's motion. Thom's interpretation of these fan-arrays perhaps represents the greatest degree of sophistication yet claimed for Megalithic man, and for good reason they have been referred to as "Megalithic graph paper".

Thom had noted that the British *lunar* sites—rather than solar sites—contained the largest upright stones (menhirs). It was after his investigations of Scottish sites that he turned his attention to the great Megalithic monuments in Brittany, especially to those of the Carnac region—a region that has been nick-named 'the Mecca of the Megalithic World".

The great French Megalithic monuments, as their British counterparts, have attracted the attentions of antiquarians and would-be decoders for centuries, and the literature is full of fanciful and less fanciful speculations as to what purpose the great single menhirs, laid out in long *alignements*, had played in the lives of ancient men.

The most impressive of all the single stones in Europe is Le Grand Menhir Brisé, Er Grah, or Mane-er-Hroeg (Fairy Stone), near the town of Locmariaquer (Plate 18). It is now recumbent and broken into five pieces, one of which is missing from the site. The stone had certainly fallen before 1727 when M. de Robien, President of the Parlement de Bretagne, made a drawing of it in the position it now occupies. Its weight, calculated in accordance to its volume and density, equals something in excess of 350 tonnes, and when erect it must have stood over 20 metres (66 feet) high. Some, nevertheless, believe that the stone never stood vertical, but that it broke during erection owing to the top end being overheavy—thus it may never have functioned in whatever manner intended by its erectors.

In Brittany there are several large menhirs still standing which range in height from 9 to 12 metres (30 to 40 feet), and menhirs ranging 7 to 8 metres (23 to 26 feet) are not uncommon. A characteristic of the Brittany monuments is the absence of stone circles like those found in Britain. The nearest example to British circles are those on a small islet at the site of Er-Lannic where two incomplete circles (cromlechs) of standing stones now form a horseshoe encroached by the sea (sea level has risen since Neolithic times). Nevertheless, both differ appreciably from British circle examples.

More characteristic of French Megalithic sites are the passage graves that reach a maximum concentration in the Carnac area between the gulf of Morbihan and the Etel River. But more characteristic still are the vast arrays of stones composed of parallel or slightly converging lines of menhirs, the most important and extensive of which also occur at Carnac ("the cemetery of the bones") and extend in an easterly direction through Kermario ("the place of the dead") and Kerlescan ("the place of the burning") for more than 5 kilometres (3 miles). Hereabout are several thousand upright stones, and they represent the greatest concentration of Megalithic remains in Europe (Plate 3).

Methodical excavation of the monuments in the Carnac region dates back to M. de Robien in the period 1727 to 1737. Many of the graves appear to have been robbed in prehistoric times, and by Gallo-Roman times several of the *allées couvertes* (covered gallery graves) were occupied and in regular use as domestic quarters—judging from the debris found inside them. This undoubtedly misled Victorian chroniclers such as Fergusson to be persuaded that the monuments were created at this later period.

Nothing quite like the Carnac alignments occur in Britain— or elsewhere. Most of the menhirs that form the rows have been at some time disturbed, particularly those resting on rock outcrops and without holes. Many were subject to misdirected restoration in the nineteenth century, and it has been frequently noted that *not in a single case* can one be sure that the present position an upright occupies is exactly the position intended by its original erectors. Many of the uprights known to have been re-erected or repositioned in recent times are denoted by a little square hole near their base which is filled with reddish cement.

The interpretation of the Carnac menhirs has often been referred to as "the archaeologists' nightmare" and has given rise to the same kind of speculative literature as that surrounding Stonehenge and other British monuments. In nearby burial mounds one finds human remains, weapons, pottery, domestic implements, necklaces, bracelets and clasps. Similar remains are found in among the rows of menhirs, but near the larger, isolated menhirs no human remains are found—even when the subsoil conditions are suitable for their preservation.

Theories put forward for the isolated Carnac menhirs range from grave memorials or grave indicators, idols for pagan worship, astronomical alignment markers, landmarks that serve like the so-called British ley markers (Chapter 12) to symbols of a prehistoric phallic cult. The latter theory is supported to some degree if related to more contemporary remains elsewhere where phallic cults are known to have been practised or still are. Local folk tales also give support to this idea (Chapter 17).

It will be remembered that Lockyer made reference to the astronomical orientation theory at Carnac formulated by Felix Gaillard and also to the work of Lieutenant Devoir. Following Devoir, several others attempted to formulate more advanced

ideas. Baschmakoff, in 1930, attributed the Brittany Megaliths
to a pre-Aryan culture which possessed a calendar dividing the
year into eight astronomically determined parts that indicated
the occasions for festivals or feasts. Baschmakoff, as an ethnolo-
gist, looked at the monuments with a different eye to that of
archaeologists or astronomers. He speculated that the rows of
menhirs and their associated carvings represented clans and their
totemic emblems. These grand designs were supposedly laid out
by an elite priestly class, echoing Lockyer's and latterly Hoyle's
similar speculations, but the construction work must have been
done by a *fellahin* division of their society. Baschmakoff's bull,
ram and serpent totem emblems have been eagerly pounced
upon by those who (wishfully) see in them indications of an
Asian-type zodiac in vogue in Europe in prehistoric times.

Thom arrived at Carnac already in possession of a fully developed astronomical model to explain Megalithic sites. Following
the knowledge acquired on British sites that the tallest stones
(menhirs) are usually lunar backsights, he decided to concentrate
first on the larger, more isolated of the Carnac menhirs. Thom,
however, now reasoned that the largest stones need not be re-
stricted to backsights: why not also foresights? It was natural
that his attention should be directed towards the recumbent
and broken Er Grah. This indeed proved to be a fruitful starting
point.

It was of course necessary for Thom to assume a position in
which Er Grah had originally stood. This ignored the possibility
that the stone may never have been successfully erected. Thom
chose the spot to be at the centre of the extreme north-west end of
the position where it now lies.

The outcome of Thom's survey at Carnac was to persuade
him that Le Ménec, Kermario and the Kerlescan stone rows,
and the associated outlying menhirs, constituted a huge lunar
observatory actually centred on Er Grah itself (Fig. 15). Applying the same rules for the rising and setting points of the Moon
as he had done with his British sites, he derived comparable
results.

Thom believed that to fix the position for Er Grah must have
involved careful observations of the Moon over several hundreds
of years. These observations would have revealed inexplicable

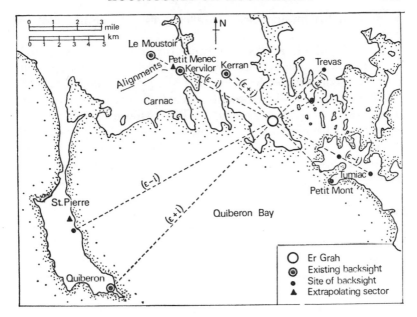

Figure 15 Er Grah, Brittany, used as a lunar foresight marker according to the ideas of Alexander Thom. The pecked lines refer to various horizon positions (azimuths) in relation to where the Moon rose and set *c.* 2000 B.C. during its inclined orbit round the Earth as seen from Er Grah (ε = ecliptic; $\pm i$ = Moon's orbital inclination above or below the ecliptic).

anomalies to the Megalithic observers owing to niggling variations caused by parallax and refraction. Thom imaginatively conceived parties of observers out at all possible places in attempts to see the Moon rise or set behind high trial marker poles. He assumed that at night the poles would need to be equipped with torches at their tops (shades of Lockyer's earlier ideas), for any other marks could not be seen until actually silhouetted against the Moon's disc. This necessitated working an earlier proto-observatory so that the astronomer-erectors could be kept informed about the swings of the Moon and the state of the 9' perturbation factor.

It is not possible to summarize all Thom's French work without omitting sections which are relevant to the final arguments, but the nub of Thom's Megalithic surveys of the Carnac sites resulted in his finding close parallels with Megalithic sites in Britain.

He believed his results confirmed his Megalithic yard, and he noted a remarkable uniformity of another measuring unit which he claimed must have been a rod equal to 6·802 (±0·002) feet (2½ MY). The sixteen-month Megalithic calendar held true, while rows of stones examined at Petit Ménec and St. Pierre were found likely to have been used as extrapolating sectors in the manner he had first suggested for similar rows of stones in Caithness. Still later surveys indicated that the cromlechs at Le Ménec associated with the stone rows conformed to his Type I and II egg-shaped rings of the kind previously studied in Scotland.

It was not until 1974 that Thom published his first Stonehenge contribution which he based on a completely new topographical survey.

As may be expected, his reconstruction of the geometry of the monument was based *a priori* on his Megalithic-yard unit. Using his now "standard" 2½ MY rod measure (2·04 metres), he found the Aubrey circle gave a circumference of 131 rods. The sarsen circle he claimed had also been laid out with the selfsame MY rod measure; its external circumference gave 48 rods and its internal 45 rods.

Coming to the sarsen trilithons, he based their setting out on two concentric ellipses 30 x 20 and 27 x 7 MY. The inner ellipse showed an integral of Megalithic rods—accurate to 2·5 —6·25 centimetres. The layout of the trilithons was also dictated by Megalithic measures; they were 1 rod wide, spaced internally ¼ rod apart and with 4 MY between trilithons.

The layouts of the Y and Z holes also attracted Thom's attention. He claimed they were not true circles but rather two spirals composed of two semicircles of different radii spaced half a Megalithic rod apart. Stretching the readers' credulity to its limits, he believed they were analogous in design to the well-known "cup and ring" marks found as petroglyphs on many menhirs.

In respect to the bluestone rings, he accepted Atkinson's ideas that sixty stones once formed the larger circle; but considered from his geometric analysis, both the larger and the smaller were less precisely laid out than the sarsen rings—this has the inference that they did not fit his own MY scheme as well as they might. Nevertheless, he suggested that the inner ring was laid out over a conjoint circle and ellipse, with the foci of the ellipse on the perimeter of the circle.

Referring to Newham's pioneer work, he argued that it looked as if Stonehenge may have been the centre of a huge lunar observatory. He believed that Stonehenge, instead of providing a lunar foresight, as he had outlined for Le Grand Menhir Brisé at Carnac, indicated a universal backsight from which distant markers on the horizon might be observed. The postholes near the Heel Stone indicated an extrapolation sector similar to those in Caithness and Brittany.

In conclusion he touched on the tricky but important problem of dates. Because new dates derived from radiocarbon/tree-ring methods were pointing to construction work at Stonehenge as beginning as early as the third millennium B.C. and not the second as had been previously indicated, he admitted that a new appraisal of the chronology was required. This might, however, be explained by assuming that the study of lunar movements began very early at Stonehenge and had extended over a period of several hundred years. And it was just possible it was as a result of this early, perhaps pioneer, work that observatories were then subsequently set up elsewhere in different parts of Britain.

It was all exciting and heady stuff, but was it *really* convincing? Some believed it was nothing more than febrile speculation. Had Thom, as Atkinson had earlier accused Hawkins of, simply overreached himself? Were Thom's monuments true moonstones, or was the whole theory simply moonshine?

12 Ley-lore and Geomancy

One of the curious by-products of Lockyer's study of British Megalithic alignments is the cult of the so-called leys and ley-hunters. The name closely associated with leys is that of Alfred Watkins (1855-1935), but it was chiefly Lockyer who provided the stimulus and background from which the ley phenomena subsequently developed. Lockyer pointed out some remarkable relations between Stonehenge and the surrounding localities which in turn had been drawn to his attention by Colonel Johnston, the director-general of the Ordnance Survey.

In his Stonehenge book, Lockyer pointed out that two straight lines could be drawn through Stonehenge which, when extended, passed through features that were probably of great antiquity. One line passed through Sidbury, Stonehenge, Grovely Castle, and Castle Ditches; the other passed through Stonehenge, Old Sarum Mound, Salisbury Cathedral, and Clearbury Ring. In addition, the lines were so arranged that Stonehenge, Grovely Castle, and Old Sarum Mound formed a "perfect" equilateral triangle. Yet another curious feature was that one side of the triangle—extended either side and aligned through Sidbury Stonehenge/Grovely Castle/Castle Ditches—was Lockyer's sunrise on the longest day at Stonehenge, viz. his adopted azimuth for the Avenue centre-line.

After noting this curious relationship, Lockyer looked for others elsewhere. In his Stonehenge book he remarked: "Such relations ... but on a smaller scale, are often to be noticed, in some cases between monuments, in others between monuments and decided natural features on the sky-line as seen from them." It is likely that these were the very words that triggered the cult of the ley-lines. . . .

Watkins, in his book *The Old Straight Track* (1925), related that he knew all about these so-called alignments before reading Lockyer's account, but there can be little doubt that Lockyer's widely read Stonehenge book was the unambiguous seminal influence. Lockyer's work triggered similar ideas in Boyle Somerville, later himself a vigorous ley-hunter.

Alfred Watkins was a native of Herefordshire. He was a keen countryside photographer, and it was on one of his rambles in his native county that he tells he first developed his ideas, which were later extended through the length and breadth of Britain—then across the globe by his later disciples.

Watkins recounts that he began to notice that beacon hills, mounds, earthworks, moats and old churches built upon earlier pagan sites seemed to fall in straight lines. Further investigations convinced him that Britain was covered with a network of straight tracks running from beacon hill to beacon hill with the way clearly marked by a mound or clump of trees on high points, by notches cut in mountain ridges, and in the lowlands by standing stones or pools carefully placed to reflect the light of a beacon and lead the traveller straight on.

Watkins claimed that some of the tracks were proven Sun alignments (another hint of Lockyer's powerful influences), others were more mundane traders' tracks, while others still were shown to be paths tracing a particular star at a certain time of year (Lockyer again!).

Watkins defined the word "ley" to describe a sighted track—"rightly or wrongly" he told his readers. He admitted that philologists believed the word (or its alternative spellings, lay, lee, lea or leigh) to mean a meadow or enclosed field of some kind. However, he suggested that its prehistoric (pre-Roman) meaning was certainly not that, but he provided little evidence to support this contention. It should be noted that in English place names, ley, and its alternative spellings, is extremely common.

Watkins seems to have arrived at his "ley" theories from experience as a practical countryman, field-naturalist and respected country photographer and—there can be little doubt—from inspiration triggered via the facile pen of Lockyer and others. However, it seemed he had always been deeply affected by the numinous ancient atmosphere of his native Herefordshire—and its half-remembered folklore. Much can be gleaned about the man from his fondness for books like W. H. Hudson's *Hampshire Days*. In the introduction to *The Old Straight Track*, Watkins quotes Hudson's strangely evocative and moving passage: "We sometimes feel a kinship with, and are strongly drawn to the dead, the long long dead, the men who knew not life in towns, and felt no strangeness in Sun and wind and rain. In such a mood on that evening I went to one of these lonely barrows. . . ."

The cult of the leys via Watkins's theories had its genesis one hot summer's day in the early 1920s. On that afternoon, Watkins recalled, he was riding across the Bredwardine Hills some 19 kilometres (12 miles) west of Hereford and stopped on a crest for a moment in order to take in the sweep of the panorama before him. It was then he noticed something which he believed no one in Britain had seen for thousands of years: it was as if the more recent surface of the great landscape had been stripped away, revealing an unambiguous web of lines linking the ancient sites of antiquity that stretched out before him. Each fell into place in the whole scheme of things; old stones, holy wells, moats, mounds, crossroads, and pagan sites obscured by Christian churches stood in exact alignments that ran on for as far as the eye could trace. In a single all-powerful visionary moment, Watkins, as a self-appointed cult leader, was witness to what one of his later disciples described as "the magic world of prehistoric Britain", but which Watkins less histrionically described as "a glimpse of a world almost forgotten when the Roman legions marched across it".

He related that, like Jim Hawkins in *Treasure Island*, he held in his hand the key plan of a long-lost fact. . . .

Watkins maintained that the so-called old straight tracks which crossed the landscape of prehistoric Britain over mountains, dales and lowland woods had decided the site of almost every kind of human communal activity. . . . Like astro-archaeological pursuits of today, the pursuits of the old straight tracks brought the investigators into contact with many of the specialist 'ologies, for Watkins remarked that one must follow where the line leads ". . . and, like the ball of thread in the legend of Queen Eleanor and the Fair Rosamond, it leads to all kinds of spots . . .".

Watkins informed his readers that following the old straight track would reveal new facts in other branches of knowledge out-side their own ken, but he remarked that he himself resisted following them—especially religion. No doubt he had in mind Lockyer's own painful experience after meddling in others' pre-serves when he wrote this, but likewise Watkins also believed that human knowledge was not built into watertight compartments.

Watkins set down his first ideas in a booklet, *Early British Trackways*; he subsequently admitted it was written somewhat breathlessly. In fact it was in print five months after he had re-ceived that first visionary clue that sunny afternoon in Hereford-shire. *The Old Straight Track*, which followed it, was the result of more mature reflection and was in print a little over three years later under the aegis of Methuen, a highly respected London publishing house. Watkins's book was certainly much influenced by Frazer's *Bough*, Lockyer's *Stonehenge* and many of Boyle Somerville's scattered writings.

When the Old-Straight-Track cult spread, and a postal club was formed, Boyle Somerville became a member and remained so until 1939 when the club was disbanded on the outbreak of World War II.

Watkins's vision-inspired theories, however, cut no ice with most archaeologists who pointed out—and continue to point out to Watkins' modern disciples—that coincidental alignments are bound to occur in a landscape like Britain's which is scattered with remains left by several thousands of years of human habit-ation. O. Crawford, editor of *Antiquity* and a colleague of Boyle Somerville, refused all advertisements for the book in his quarterly journal, believing, like most of the other influential archaeolo-gists, that Watkins's theories were pure nonsense and could rightly be committed to the lunatic fringe of archaeology.

In spite of its archaeologists detractors, Watkins's *The Old Straight Track* was read by a wide public and went through several editions. In the 1948 edition it appeared in Methuen's list incongruously alongside books such as F. E. Zeuner's monu-mental *Dating the Past*, Grahame Clark's *Archaeology and So-ciety* and C. F. C. Hawkes's *The Prehistoric Foundations of Europe*. The book eventually went out of print and was then diplomatically dropped from Methuen's list. In 1972 it was re-surrected by the Garnstone Press, a publishing house specializing in popular books with strong hypermystical overtones. In this

L

edition it was prefaced by the self-confessed flying-saucer enthusiast John Michell.

For the wayfarer who likes to keep his eyes open and his senses alert, Watkins-style ley-hunting provides an innocent enough pastime for country excursions. Watkins's message, with its ever-enquiring schoolboy appeal, tells the would-be ley-hunter to keep his eyes wide open when cycling or motoring whenever "on a bit of straight road" for signs of any marker, hill point, church, mound or earthwork—for such an observation almost certainly would lead to the discovery of a ley through the point and on the road.

In an appendix, "Ley-Hunting", Watkins provides much information and advice in the vein of Lockyer's "Astronomical Hints for Archaeologists", contained in his Stonehenge book. Watkins stressed the importance of both indoor map and outdoor field-exploration. He was right too when he said that many mounds, ancient stones and earthworks were missing from large-scale maps, such as the 6-inch to 1-mile series. He also provides useful hints concerning compasses, glass-headed pins, maps, drawing boards, T-squares, circular protractors, etc., in fact all the paraphernalia that a would-be ley-hunter requires for his field-studies.

After equipping oneself with 1-inch maps (now presumably replaced by the metric series), Watkins tells his readers to look out for: ancient mounds ("which are called tumulus, tump, barrow, cairn, or other names"); ancient unworked stones (but *not* those marked as boundary stones); moats; traditional or holy wells; beacon points; crossroads with place-names, and ancient wayside crosses; churches of ancient foundation and hermitages; ancient castles, and old "castle" names.

When these objects were located, they were to be marked in as a ring on the map. When a mark point was found (or other indication such as a mound or stone), the ley-hunter was to place the straight edge against it and then move it to see if *three* with ringed points could be found to align—or alternatively two ringed points and a piece of existing straight road or track. If this proved possible, a pencil line was now required to designate provisionally the potential ley.

In following up Watkins's instructions there are Sherlock Holmesian overtones. He tells his readers that faint traces of an

ancient track or earthwork were most easily detected when the
Sun is low and on one side, as in late evening. Winter, he maintained, was an ideal time for ley exploration owing to the absence
of leaves on the trees, but he provided a cautionary warning when
he remarked that a great multiplicity of leys in a small area
would "surprise" and perplex the ley-hunter, but added that it
was a fact that had to be accepted.

But how scientific is ley-hunting? Notwithstanding the criticism by archaeologists, many of Watkins's ideas do sound quite
plausible. Orientation ideas based on sight notches in distant hills,
traders' tracks, beacon sites aligned to tracks, *some* Sun alignments, and Christian churches erected on older pagan mounds
all have a smack of verisimilitude. It is Watkins's more hyperspeculative ideas—his ancient men-of-the-leys, the so-called Dod-
man surveyors who supposedly marked out tracks and alignments
in prehistoric times, and Watkins's reference to the use of sighting
staves and tenuous archaeological links with Babylonia, Josephus,
Moses and Tutankhamen—that invoke the first scepticisms and
uncertainties in discerning readers.

Some of Thom's ideas about Megalithic alignments are not so
far removed from those of the old straight track. Indeed, after
reading what Thom had to say in the 1960s, there were those
who recalled Watkins's similar ideas via Lockyer and Boyle
Somerville. Could it be, it was wondered, that Thom had also
come under the influence—even subconsciously—of Watkins's
straight-track theories. Watkins had first cited hill notches to
mark sight lines, but it was Boyle Somerville rather than Lockyer
who developed the orientation ideas based on far distant hill
summits. Boyle Somerville searched out numerous alignments that
sometimes extended through an alignment marked by a cairn or
earthwork and then projected fortuitously through an abrupt
gap in the distant hills. He developed these ideas in several long
articles on the subject, one of which—and now perhaps a classic
of its kind—was printed in the very first issue of *Antiquity* (1927).

In "Orientation" Boyle Somerville discussed the original meaning of the word, and how modern usage had changed it. He
stressed that the orientation found in monuments of antiquity
was no new discovery, but that its existence was still largely
doubted. He maintained that the connection between Death and
Orientation was well proven—citing the fact that the Christian

custom of laying the dead in the ground with the feet towards
the east still existed. Or in other words, these interments were in
fact "orientated".

Boyle Somerville had some interesting ideas to account for the
believed orientation of long barrows (and various kinds of passage graves). Nearly all of the long barrows are directed to some
easterly point, but some are markedly northward or southward
of east and do not follow a precise west-east orientation. Recent
ideas about the Newgrange Megalithic passage grave in Ireland
(*c.* 3000 B.C.), which appears to be orientated to receive the Sun's
rays at precisely midwinter solstice, lends general support to ideas
that some funerary chambers are orientated structures (Fig. 16).
Boyle Somerville himself believed that Megalithic funerary
chambers (as, for example, that of Bagneux, near Saumur in
France) were orientated to important prehistoric calendar dates.
At Bagneux (Fig. 1), Somerville maintained it was orientated to
the rising Sun on 8 November or 4 February—calendar dates

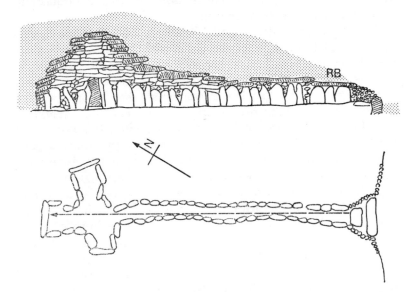

Figure 16   Passage grave at Newgrange, County Meath, Ireland, which
has been radiocarbon dated to 3100 B.C. plus or minus 100 years (corrected
date). It is claimed that this structure was orientated by its builders so
that precisely at midwinter solstice the rays of the rising Sun (dashed line)
shone along the passage through the roof box (RB).

(half-quarter days) about midpoint between the winter solstice and the equinoxes.

Boyle Somerville was under no doubts about the Sun's importance as an "orientation calendar", and this idea is certainly borne out by similar findings among neoprimitive societies.

But often Boyle Somerville, like Lockyer, was sometimes too receptive and a little too credulous and uncritical about the whole concept of orientation, and his ideas were clearly not always endorsed by his colleagues at the Society of Antiquaries.

Among his more sober beliefs were that in a circle, the stones to be employed for the purpose of fixing the alignments were usually indicated by being considerably larger than other stones of the circle. The chosen foresight, or the stone nearest the Sun in taking the observation, was engraved all over with cup-mark petroglyphs. In two cases he noted that additional standing stones were placed at a short distance outside the actual stone circle to form a third stone on the alignment. This he claimed must have been intentional to the builders' purpose so that there could be no doubts as to the line to be followed for the orientation. Indeed, it is from a close study of Boyle Somerville's writings one can see the genesis of some of Thom's ideas. In turn it is of interest to note that Thom's ideas in particular— derivative of one of the Old Straight-Track Club members—have been eagerly pounced on by the vigorous band of neo-straight-trackers typified by the writings and thoughts of John Michell.

In Michell's *The View over Atlantis* (1969)—a stable companion to the reissued *The Old Straight Track*—Thom's, Lockyer's and Boyle Somerville's work is represented as providing strong confirmatory proof of many of Watkins's ideas, and included are more recent "interpretations" of Watkins's basic thread formulated by John Michell himself.

Michell incorporates an account of pseudo-pyramidology (endorsing its ideas), and by manipulating Thom's Megalithic yard, he equates it with all manner of numerical and metrical puzzles of the ancient world and lards it with the seemingly obligatory mystical overtones. In a remarkable chapter entitled "The Alchemical Wedding" he tells his readers that the Great Pyramid was in fact an instrument of alchemy, and this could be proved by a study of the Pyramid's numbers and the principles which they represented—thus even upstaging the hyperspecula-

tive fancies of pseudo-pyramidologists such as Taylor and Smyth
(Chapter 14). The outcome was that the Great Pyramid was
constructed to fuse two elements: celestial and terrestrial. It
was in fact the instrument of inspiration. From this union gestated the spirit of God in men and the establishment of the New
Jerusalem on Earth.

Woodhenge (Plate 2) was supposedly laid out according to a
plan derived from the magic square of Mercury. The prox-
imity of Woodhenge to Stonehenge was in line with sound cosmic
reasoning, for Woodhenge was less than 2 miles from Stonehenge, "the former solar capital".

Michell's metrical schemings are breathtaking. He believed
the whole of prehistoric science to be succinctly expressed in
his so-called Great Pyramid equation: $1080 + 666 = 1746$ (a
numbers game to beat all the Stonehenge numbers games!). In
the same vein he relates that the Pyramid was constructed to
represent the four principal linear units of antiquity: the foot,
yard, cubit and Thom's Megalithic yard; he then proceeds to
show, in good old-fashioned Q-E-D-style, how this can be deduced via the construction of two circles each with a diameter
of 555 feet and a circumference of 1,746 feet. This excursion
into classical metrology makes Taylor's and Smyth's Pyramid-
inchology sound like nineteenth-century dogma—yet an ever-
credulous lay-readership laps it up with apparent gusto and
demands more fare of this kind from its author.

Michell's Megalithic investigations naturally include Stonehenge, which he calls the "New Jerusalem", and Glastonbury—
also referred to as the "New Jerusalem". Using Thom's Megalithic yard unit in his 'alchemical fusion", he endeavours to
upstage its inventor in his suggestions for a geometrical layout
of Stonehenge by providing a graphical construction of a metrical scheme uniting the British monument with the Great
Pyramid. For good measure he throws in the old idea that
Salisbury Plain was a giant orrery. Silbury Hill is cited as being
erected by a former race of giants. Lichfield Cathedral is related
to the magic square of Mars, and literally and metaphorically
no stone is left unturned in his grand tour. Even an earlier
suggestion by Hoyle that drum beating may have been used at
Stonehenge for disseminating information at high speed is
dragged in to demonstrate that ". . . stone levitated by sound

could become a flying chariot moving along the line of a certain magnetic intensity, whose course was marked out on the ground by alignments of stones and earthworks, linked by raised causeways and rides through the forest . . .". Indeed under the aegis of Michell, Watkins's old-straight-track theories were fashionably updated to conform to claptrap space-age cults.

With the reprinting of Watkins's book and under Michell's stimulus, the neo-straight-trackers have become a very active body. The editor of *Antiquity* again refused a straight-track advertisement; this time not for Watkins's book but for a cult magazine, *The Ley-Hunter*, which apart from leys covered topics as diverse as bats, wishing stones, Old Mother Midnight and even an article evocatively entitled "Why Flying Saucers followed the Leys". When a somewhat credulous journalist suddenly "discovered" the leys for himself and was rash enough to write about it in a leading influential British Sunday newspaper, there followed a phenomenal postbag on the subject. In reply, one sceptical correspondent wrote that he had discovered about fifteen country pubs which followed a straight line; another sceptical reader came up with an "educational" alignment for half a dozen schools. One of the best replies received was from a correspondent who discovered some forty alignments of telephone call-boxes in the Chiltern Hills (a ley-hunters' paradise). Another ingenious ley-hunting experience was sent in by an anonymous Oxford don, who, with tongue firmly in cheek, recounted how he had discovered that all the Roman Catholic churches in inner London formed a perfect logarithmic spiral.

Of course, there were also correspondents whose attitude to the ley-phenomena was not always clear. Someone in Cornwall discovered a global ley which began on an alignment composed of a dozen or more West Cornish churches and prehistoric hill forts and then somehow fell in line with Rome, the Valley of the Kings (Egypt), and a major concentration of Aztec and Maya pyramids.

An ever-present problem facing the whole of Megalithic speculation is separating the fact from the fancy. There are several well-documented examples where Christian church sites are purposely involved in, or are non-accidentally related to, Megalithic or prehistoric pagan sites.

One of the most interesting of British Megalithic/Christian sites is at Knowlton in Dorset where the church is erected inside a henge monument. In Cardiganshire (Wales), at the church of Yspyytty Cynfyn, three menhirs form a circle and are incorporated in the circular wall of the churchyard. Only 32 kilometres (20 miles) away is the Church of Llanfairpwllgwyngyll where a Megalith lies under the pulpit. In Yorkshire, at Rudston (origin probably "Rude stone" or, as some believed, "Red-stone" or "Rood stone"), an impressive menhir 8 metres (26 feet) high —the tallest in Britain—still dominates the churchyard and stands only 4 metres (12 feet) distant from the church walls (Plate 19). This stone is associated with an old East Yorkshire legend similar to the Friar's Heel legend of Stonehenge. The whole area round is rich in prehistoric remains including three interesting cursus-like features which, when viewed from the church tower, appear to lead into the valley of Rudston as trackways.

The menhir of Rudston is also of interest in that it is a "foreign" stone to the district. It is likely that this huge gritstone was man-hauled from an area some 16 kilometres (10 miles) to the east. Some believed its possible original name "Rood stone" is formed from the Old English 'rood" or "cross" and "stan" meaning stone. It has been suggested that the "rood" element relates to the fact that the menhir may have had a cross-head affixed so as to Christianize it—possibly by Anglo-Saxon missionaries. In the churchyard is another, smaller upright slab about 1 metre (3 feet) high that now stands in the north-east of the churchyard, but originally it stood to the east of the large menhir, and the two may have lined up to provide some significant orientation now unfortunately lost.

Similar to the Rudstone menhir are three gritstone menhirs— the Devil's Arrows—found at Boroughbridge, some 65 kilometres (40 miles) distant to the west. Petrologically these stones originate from the same beds as that of the Rudston menhir. They were once believed to be the sole survivors of a great stone circle which stood there, but it now seems likely they are remnants of a stone avenue like those at Avebury in Wiltshire and Shap in Cumberland. As the name implies, this is yet another monument dedicated to Old Nick himself. One story says they are three of the cross-bolts—turned to stone—which he shot at a nearby

Christian missionary settlement. The three gritstones of Borough-bridge and the one at Rudston are marked by curious flutings, earlier believed to be purpose made by their erectors, but there is little doubt they are the results of weathering over 4,000 years. The top part of the Rudston menhir was actually dressed in lead in 1773 to protect it from the weather, but this was later removed. Another curious feature of this latter stone is its reported depth below ground. According to an experiment conducted by Sir William Strickland in the late eighteenth century, there is as much stone stump hidden below as is showing above.

One man who looked closely into the whole question of British pagan/Christian sites was Lyle Borst, an American professor of civil engineering and astronomy. His work is highly contentious, and he is yet another who was apparently motivated by Lockyer's and Penrose's earlier theories in addition to Thom's ideas for standard Megalithic units. Like Lockyer, Borst related that his interests developed during a visit to Greece where he initially travelled to study ancient metallurgy in the 1960s. One afternoon he and his wife (as tourists) visited the Temple of Hera at Argos, built about 500 B.C. and dedicated to the Vestal Virgins. He noted that the axis of the later temple was different from that of the earlier one destroyed by fire. This shift Borst claimed could be attributed to the precessional shift of the star Spica; for he concluded that both temples had been dedicated to the rising of this particular star, and the changes in axis were caused by the precessional shift between the two construction dates. He was back where Penrose left off in Greece seventy-odd years earlier.

Borst now decided to extend his search. After analysing the architectural plans of the cathedrals at Canterbury, Wells, Winchester, Gloucester and Norwich, and the churches of Knowlton in Dorset and Wing in Buckinghamshire, he claimed to have discovered what he described as "Megalithic designs of an explicit kind". These ideas follow much in the vein of Watkins's straight-trackers. He relates that in his Megalithic studies he visited each site in turn and came to the conclusion that later Christian structures showed the same essential character as Stonehenge, Woodhenge, Arminghall (the Megaxylic henge site in Norfolk) and five lesser stone rings described by Thom as egg-shaped rings of Type I. He believed that Lincoln Cathedral

showed evidence of a different Megalithic pattern, typical of
Type-II rings. He contended that his novel study of cathedral
architecture shed new light on the geometry of henge monuments and that it really is the study of henge monuments and
long barrows which might explain the reasons for so-called peculiar features in cathedrals.

Borst's approach to the intriguing pagan/Christian Megalithic site problem is certainly a novel one. Unfortunately his
ideas and methods are rather arbitrary and often rely on doubtful evidence; generally his thesis is unacceptable to those archaeologists who have specialized knowledge of early churches and
Megalithic monuments.

Basing his study on acceptance *a priori* of Thom's Megalithic
yard, he claimed to have found unequivocal traces of it in all
the sites chosen for study. Only infrequently, however, did he
note traces of the half-yard or other fractions of it sometimes
cited by Thom and others. Instead he claimed to have found
the larger unit 6 MY (5·03 metres; 16·2 feet). Borst maintained
that this 6-MY "unit" was no accident, for it relates very nearly
to the length of the English rod of 16·5 feet (5·06 metres) and
that for most purposes the two units could be used interchange-
ably.

He tried to show that the processional path of a cathedral
is usually 1 rod wide, but that the distance between side chapels
is an integral number of Megalithic yards—although rarely
multiples of six. Leaning on Thom's evidence about the Megalithic use of the Pythagorean triangle, he believed it indicated
a ritualistic value to the Megalithic cultus, and those present in
cathedral places provided the strongest evidence that Christian
cathedrals rest on henge monuments.

Borst composed a list of both "Megalithic Sanctuaries" and
"Church Sanctuaries" with all the supposed relevant inbuilt geometric qualities. Among the Christian Sanctuaries, Wing Church
is the only one he claims with a simple 3:4:5 Pythagorean-
triangle construction. Wing, even without Borst's ideas, is potentially a very interesting site in its own right. It is one among
only three surviving Anglo-Saxon churches that show architecture based on the Roman *basilica*, or law court, where the apse
is semi-circular or polygonal. Beneath the apse at Wing is a

crypt of Saxon date (probably fifth century or earlier). Borst contended that an oval based on a 3 : 4 : 5 MY triangle fits the crypt outline as well as any smooth figure could be expected to fit the irregular polygonal structure. Since the geometrical design at Wing is simple, it was therefore presumed to be earlier than that of the more involved Megalithic geometry of the great churches.

The nub of Borst's thesis was of course that the church builders followed the sanctuary patterns laid out by the Megalith builders, and in addition that they still showed signs of the old stellar orientations given them. Wing, he believed, was orientated to Bellatrix (sometime between 2300 to 1500 B.C.), and Canterbury Cathedral to Betelgeuse at around the same period. Wing indeed may well have been a pagan/Megalithic site, for there is good evidence of occupation in the area going back to well before Neolithic times, but the evidence for stellar orientation is very doubtful and at best is only conjectural. Borst claimed that Wing was contemporaneous with the Megaxylic site at Arminghall. Excavations there have disclosed eight postholes in the form of a horseshoe with a circular inner and outer ditch and intervening bank (Plate 4). Borst considered the setting-out pattern to be based on a major radius of 8 MY of a 6 : 8 : 10 MY triangle—for this fits the geometrical pattern reasonably satisfactorily. He admitted, however, that the pattern was not perfectly symmetrical, and some latitude was possible in positioning the oval. He believed too that the Nidaros Cathedral at Trondheim in Norway—which has a similar octagon—was related to the Arminghall geometry.

Borst extended his studies of the Megalithic yard to chambered long barrows and, of even more interest, to discussing the so-called geometry hidden in Stonehenge where he uses Stations 92 and 93 to form an isosceles triangle with the Heel Stone, providing for Pythagorean triangles of 120 : 50 : 130 MY. He showed how the sarsen circle, the bluestone ring, the great trilithons and inner bluestones can be related by egg-shaped constructions and MY geometry. It is of great interest to compare his Stonehenge geometry with that of Thom's later attempts (c. 1974.) The two are totally at odds.

Among the most remarkable triangles Borst reconstructed were

12 : 72 : 73 which he claims to have found in the three English cathedrals of Canterbury, Norwich and Gloucester—and in the Finnish cathedral at Turku.

According to Borst's general ideas, Megalithic/Christian geometry could be expected to show progress from the simple to complex. The Trondheim Cathedral would be representative of the oldest. The sites hidden below the church at Wing, the monument at Arminghall and Turku Cathedral are supposedly of comparable age (c. 2500 B.C.); while the cathedrals using 12 : 72 : 73 (Canterbury, Norwich and Gloucester) were among the most recent. It was this conclusion that led him to claim that the Megalithic cultus was undoubtedly Scandinavian in its earlier form. A view unendorsed by all present-day archaeological thinking.

13 New Archaeology and the Neolithic

Before the late 1960s the traditional view of British prehistoric culture was to attribute much of it to a European or Eastern Mediterranean influence via what can be described as the "invasion hypothesis". Many archaeologists and prehistorians could not believe in Stonehenge without invoking diffusionist influences from Mycenae (or elsewhere), consequently the thesis of "Wessex without Mycenae" was held to be an archaeological heresy.

It has since been argued that British prehistorians were so anxious to avoid ascribing any invention or innovation to their own island forbears that there developed an invasion neurosis. Thus in the first half of the twentieth century especially, every change, every development of any kind, was ascribed to overseas influence, preferably by the process of invasion; simple culture contact was not deemed sufficient. It was this inhibition which prevented recognition of any kind of "self-willed" prehistoric innovation in Britain as having sprung from within.

But the invasion-diffusionist hypothesis was not formulated without good reason. After all within historic times Britain *had* suffered several major invasions plus minor infiltrations, and there was every reason to believe that in prehistoric times Britain had suffered similar incursions. The extreme hyperdiffusionist view of the origins of British culture was replaced in the 1920s by Gordon Childe's more sober modified diffusionism with its thematic "The irradiation of European barbarism by Oriental civilization". But even this still carried overtones of the older hyperdiffusionist ideas. The attitude towards Stonehenge III typified this point when J. F. S. Stone remarked *c*. 1958 ". . . I feel sure that we must look to the literal civilizations of the Mediterranean for the inspiration and indeed for the actual execution. . . ." There were few dissenters.

In the 1960s the firmly entrenched diffusionist arguments began to be seriously questioned. This coincided with the first rumblings of the so-called "New Archaeology", nicknamed more aptly "New-think" or "New-speak" Archaeology. New Archaeology, like the analogous New Geology of seafloor spreading, came about by the widespread adoption of newer scientific techniques and technologies following World War II. This caused a minor revolution in the whole field of scientific methodology. In particular, the enormous success of the International Geophysical Year (IGY) in 1957-8 led to the reintroduction of an inter-disciplinary approach to solving scientific problems and provided a model of co-operation for the future. British archaeology began to move with the times in the early nineteen sixties.

New archaeology owes much of its *raison d'être* and subsequent impetus to radiocarbon dating. No other new scientific tool has made such an impact on archaeology—on the absolute chronology of the European Neolithic particularly—since the development of the stratigraphical techniques of the earlier "New Geology" of 1780-1830.

Radiocarbon was first recognized in 1939 when Serge Korff of New York University was conducting research into cosmic rays. This material has an atomic weight of 14 instead of the normal 12 of carbon, and for this reason it is referred to as carbon-14 (C-14). The first to find radiocarbon in nature was W. F. Libby, the American nuclear chemist. Libby knew that cosmic rays, which bombard the upper atmosphere, produce large numbers of neutrons. He reasoned that when these collide with nitrogen atoms in the atmosphere, some of them are transmuted into radiocarbon. Nitrogen is changed to carbon by replacing one of the positively charged protons in the nucleus of the nitrogen-14 atom with an uncharged neutron of almost the same mass. It was Libby's belief that radiocarbon combined with oxygen to form carbon dioxide which is diffused throughout the atmosphere. Plants absorb carbon dioxide by the process of photosynthesis. Plants in turn are consumed by animals and humans, and as a result radiocarbon is acquired in all their tissues.

But what happens to radiocarbon when a living organism dies? It is obvious that death would stop further intake of radiocarbon. Libby found that what remained in the tissues after death slowly leaked away. The carbon-14 atom in fact is unstable and throws out its negatively charged electrons and becomes stable nitrogen. It was this characteristic which Libby realized could be put to good use.

Libby's calculated value for the breakdown of C-14 to nitrogen was a half-life of 5,568 (plus or minus 30) years. Thus Libby realized that by determining the amount of radioactivity left at any point—as others had done using the longer half-life of uranium to date rocks—and measuring this amount against a calibrated scale based on the radioactivity of modern carbon, it would be possible to gauge the age of the host substance. It was in this way that radiocarbon dating (C-14 dating) was born.

Although carbon makes up only 0·12 per cent of the Earth's crust by weight, its importance to man is very great. It is necessary for all life. Consequently it is found in the living material of all animal and plant bodies, in practically all fuels, paper, wood, textiles, and the food we eat. More compounds of carbon exist than do compounds of any other element.

Libby found that any organic material is suitable for radiocarbon dating—wood, flesh, bone, antler, peat, excreta, grain, even beeswax. Each substance can be made to reveal its age. To check out the theory, Libby first experimented with objects of *known* chronological age, but some early results were disappointing. Nevertheless, when laboratory techniques were refined, it was generally accepted that Libby's method might provide radiocarbon dates accurate to within a few per cent of the true value.

Many famous objects were checked out. The Book of Isaiah, from the Dead Sea scrolls, was dated at 2,050 (plus or minus 100) years. Charcoal from the Lascaux Cave in France, where Cro-Magnon Stone-Age man had executed his fine wall-paintings, gave up a date of 15,516 (plus or minus 900) years. More mundanely, but of great interest, some bread carbonized from the Pompeii disaster of A.D. 79 gave up its age unambiguously.

Another test was to check against the date for the Babylonian King Hammurabi—a date not known with exactness by traditional calendar-dating methods. Hammurabi's date is also a subject closely related to Velikovsky's controversial date for the Venus tablets of Ammizaduga (Chapter 15). Libby's results in the 1950s finally gave a figure for Hammurabi of *c.* 1750 B.C.—plus or minus a century. Libby also attempted to provide conclusive evidence for one of the stickiest unresolved problems in Mesoamerican archaeology—the exact correlation of the Maya calendar with the Western calendar which is still subject to controversy. His result (451 B.C. [plus or minus 110 years]) indicated that the Spinden correlation of 481 B.C. seemed to provide a better fit than the Goodman-Thompson correlation of 741 B.C.

In general practical usage Libby's radiocarbon-dating method was subject to contamination problems that sometimes gave anomalous results, but the method was accepted as accurate enough. Nevertheless, it was clear *something* was wrong. . . . Libby had assumed that carbon-14 had been in the atmosphere in similar amounts through time; in other words it was assumed that a more or less steady flux of cosmic rays had produced a constant proportion of carbon-14 relative to other isotopes of carbon. But this assumption has proved to be an oversimplification. It is now recognized that cosmic radiation intensities have been variable at different periods in the past. For example, periodic outbursts from the Sun and other astronomical bodies such as novae, supernovae, pulsars, quasars and enigmatic X-ray bodies may have significant effects on the intensity of cosmic radiation falling through the atmosphere. It has also been shown that lightening bolts can enhance the level of carbon-14 in wood. With many Egyptian artefacts, radiocarbon methods provided chronological fixes that were *later* than historical calendar dates. This was suspicious because Egyptian calendar dates had long provided archaeologists and historians with reliable chronological fixes; and the Egyptian calendar had long been reckoned as the only intelligent calendar to have existed in ancient times.

Radiocarbon dates for elsewhere seemed all right if one made assumptions from evidence obtained from other prehistoric studies. For example, dates for European Megalithic societies seemed just right if equated with assumed dates derived from prehistoric studies. A date of about 2400 B.C. seemed right for

16 (*above*) The West Kennet Avenue leading to Avebury from the south.

17 (*right*) William Stukeley's contemporary sketch (*c.* 1724) showing the 'fire-and-water' method of destroying sarsens at Avebury.

18 Le Grand Menhir Brisé, Er Grah, Brittany, now lying in four pieces.

19 The Rudstone monolith, East Yorkshire. This very impressive menhir is 8 metres (26 feet) high and is the tallest in Britain. It is likely that Anglo-Saxon missionaries deliberately chose this site for a church in order to Christianize the pagan stones.

20 The Great Pyramid of Cheops, and a section through it drawn by Piazzi Smyth showing the Entrance Passage orientated towards the pole star Alpha Draconis *c.* 2170 B.C.

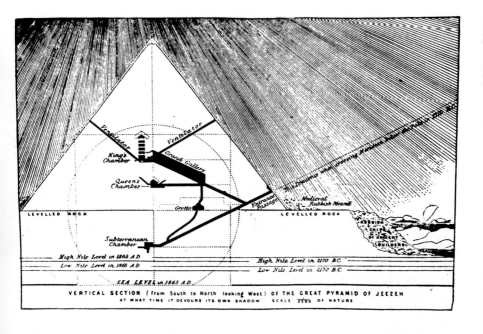

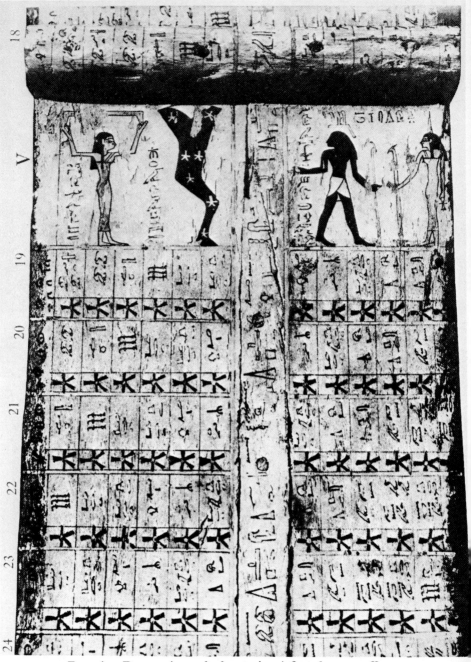

21 Egyptian Decans (star-clock asterisms) found on a coffin *c.* 2100 B.C. Depicted (top, left to right) are sky-goddess Nut, the Ox's (or Bull's) Foreleg (Ursa Major), Orion and Sothis (Sirius).

22 Egyptian star-clock diagram of the Rameses period *c.* 1200 B.C.
The large-eared astronomer-scribe depicted is the so-called target
scribe. Another scribe facing (not visible) would call out the hours
of the night in relation to how the stars shifted relating to some
anatomical feature of the target scribe, e.g. '11th hour, the star Sothis
over left eye'.

23 Egyptian sky-goddess Nut – a direct descendant of the Earth-
mother goddesses of the Upper Paleolithic.

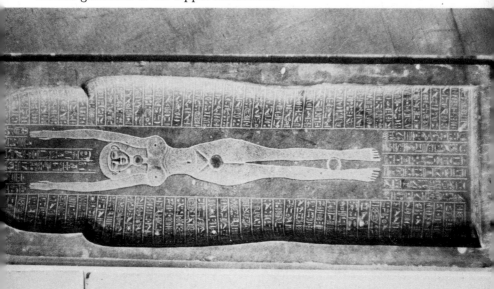

24 (*above left*) Babylonian tablet K160 – one of the controversial Venus Tablets of Ammizaduga (*c. before* 1500 B.C.) recording detailed observations of the appearances and disappearances of the planet Venus.

25 (*above right*) A Babylonian 'boundary' stone (*kudurru*) showing (top, below the serpent, left to right) the triad of Venus, the Moon, and the Sun. Below are other divine emblems including the Scorpion.

26 (*right*) The Aztec Calendar (or Sun) Stone designed to symbolize the Aztec universe. Centre is Tonatiuh – the Sun, flanked by four cartouches providing the dates of the four previous ages of the world. Also included are the names of the twenty calendar days, symbols for the heavens, signs for stars and two fire serpents representing the Year and Time.

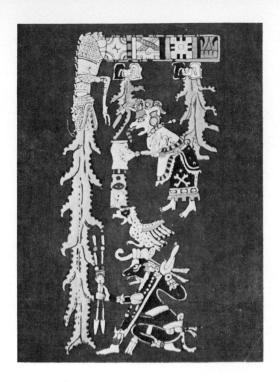

27 Facsimile of the last page of the Dresden *Codex* showing three rivers pouring from the sky, and various glyphs. The four squares at the top *may* be four constellation squares or possibly (left to right) the planets Venus, Mars, Mercury and Jupiter. At the start of the middle river there may occur the Maya glyph sign for a solar eclipse, and from the right-hand river the glyph for a lunar eclipse. However, these interpretations are by no means certain.

28 Bas-relief from Laussel *c.* 30000 B.C. This faceless Venus holds a bison horn inscribed with thirteen lines which may represent the 'round' lunar-month count of the solar year – or the number of days from a sighting of the new crescent to Full Moon.

29 (*above left*) At Avebury several large Megaliths suggest Earth-Mother cum-fertility concepts. (*above right*) Chalk fertility-goddess of the Neolithic age from a British site. (*below*) A male and female pairing(?) in the West Kennet Avenue.

Iberia and likewise dates of 1620 to 1720 B.C. for the main structure of Stonehenge.

Nevertheless, a reassessment was necessary when it was apparent that radiocarbon datings in prehistoric times were in serious error. The solution to the difficulty was resolved by falling back on tree-ring dating—using the science of dendrochronology. This proved the salvation for the radiocarbon method. In particular the role played by the bristlecone pine (*Pinus aristata*, later renamed *Pinus longaevia*) was very significant. This tree is found in the White Mountains of California, and the oldest living example is 4,600 years old.

Earlier in the twentieth century, the American astronomer A. E. Douglass pioneered a scientific method of tree-ring dating. Douglass noted that trees of certain species showed marked variations in ring width, reflecting wet and dry years. This he found especially true of the Rocky Mountain Douglas fir and some other pines. By coring trees with a simple instrument, growth rings could be checked against those of neighbouring trees. By this method it was possible to trace missing rings, extra rings, and other growth irregularities, and so date the rings exactly. By this method it was found possible to date the time the prehistoric Americans built their pueblos.

Douglass's technique was later applied to the bristlecone pine. Long time spans can be cross-calibrated using many tree samples of old living trees and dead wood which overlap in age with samples from younger trees. This is possible because of the recurring characteristic rings brought about by various weather conditions. Trees in the same area are affected in much the same way, therefore all carry the same signature. In this way bristlecone pines have provided a chronology going back for some 8,200 years.

The new breakthrough in dating came about because the bristlecone pine rings provided samples of wood that could be dated by counting tree rings *and* by measuring their carbon-14 content, and the two results could then be compared. When this was done, it yielded results so surprising that the whole correlation method was immediately called into question. If one accepted the C-14 correction indicated by the dendrochronological studies, the whole structure of prehistoric archaeology in Europe was upset.

M

A check was made : an independent tree-ring calendar was constructed using different wood samples. But the results were the same; the two calibrations agreed exactly. These results also confirmed that contrary to previous belief, each tree ring does not correspond to one year. It also confirmed that large discrepancies observed between dendrochronological and radiocarbon ages could not be explained by major systematic errors in tree-ring dating.

For prehistoric studies, particularly for the archaeology of North-West Europe, the consequences were far reaching. The correlation showed that radiocarbon dates before 1000 B.C. are much too young. In North-West Europe the recalibrated dates showed that the Megalithic tombs, once believed to have been built *after* or contemporary with the pyramids, sometimes predated them by two whole millenniums. Instead of European Megalithic societies having been influenced by the ancient Egyptians and others from the "East", it was seen that early European Neolithic societies had evolved independently, and that their ideas were mostly the subject of local innovation rather than ideas which had arrived from overseas by invasion or cultural diffusion.

Nevertheless, there are still several problems to be faced with radiocarbon dates. The Libby half-life estimate of 5,568 years is probably in error. However, at present, so there can be a uniformity of results, Libby's original value is still cited. In the future, when the exact half-life has been determined, it will then be easy to apply a conversion factor to bring all the dates into line.

The new calibration curve has resolved the puzzling Egyptian radiocarbon dates; these have now fallen neatly into place with traditional historical calendar dates. But for Megalithic Europe, the new calibration provided no such reassurances, for it put back many Megalithic tombs to a date earlier than the pyramids. When in 1930s Gordon Childe fixed the beginning of the earliest European Neolithic to about 2700 B.C. and that of Britain and Scandinavia to about 2400 B.C., everyone agreed that this estimate looked about right. When the new chronology indicated that some Megalithic structures like Newgrange in Ireland were built *c.* 3100 B.C., it was realized that Childe and others had got it wrong, and that the whole of European Neolithic prehistory needed rewriting.

The dates for the *late* building phase of Stonehenge III are not so dramatically affected, and this phase is now set around 2000 B.C. But culture-wise the new chronology set the completion date of Stonehenge at least four centuries *before* the Mycenaean civilization of the Aegean *began*.

Thus the old speculations and the chronology of prehistoric Europe have been turned upside down. Many of the so-called Mediterranean innovations supposedly carried into Europe by diffusion are now found *earlier* in Europe than in the East, and all the assumptions that became the archaeological dogma over the previous half century were not substantiated. One principal effect of the upset chronology has been to invalidate each of the three routes by which these influences supposedly reached Britain and the rest of Europe, i.e. from the Aegean to Spain; from the Aegean to the Balkans; and from Mycenaean Greece to Central and North-West Europe. What is more, it is now beyond doubt that in the sixth and fifth millenniums B.C., Balkan societies were as complex as any in the world—perhaps even more so.

One of the crutches on which the diffusionist origins of Megalithic culture rested was that the earliest Megalithic tombs in mainland Europe were supposed to be found on the Iberian peninsula. From here the Megalithic culture was believed to have spread northwards to Brittany and then to Ireland. The final stage of the northern arm of this diffusion movement was again supposedly represented by the great Megalithic tomb at Maeshowe in the Orkneys. Several influential books still in wide circulation have maps that glibly depict in broad arrows these supposed lines of migration relating how various parts of Europe were "colonized". In Iberia the Megalithic settlements were considered to have been Aegean colonies that had become established after exploratory trading voyages. The archaeological evidence seemed to give ample support to this idea: they had similar knowledge about smelting ores; similar fortifications; and, most significantly, burial in Megalithic tombs. Taken together the corpus of evidence seemed to provide an impressive dossier, and even the earliest C-14 dates did not conflict with it.

In Britain some of the strongest arguments for Mycenaean diffusion rested on artefacts such as dagger hafts of which similar patterns are also found in Mycenae. When Atkinson discovered the dagger carvings at Stonehenge, this finally seemed to clinch the theory. Additional evidence was the famous Rillaton cup from Cornwall that was very similar to two gold cups from a Mycenaean grave; and there were the blue (Egyptian) faience beads and double axes unquestionably long considered Mycenaean.

After the results of the new radiocarbon-dating calibration, these artefacts were subject to further examination. The pundits hesitated, there was doubt, then a face about. The Rillaton cup was suddenly attributed directly to British culture; the faience beads were found to be of a different composition to *similar style* beads from the east Mediterranean. Actual undisputed Mycenaean imports in Early Bronze Age contexts turn out to be very rare in Britain *and* the rest of Europe, except for southern Italy. The famous double axes appeared to have very doubtful pedigrees archaeologically and may have been brought from the Aegean area at a much later date; certainly none can now be admitted to have originated from prehistoric contexts in Western Europe. Almost overnight, Gordon Childe's beautiful "Oriental irradiation" theories that had swayed opinion for so long were found to be without substance. Today it is impossible to build up a reliable chronological development for the Early Bronze Age of Central Europe on the basis of direct cultural links with the Mycenaean world. The once believed-in Early-Bronze-Age Mycenaean-inspired Wessex culture, so closely associated with later development of Stonehenge, seems without doubt to have evolved naturally from a British native Megalithic culture. Thus, until contrary evidence is forthcoming, the *final* design of Stonehenge can now truly be claimed as a native innovation of the Neolithic aborigines of Southern Britain.

Considering Europe as a whole, it is possible that European Megalithic cultures evolved independently in several centres—products of separate culture foci. Brittany possessed Megalithic tombs before 4000 B.C., Britain and Denmark before 3000 B.C. Egypt as a source of Megalithic inspiration can now be dismissed outright, for nothing there is found in stone before 3000 B.C., and likewise with Babylonia. A separate culture focus for each

Megalithic centre is borne out by individual stylistic fashions reflected in Megalithic architecture. Yet even so, few disciples of the New Archaeology would deny that *some* diffusion via "culture creep" from one group to another must surely have been influential to a degree in Neolithic Europe. A parallel of this can be seen in the spread and influence of Babylonian astronomical ideas, first to India and then to China. A more modern parallel of culture diffusion is that provided by Galileo's first telescope. Galileo did not invent the telescope. He never saw the instrument made by the Dutch spectacle-makers, but when he *heard* about the idea, he immediately saw its possibilities and then set to work to construct something much superior—and succeeded.

It was Frazer who put diffusion in a commonsense light when he said : "No one claims that Christianity originated in Scotland : it reached there by diffusion."

But independent innovation of a particular idea by peoples divorced in time or geography, or both, occurs more often than one supposes. No one would now claim—except perhaps the most ardent hyperdiffusionists—that the almost identical methods to tie timber piles used by the Mesolithic Lake Dwellers and the contemporary Polynesian races is anything more than the example of human minds working alike to solve a particular problem.

14 Piazzi and the Pyramid

The ancient Pyramids of Egypt form somewhat of a long cluster-
ing group ... there are none to equal the combined fame and
antiquity of the several stone pyramids near Jizeh [Giza], in view
of the ancient Memphis, and not far from the present city of
Cairo ... But amongst these Jizeh Pyramids, again, there is one
that transcends in importance all the rest; one that has been
named for ages past " the Great Pyramid"; and which stands out
distinct and distinguished from all its fellows, by its giant size,
its wondrous internal structure, its superior and even exquisite
finish, the deep mysteries of its origin, and the hitherto inscrutable
destiny of its purpose ... Under whose direction ... and for what
purpose was the Great Pyramid built ...? This is indeed a mystery
of mysteries, but a noble one to inquire into. ...

Our Inheritance in The Great Pyramid (1864)
C. Piazzi Smyth.

It is recorded in history books that Napoleon Bonaparte before
the Battle of the Pyramids in 1798 addressed his troops with the
stirring message : "Think of it soldiers, from the summit of these
pyramids, forty centuries look down upon you." It is not recorded
whether Napoleon ever climbed a pyramid himself, but it was
Napoleon who cited the interesting statistic that the three Giza
pyramids contained sufficient stone to erect a defensive wall
(3 metres high and 30 centimetres wide) round the whole of
France. But whether it was Napoleon himself who made the
calculation is doubtful. It was more likely his friend the mathematician Gaspard Monge, who was included among the savants
of Napoleon's great scientific Commission despatched from

France to unlock the age-old secrets of Egypt.

Napoleon's Commission did not resolve the question of the pyramids. Indeed, it complicated it. Even today the question of the purpose of the pyramids is still a subject fraught with academic contention. . . .

When John Greaves, professor of astronomy at Oxford, wrote his *Pyramidographia* (1646), he reviewed, for the sake of his readers, all the old theories trotted out about the Egyptian pyramids which had come down since ancient times. These included the weighty judgement of Aristotle who believed them "the works of Tyranny"; while the Roman scribe Pliny believed them to have been built partly out of ostentation and—more subtly— as a means of keeping the *fellahin* in employment "to divert them from Mutinies and Rebellion". Pliny may well have been close to the truth, and this latter view of the pyramids' prime purpose has been echoed again by several modern pundits who unfortunately have not given prior credit to the astute old Roman.

As early as the fourth century, Julius Honorius had advanced the idea they were simply the granaries created by Joseph for storing wheat against the seven lean years. This biblical connection set an early precedent that was later to blossom more fully with the colourful idea that the Great Pyramid itself was nothing less than a Megalithic masterpiece of God's creation—a veritable "Bible in Stone".

Medieval Arab scholars had other ideas and forwarded beliefs that the pyramids were built by wise old men as either refuges against judgements of the Almighty or protection against inundation and fire. These theories continued to be bandied in serious literature until comparative recent times.

Greaves also cited the ideas that they were designed as astronomical observatories. As a thoroughly practical man, he remarked:

> . . . But that these Pyramids were designed for observatories . . . is in no way to be credited . . . Neither can I apprehend to what purpose the priests with so much difficulty should ascend so high, when below with more ease, and as much certainty, they might from their own lodging hewn in the rocks, upon which the Pyramids were erected, make the same observations . . .

Greaves was quite emphatic they were sepulchres and that

"the true reason for the pyramids depends upon higher and more weighty considerations . . . And this sprang from the Theology of the Egyptians, who believed, that as long as the Body endured, so long the Soul continued with it".

But there were those who believed Greaves was mistaken. It was known from Greek texts that the earliest astronomy related to the civilizations of the Chaldean-Babylonians and the Egyptians. From these two civilizations the Greeks themselves were supposed to have derived much of their own astronomy. It was recorded in some Greek texts that the priests of Thebes had claimed that they were the originators of exact astronomical observation. Herodotus, who was the first to comment on the pyramids, wrote that geometry, leastwise that part of it involved in land measurement, was invented in Egypt; this having been necessary because the Egyptians had to redefine field boundaries after the annual inundation of the Nile. Diodorus Siculus wrote that the Egyptians claimed to have taught astronomy to the Babylonians. Yet it was Josephus (A.D. 37-100), the Jewish historian, who claimed the opposite and wrote that the patriarch Abraham was a Chaldean and taught arithmetic and astronomy to the Egyptians, who in turn passed on their knowledge to the Greeks.

These strongly partizan arguments about who were the first astronomers raged up to modern times. When the influential classical scholar George Cornewall Lewis wrote his epic *Astronomy of the Ancients* in 1862, he devoted much of its 526 pages to examining in turn all the partizan arguments. Although he did not realize it himself, his conclusions were obsolete even before his book was published. Already there were tablets from Babylonia—then inscrutable—which were soon to shed an entirely new light on the origins of scientific astronomy (Chapter 15).

Some of the most intriguing arguments surrounding ancient astronomy concerned the claims of Diodorus Siculus who said that the Chaldeans at a very early period were able to predict the occurrences of eclipses as well as the return of comets. According to Herodotus it seemed that Thales had successfully predicted an eclipse of the Sun which put an end to the battle between the Medes and Lydians sometime between 652-585 B.C.

These claims were accepted at face value by many European scholars before the middle nineteenth century. But there were doubters. If these claims were true, then the Chaldeans indeed possessed a very advanced astronomical knowledge—especially about comets—for it was not until Newton had formulated the laws of gravitation and Halley successfully had applied them and predicted the return (in 1759) of the great comet that now bears his name that European astronomers were really sure they understood the dynamics of cometary motion.

The difficulty about accepting or denying these claims in the eighteenth and early nineteenth centuries was that no one could be absolutely sure about the nature of Babylonian or Egyptian astronomy for the simple reason that cuneiform and hieroglyph texts were inscrutable; and apart from second-hand and third-hand redacted Greek texts, no other philological sources were available. It was not until Champollion deciphered the hieroglyps around 1820 and Rawlinson finalized the decipherment of cuneiform in the 1830s that scholars could consult directly any written evidence to check claims made by Greek authors.

Many of the savants who accompanied Louis Napoleon's great expedition in 1798 were themselves convinced that the massive stone pyramids and some of the temples held a hidden and advanced astronomical science going back some thousands of years before the time of Christ.

Apart from the inscrutable pyramids whose exactitude in their setting out to the principal cardinal points had deeply impressed the scholars, some of the tombs and temples showed more obvious astronomical content. One of the most intriguing was the temple of Isis-Hathor at Dendera discovered in 1798 by General Desaix while pursuing the broken remnants of Murad Bey's army. Incorporated in the architectural decoration of the temple were found a series of unusual carvings. In a hidden room the ceiling centre-piece consisted of a $2\frac{1}{2}$-metre (8-foot) round carving depicting what appeared to be a plan of the heavens in symbolic signs, including a few recognizable signs of the zodiac (Fig. 17). For this reason the monument was given the name the Round Zodiac of Dendera—although in actual fact the depiction is not a zodiac in the usually accepted meaning of the word. Along the walls of a lower chamber of the temple was found a rectangular depiction even more ambiguous than the upper one, now usually referred to as the Rectangular or "Square" Zodiac of Dendera, but again it is not strictly a zodiac. The

Figure 17 A facsimile of the Round Zodiac of Dendera. The original of this intriguing depiction of the heavens dates only from the Ptolemaic period, but it is partly based on earlier Egyptian sky maps going back to the third millennium B.C. Among the wholly Egyptian asterisms and stars few can be identified with absolute certainty. The Ox's Foreleg (Ursa Major) is centre, while Orion is the royal figure standing under the Bull's hoofs. Sirius is represented as a Cow lying in a boat. The more enigmatic decans (figures with stars) are seen portrayed along the circumference inside the sky sphere supported by gods and goddesses.

figures were sketched by the artist Denon and later reproduced as an engraving in his great work *Travels in Egypt during the Campaign of General Buonaparte.*

The discovery of these celestial carvings was heralded as a thrilling discovery for science—something that might provide a breakthrough to understanding the ancient cosmic secrets of the early Egyptian civilization. At the time they generated as much interest among scholars as did the later findings of the Rosetta Stone. It was believed that an intense study of the zodiacs and the mysterious engravings—vaguely similar to engravings already found in tombs and temples—would confirm what the savants had suspected: it would prove the Egyptians knew about the sphericity of the Earth long before the Greeks knew it; it would confirm that the ancient Egyptians recognized and measured the obliquity of the ecliptic and its periodic changes; and it would reveal that the Egyptians knew the real reason why eclipses occurred. It was just supposed that the zodiacs might even provide a built-in method of calculating eclipses—thus predating knowledge then believed possessed only by the Babylonians in the last millennium B.C.

But it was the finding of the Rosetta Stone (in 1799, and finally deciphered in the 1820s) which eventually pricked the bubble of speculation surrounding the zodiacs when it provided the key to hieroglyphic texts.

In the so-called "Square" Zodiac many of the signs contained in it are intermixed with mythological personages—some sailing in boats. No one at first could make sense of it; then it was recognized that it depicted the Sun's course during the day— the twelve solar positions occupied by the Sun each hour from rising to setting (represented by twelve boats).

But it was the Round Zodiac found on the ceiling of the secret room above the main temple that attracted most attention. Like the Rosetta Stone the French saw it as one of the great archaeological prizes of its day. The Rosetta Stone had been surrendered and irretrievably lost to the British in 1801. Loyalist Frenchmen now wanted the Round Zodiac for France. It had been discovered by a Frenchman and deserved its place in one of the archaeological show-cases in Paris as a fitting trophy of Napoleon's Expedition.

The story of how the French Deputy M. Sebastian Louis

Saulnier, man-of-wealth and antiquarian, enlisted the aid of the French traveller Lelorraine to go to Egypt and hack out the Round Zodiac from the temple ceiling is one of the great (yet disheartening) stories of Egyptology. Today, disparagingly, we look down our noses at the antiquarian trophy-hunters of yester-year, but it was a different age with different standards. It is quite certain too that had not the French taken it from under the eyes of the British, it would soon have disappeared from Egypt to reappear in the basement vaults of the British Museum. Lelorraine pipped the British attempt to steal it—by the notorious Consul, Henry Salt—by a matter of a few days. Today it stands on the stairs of the Louvre while, sadly, at Dendera only a replica of it hangs on the ceiling.

Many of the ideas about the fabulous antiquity and profound nature of Egyptian astronomy had been fostered by savants such as Charles François Dupuis (1742-1809), who had helped Napoleon create and then organize his great Commission to explore Upper Egypt. Another who followed this line was Jean Baptiste Biot (1774-1862)—a Lockyer of his age—who became very interested in the Dendera zodiacs and made several attempts to decipher them. Biot was a scholar and a scientist of the first order—although he failed to decipher the zodiacs completely, he believed that the sculptures they contained were conclusive proof of the great antiquity of Egyptian astronomy.

When Champollion tackled the decipherment of the Rosetta Stone, where the Englishman Thomas Young left off, and finally cracked the secrets of its part-hieroglyphic inscription, the result was that the inscription accompanying the zodiacs could then be read. It was with shock surprise that the savants learnt that the temple related to the Ptolemaic period of Egyptian history —as recent as about 30 B.C. So much for the great antiquity of Egyptian astronomy, smiled the critics, and the Greek scholars were not slow in reiterating their view that whatever astronomical knowledge the Egyptians had possessed had been obtained from the Greeks or Babylonians. They were right on one point. The Egyptians certainly inherited all the late-period horoscope nonsense from the Babylonians and the Greeks, but they were wrong about the rest.

Meanwhile the largest Megalithic works of the ancient world —the pyramids—continued to attract widespread attention, and

Champollion's work did not settle any of the old contentions surrounding them. The inscriptions on the pyramids provided no clear evidence about what purpose they served the pharaohs who built them other than the obvious one of sepulchres.

The inside of the Great pyramid was not penetrated until Caliph El Mamoun broached it in A.D. 820 when some believed he found the undisturbed gold- and jewel-bedecked body of Cheops—a pharaoh of the fourth dynasty. Tradition has it (but on poor authority) that part of the treasure included a ruby the size of a hen's egg which shone as a flame. Most authorities consider the whole story of the treasure-find a colourful myth, and that the Great Pyramid was emptied of its contents by tomb robbers way back in ancient times.

Since the Renaissance the Great Pyramid had been deeply involved in countless occult traditions concerning the heavens, and Greaves's book and his forthright opinions (c. 1646) did little to influence the committed. In 1693 we find the astronomical ideas being pushed again by Carari and de Chazelles, who put forward the theory that they were both tombs *and* observatories.

Like Stonehenge which at one time was beset with various "sun-dial" theories, it was inevitable that comparable ideas would be attributed to the Great Pyramid, and the first on record is that of Paul Lucas in 1714. Lucas's theories embraced the belief that the architecture of the design was arranged to mark out the solstices. Biot himself was convinced that whatever else was the Great Pyramid's prime purpose, it also served as an immense gnomon for the determination of the equinoxes. In 1853, Mariette, the French Egyptologist, following Biot's instructions, claimed he had determined the time of vernal equinox within twenty-nine hours. He wrote later :

... With or without intention by the Egyptians who built the Great Pyramid, it has, since it existed, functioned as an immense sundial which has marked annually the periods of the equinoxes with an error of less than one day, and those of the solstices with an error less than a day and three quarters.

Nevertheless, it is not generally appreciated that *any* object carefully orientated north-south (as is the Great Pyramid), and

given the right (coincidental) geometry and casts shadows, may
be used to act as a sun-dial or gnomon. It is this exact orientation of the Great Pyramid to the cardinal points which triggered the whole business of the search for astronomical significances and its so-called metrical and mystical truths.

John Taylor, an eccentric London publisher, has been called
"the Father of the Pyramid mysteries". Surprisingly for one who
devoted thirty years of his life to formulating his theories he
never visited Egypt once. The culmination of his three decades
of thought about the problem was a book entitled *The Great
Pyramid: Why was it Built? And Who Built it?* (1859).

In a nutshell, it was Taylor's belief that the Great Pyramid
was part of God's plan, and he supposed it incorporated all kinds
of deliberate mathematical truths in its design. For example, he
claimed: "... The coffin in the King's Chamber ... was intended to be a standard measure of capacity and weight for all
nations; and certain nations did originally receive their weights
and measures from these."

But according to Taylor the builder of the Pyramid was not
an Egyptian but an Israelite, perhaps Noah himself, acting again
under divine orders. Thus: "He who built the Ark was, of all
men, the most competent to direct the building of the Great
Pyramid. . . ."

But Taylor's best remembered observations are his two pro-
positions concerned with *pi* and the so-called unit-inch sacred
cubit. The first proposition was that, in its original condition, the
Great Pyramid's height "was twice its base, as the diameter to
the circumference of a circle". Or, using Taylor's numbers:
vertical height of the Pyramid = 486 feet; breadth of base 764
feet, therefore: $486:1528::1:3 \cdot 144$.

His second proposition concerned the sacred cubit—thought
by Taylor to be *about* twenty-five British inches. This Taylor
claimed was the same cubit used by Noah in the construction of
the Ark and was based on the length of the Earth's axis divided
by 400,000.

A large public following could not resist such persuasive arguments, for the pious Victorians were ripe for such metrical
messiahs who believed in their bible. Was it more than coincidence that John Taylor's book appeared in 1859, the same year
as Darwin's *Origin of Species* which the Church decried? Fore-

most among the converts was Charles Piazzi Smyth—Astronomer
Royal for Scotland. Piazzi was a powerful, influential figure in
world astronomy when he took up his pyramid interests. Taylor
began to correspond with him, and soon Piazzi became fascinated by the new Pyramid theories—then totally beset by them.

Piazzi was son of the distinguished Vice-Admiral Smyth
known in British navy circles and at the Royal Geographical
Society as "Mediterranean Smyth". The family was directly related to a loyalist emigré who fled from New Jersey to England
after the American Revolution, and who in turn had been a
direct descendant of the famous Captain John Smith now remembered for his classic *History of Virginia* (1624).

Admiral Smyth had a distinguished career in the navy after
having risen from the ranks. In turn he had been president of
the Society of Antiquaries, the Royal Astronomical Society and
the Royal Geographical Society. Piazzi had received this particular forename as a direct result of his father's passion for
astronomy. During the Napoleonic Wars the Admiral was sec-
onded to the Mediterranean, and it was this which took him to
Palermo in 1813 where he met and became a good friend of
Giuseppe Piazzi, discoverer of the first asteroid (named Ceres at
the insistence of Piazzi after the Neolithic fertility goddess of
Sicily). When a son was born to the Admiral, it seemed natural
that he should honour his good friend the Italian astronomer.

While the Admiral's astronomical ideas were conventional, his
antiquarian-cum-archaeological ones were less so. The Admiral
was much enamoured by the views of the British eccentric antiquarian Kingsborough—author of the nine folio *Antiquities of
Mexico* (1831)—who had become obsessed with the idea that
the New World had been reached by ancient voyagers from the
Old World (the Lost Tribes of Israel). Piazzi, from childhood,
was much under his father's influence, and at home he lived
constantly exposed to the heady intellectual atmosphere of astronomy laced with Egyptology and diffusionism.

Piazzi Smyth took over where John Taylor left off. By the
time Smyth's book *Our Inheritance in the Great Pyramid* was
published in 1864, Taylor was dead. In his preface Smyth wrote
he had arrived at much the same results as Taylor "though by
a different road".

Smyth's particular metrical obsessions were to hinge on the

sacred cubit and his belief that the length of the British Imperial inch was derived directly from it, plus the "discovery" of the hidden truth that the base of the Great Pyramid divided by the width of a casing stone equalled exactly 365—or the number of days in the year. Since the width of a casing stone was about twenty-five inches or slightly more, this *also* related to the length of the sacred cubit. One twenty-fifth of this cubit was about what Smyth now called the "Pyramid inch". He believed it was no chance accident that this inch was near to the British inch. It was incorporated in the Great Pyramid "the result of settled intention and high purpose, arranged from the beginning of the world". Proof again was that twenty-five such unit inches once formed the sacred cubit of the Jews "and was specially maintained by them for important purposes, in antagonism to the measures of profound nations, during all the period of Divine Inspiration to the chosen of their race".

Smyth deduced that the Pyramid's measurements, including the various internal passages, symbolized different periods of time in world history, measured from the date of the building of the Pyramid which, on astronomical grounds, he assigned to 2170 B.C., but so far no Egyptologist has conceived so recent a date for its construction.

It was the no-nonsense establishment figure of Sir John Herschel who reintroduced the astronomical element into the Great Pyramid after the first only part-successful efforts of Napoleon's savants. Back in 1836, Herschel had noted that the north-facing entrance to the Pyramid was curiously aligned to the star Thuban (Alpha Draconis) about 2160 B.C. when this star was the pole star (now removed from this position owing to precession). Had the very sober Herschel then known what significance was later to be placed on this curious (coincidental?) observation, he might well have kept his own counsel. On reflection the discerning student of astro-archaeology may arrive at the conclusion that much of today's doubtful Megalithic-alignment theory is derivative of Stukeley, Biot and Herschel.

Another well-known nineteenth-century astronomer who became interested in Pyramid speculation—but avoided Smyth's metrical obsessions and biblical overtones—was Richard Proctor, a popular author of the period. While not accepting Smyth's ideas, he nevertheless had little doubt that at least *one* architec-

N

tural feature in the Great Pyramid was astronomical. Proctor concluded that the entrance "tunnel" aligned to the Egyptian pole star (Alpha Draconis) was not intended for use *after* the Pyramid was built, but that it was used during the period of the Pyramid's construction to allow the architect to obtain a true northward orientation. This was a novel idea, but in practice there are much easier means of setting an exact north orientation, and we can be sure the contemporary Egyptians realized this themselves.

Proctor was certain that it had also been the intention of the Egyptian master-builder to set the Great Pyramid so it would straddle latitude 30°N exactly. Substantial proof of this Proctor maintained was that the final error in siting was only 1′ 9″ of arc (or 1 mile 570 yards; 2·2 kilometres) south of the 30th parallel. The small error was significant and showed that it was unlikely the Egyptian surveyor-astronomers knew about the necessary corrections for atmospheric refraction—the error was about what one could expect if correction for refraction had been left out.

Proctor, looking south from the Pyramid, noticed that there might be alignments associated with the southern (ventilator-shaft) passage. He believed there could be, and that it was the star Alpha Centauri whose declination coincided with the angle of the passage round about the period 3300 B.C. But this figure is about 700 years too early for the date of *c.* 2600 B.C. nowadays given this Pyramid. Yet another arbitrary stellar alignment was cited on a line perpendicular to the Alpha-Draconis line, and this carried to Eta Tauri, one of the Pleiades cluster stars.

Thus gestated a tangled web of hyperspeculation about Pyramid alignments in which several influential astronomers became involved, including the Astronomer Royal for Ireland, Dr. Brunnow. Another was the later very controversial figure of Percival Lowell, one of the champions for the existence of Martian canals, not finally discredited until the US Mariner flights to the planet in the 1960s.

Piazzi Smyth ruined his career and reputation with his obsession for biblical truths mixed with metrology. His peers could turn a blind eye to his obsessive religious zeal—that was a man's own prerogative—but they would not assist him in his disseminating anti-scientific propaganda concerning God's so-called metrical truths. When in 1874 the Royal Society refused to publish the latest paper on his metrical discoveries, he resigned his Fellowship in a fit of pique, and from then on his status as a recognized man of science declined.

It was Flinders Petrie who finally exploded the last shred of any verisimilitude that lingered with the establishment about pyramidology. Petrie began his career as a land surveyor; and after writing *Inductive Metrology* (1875) and then *Stonehenge* (1880), he turned his attentions to Egypt at the request of his father. Petrie's father—an engineer and chemist—had been one of Taylor's and Smyth's god-fearing converts, and as many others of the period he had been completely infatuated and beguiled by the strong religious overtones that went hand in hand with pyramidology.

The younger Petrie remained in Egypt from 1880 to 1882, spending nine months in Giza surveying the pyramids and amassing the data that was to finally damn Taylor's and Smyth's theories. Petrie's own pyramid labours resulted in the publication of *The Pyramids and Temples of Gizeh* (1887), which provides a landmark in the history of Egyptology. From then on he was an archaeologist with an overriding interest in Megalithic monuments, but his early career in land surveying and interests in metrology stood him in good stead for the rest of his life. In the fashion of some present-day astro-archaeologists, he had a predilection for playing the numbers game—and not always with tongue-in-cheek. On one occasion when Petrie was recounting the significance of the Egyptian royal cubit (20·62 inches) he threw in for good measure the interesting fact that the diagonal of the square of this cubit ([the double remen] $= 29 \cdot 161$ inches) "... is almost exactly the natural length of a pendulum which swings 100,000 times a day; at the latitude of Memphis this would be 29·157 inches...". This snippet of Petrie's was undoubtedly the very story which gave rise to a letter in *New Scientist* that the length of the Megalithic yard was perhaps determined by the discovery of isochronism of the pendulum, i.e. employing suitable foresight and backsight markers in the meridian for the successive meridian passage of two specific stars. For example, the MY would give about 150 swings between the passage of Epsilon and Zeta Orionis (two of Orion's Belt stars). In such a method the correspondent suggested that the number of swings could be quoted for a rope of correct length.

Some interesting asides of Petrie's character and his prowess as a surveyor as well as an improvisor are provided in Mortimer Wheeler's autobiographic book *Alms for Oblivion* (1966). Wheeler recounted that in 1925 Petrie spent a holiday with him at Brecon in Wales while Wheeler was excavating a Roman fort. Petrie decided to busy himself surveying stone circles and other Megalithic monuments in the surrounding country. Wheeler asked Petrie how he proposed to do this work and with what instruments? Wheeler recalled:

> ... a look of ineffable cunning came into his eyes as he produced a single slender bamboo pea-stick and—a visiting card. The pea-stick, he said, planted in the ground gave him the line, whilst the visiting card, sighted carefully along two of its sides, gave him a right angle. At night after dinner, by the light of an oil lamp, he would get out a notebook containing lists of measurements resulting from his day's work in the field, and, with the help of a logarithm-table, would ultimately reduce them to a schematic diagram.

Wheeler in recounting this anecdote said that it illustrated the paradoxical character of Petrie. By incredible ingenuity he was often able to solve complex problems and render them simple and surmountable; yet, at other times, simple problems might be tangled into inextricable complexities.

Today Petrie is best remembered as the British giant of Egyptology, and most archaeologists prefer to forget (or are unaware of) the great master's own metrical aberration: the so-called "Etruscan foot". This was the unit of measurement that he evolved to fit the theories surrounding his grand scheme for relating hill figures. In his *Hill Figures of England* (1926) Petrie believed that the Whiteleaf and Bledlow crosses, the Long Man of Wilmington *and* Stonehenge could be shown to belong to the same primitive period and were set out with the same unit. For example, it was his notion that the base line of the Whiteleaf Cross, which he measured as 386 feet in length, was the exact diameter of the main sarsen circle at Stonehenge, approximately 400 Etruscan feet. Petrie had in fact simply fallen into the same obsessional trap as had Smyth with his Pyramid-inch theories.

In spite of Petrie's pyramid labours, the cult of pyramidology continued to flourish among the naïve and credulous and is still actively with us in what has been aptly called the lunatic fringe of archaeology. The truth is that people will believe what they want to believe. . . . Petrie recounted the story that he once found a zealous disciple of Smyth's busily attempting to file down the particularly significant granite boss of the vestibule of the Great Pyramid to suit the exact size that theory demanded. John Taylor had given the inspiration for the cult, and Piazzi Smyth had tried to give it scientific verisimilitude. The farrago of metrical nonsense they created has provided their disciples with a gold-mine of pyramid lore to arrange and rearrange to suit age-to-age changes in fashion. In many respects pyramidology foreshadowed the pseudo-scientific cult of Velikovsky that began to plague science in the 1950s (Chapter 15).

Following Smyth, many other names appear in the story of the pyramid cult. Two brothers, John and Morton Edgar, journeyed to Egypt in 1909 to make measurements of their own and discovered new truths and prophetic teachings in the architecture of the Great Pyramid which resulted in a two-volume work, *The Great Pyramid Passages and Chambers* (1910-13).

But the culmination of pyramid pseudology and the "Pyramid-idiots" was a book entitled *The Great Pyramid: its Divine Message* (1924) authored by D. Davidson and H. Aldersmith. This book and its subsequent editions was indeed the very pinnacle of pyramidology. The authors deemed it wise to discard some of Smyth's obsolete and often suspect measures and cunningly fell back on Petrie's authenticated ones, manipulating them in arbitrary fashion to suit their theories. Even Stonehenge was dragged in to provide substance for arguments. They invented a whole new battery of geomancy and bizarre formulae for a new corpus of Pyramid prophesies. A great war was predicted for 1928 and the Second Coming of Christ in 1934. When these prophesies were not fulfilled, Davidson, apparently unruffled, replayed his Pyramid numbers game and discovered that 1953 was to be the actual year the world would end. Although we can now smile at this whole saga of Pyramidology, there is still a credulous Bermuda-Triangle-enamoured public who takes it seriously.

What then was the *true* extent of Egyptian astronomy? A search of the archaeological record reveals little evidence of a true scientific astronomy of the kind claimed for Megalithic North-West Europe. Contrary to traditional belief, there is no evidence that eclipse-prediction methods were known at any period right up to Ptolemaic times. Even reference to eclipses in written documents or inscriptions is very sparse.

Nevertheless, in all periods the Egyptians were much concerned with calendars and time as would be expected of an agrarian society. There is good evidence that in pre-dynastic times the calendar was a lunar-based one. From the earliest dates we can glean references to the determination of the time of night by star-group risings from the enigmatic Egyptian decans—so named from the Greek *dekan* (ten) because they are believed to represent 10° divisions of the sky.

These star-group decans (twelve-hour star-clocks) are *reproduced* on paintings on coffins relating to the Middle Kingdom 2100 to 1800 B.C. (Plate 21). Later there were more elaborate star-clocks like those reproduced in the Rameses' tombs (Plate 22). These early star-clocks were continued as decorative motifs in funerary contexts long after they served any practical usefulness as timekeepers (owing to precession). We can guess that after the Rameses' period there was a decline in Egyptian astronomy which may well have achieved a high peak of attainment round the time of the building of the Giza pyramids *c.* 2700-2600 B.C.

Many of the astro-depictions found in funerary contexts included serious copying errors perpetuated by artists who, we can be sure, had no pretentions to technical astronomical knowledge themselves, and perhaps even their scribal masters at this time were no better. It is also clear that these astro-depictions were repeatedly copied from sky charts originally compiled by knowledgeable astronomer-scribes as early as the Old Kingdom. None of these originals have unfortunately come down to us in the archaeological record.

The old Egyptian stellar asterisms are very difficult to reconcile with those constellation figures inherited from Babylonia which still form the basis of contemporary constellations. The early interpreters of the zodiacs of Dendera and Egyptian star asterisms, found in funerary contexts, made the error of believing that the Egyptian astronomers depicted the heavens in proportion, and to scale, just as the makers of modern planispheres and zodiacs attempt to do. It is now apparent that all Egyptian sky charts were highly schematic in form and often grossly distorted —sometimes with constellations positioned in the wrong order to suit the convenience of the artist. But it is now clear that the French savants were right about the great age of Egyptian astronomy, and certainly we can be sure the decanal figures and the other strange asterisms date back to *at least* the third millennium B.C. Few sure identifications of Egyptian stars and star groupings can be made. Only the star Sirius and the constellations of Orion and Ursa Major can be said to be positive identifications (Plate 21).

The Pyramid Texts provide clues and clear insights of how emotionally and spiritually involved the Egyptians were with the numinous celestial vault that hung above them. This was considered the natural world rather than the world of the daylight earth plane—quite opposite to the concept of present-day mankind. The old texts provide clear examples of what Neolithic man in Egypt (and likely elsewhere) felt about the gods and the cosmos. Osiris was a supreme god. His son Re, the Sun-god, had power over darkness—equated with powers of life and death. Osiris himself was sometimes considered to live on in the annual sprouting of the grain or in the Nile floodwaters which personified the fertility of the land. He was also the Moon or the constellation of Orion, and his sign is depicted with Orion (Plate 21).

Osiris was also associated with the nether world and the Egyptian Cult of the Dead. It was the deadman's greatest wish that he be absorbed into the great rhythm of the Universe— either as an eternal passenger aboard the Sun-boat Re; or among the circumpolar stars; or to seek rebirth with the Moon in his boat which like that of Re sailed over the sky-back of Nut, the great sky-goddess (Plate 23). The Pyramid Texts refer to the Cosmic Heavens as a place of beautiful roads where the dead king accompanies Orion who is guided by Sirius, the Dog Star (Plate 21). In the Coffin and other Egyptian texts there is written much cosmic poetry that was echoed again by the Egyptian astronomer Ptolemy *c.* A.D. 150 when he wrote: "I know that I am mortal and the creature of a day, but when I search out the many rolling circles of stars, my feet touch the Earth no longer, but with Zeus himself I take my fill of ambrosia, the food of the gods."

It is in Egyptian texts where we also glean insights into how ancient man was totally and emotionally involved with Nature's processes. The course of the Sun, the rising and setting of the stars, and the swing of the Moon became firmly ingrained in him as part of a farmer's theology and unshakeable creed.

It is not surprising that the later Egyptian calendar was strictly an agrarian one which consisted of three seasons each of four months. It began initially with the heliacal rising of Sirius at dawn because this coincided with the flooding of the Nile—the prime event in Egyptian life. Although it seems certain that the earliest Egyptian calendar was a lunar-based one, the one that superseded it was based on the civil year composed of twelve months of thirty days each and five additional days at the end of each year. Sirius was known as Soth, and therefore the calendar based on it was called the Sothic cycle. The trouble is that the 365-day calendar is really too short with the result that in intervals of 1,460 years the seasons shift entirely through the months. Nevertheless, it is from Egypt that we derive our modern calendar, but it is from Babylonian astronomy we derive the sexagesimal system (of minutes in the hour based on the number 60).

Although the Bible-in-Stone ideas have been thoroughly discredited and Lockyer's later ideas for stellar alignments contained in Egyptian temples are considered at best unproven, one must not fall into the trap that certain stars were not significant to the Egyptians in the directional sense. The northern stars were likely very significant in the context of the Cult of the Dead and the equatorial and southern stars in the context of clock-stars (Plate 22). In the Pyramid Texts a king becomes a star as well as the Sun when he ascends the sky after death to gain union with the gods. The Great Bear, known as the Bull's Foreleg and the "Imperishable", was a very important asterism; important too were the entire northern circumpolar regions which were greatly revered. In the Pyramid Texts we read that the goal of the deceased was the region of Dat, in the northern part of the heavens. He who joined the (northern) circumpolar constellations (visible throughout each night of the year) would live for ever. A king's house in the sky could never be destroyed, and in the *Book of the Dead* we read that the stars themselves aided the dead man until Nut, the great sky-goddess, uncovered her arms to receive him. . . .

Perhaps then, in the context of the Cult of the Dead, there may indeed be significance in the entrance passage of the Great Pyramid *facing* northwards since this was the most important direction for Heaven, and several of the other pyramids at Giza have north-facing passages.

Whatever the importance of the entrance passages, it is clear that the pyramids—particularly the pyramids at Giza— were engineered by men of genius like the men who built Stonehenge, Avebury and the Megalithic monuments at Carnac. Unlike the anonymous Megalithic masterminds of North-West Europe, some of the names of the pyramid designers are known. One of these was the polymath-priest Imhotep, architect-astronomer and father of medicine. It is known that Imhotep was vizier of Pharaoh Zoser of the 3rd Dynasty (*c.* 2778 to 2723 B.C.). He is supposed to be the designer and supervisor of the first Step-Pyramid at Sakkara where his name appears inscribed on Zoser's statue. He held many titles including "supervisor of all things which heaven brings, the earth creates and the Nile brings". He apparently stemmed from a priestly hierarchy, for Kanofer, his father, is recorded as "chief of the works of the south and the northland". Two thousand years later, in *c.* 525 B.C., Imhotep re-emerges raised to the status of an Egyptian god.

Although a shadowy historical figure, Imhotep provides astro-archaeology with a reassuring firm model for the kind of master-mind found living in the third millennium B.C., and there is little reason to doubt he had his mirror-image counterparts in North-West Europe at around the same period.

15 Venus and Velikovsky

When in the month of Sabatu on the
15th day Venus disappeared in the west, was invisible
for 3 days and appeared again on the 18th—
castastrophies from kings, Adad will bring rain,
Ea underground water, kings will send kings greetings. . . .
  Inscription on a Babylonian clay tablet *c*. 1646 B.C. (?)

In a study embracing Megalithic cultures the inclusion of Babylonia—primarily a region of mud-brick cultures—may seem at first sight a strange incongruous choice. Nevertheless, because the Babylonians from earliest times were involved with astronomy in various guises, no study citing the earliest astronomy of mankind would be complete without reference to those whom many Greeks believed to be the true fathers of this science. Furthermore there are the pseudo-scientific theories of Immanuel Velikovsky concerning the planet Venus which provide a strong thematic link between Babylonia and the mystery of the Megaliths.

In the past great weight was given to the importance and primacy of Babylonian astronomy by ancient authors, and although there were strong counter-claims that astronomy may have been founded in Egypt, consensus weighed towards its coming from one of the ancient mud-brick cultures of Mesopotamia. One man responsible for providing this opinion was Berosus, himself a Babylonian. Berosus is another shadowy figure in astronomical history, but it is known he was born in the reign of Alexander the Great and later became a priest at the temple of Bel-Marduk in Babylon. He was invited to Greece to form an astrological school on the island of Kos and became very influential in Greek astronomy and astrology. It is known he wrote several books including a great history *Babyloniaka*, of which only fragments survive in the works of Josephus, Eusebius and Syncellus. Nevertheless, Berosus as a source of scientific astronomy is disappointing, for the fragments attributed to him all consist of astrological or mythological references chiefly relating to ancient cosmological legends.

Berosus is now best remembered for his Babylonian king-lists extending from before the Flood to Tiglath-Pileser III. As a list it has been of use to historians in fixing the relative chronology of Babylonia, but since it extends back 36,000 years, as Berosus claimed, it needs to be taken with the proverbial pinch of salt.

When George Cornewall Lewis wrote his definitive *Astronomy of the Ancients* in 1862, the extent of scientific Babylonian astronomy was not yet appreciated. Although tablets with cuneiform inscriptions had arrived in France in 1846, having been excavated from the ruins of Khorsabad by the French consul Paul Émile Botta, and tablets from King Assurbanipal's library at Kuyunjik had been excavated by Austin Henry Layard in 1849–50 and sent back to London by the crateful, the true content of most had not been recognized.

Cuneiform had been partly disciphered by Georg Friedrich Grotefend about 1802 and then independently by the Frenchman Eugene Burnouf and the German Christian Lassen in 1836 and then by Henry Rawlinson in the mid and late 1830s. Yet it was not for several more years that scholars with the necessary technical background recognized what the classical scholars had missed or misunderstood.

First to recognize Babylonian astronomy inscribed on clay tablets were the German scholar Julius Oppert and the British biblical scholar A. H. Sayce. It was Sayce's re-translation in 1874 of a clay tablet first deciphered in 1870 by Rawlinson and George Smith (who later dramatically found the famous Flood Tablets) which began the long-contentious saga of the interpretation of the so-called Venus Tablets found in the ruins of Kuyunjik (ancient Nineveh).

The discovery of King Assurbanipal's library (*c.* 650 B.C.) in the ruined palace of King Sennacherib at Nineveh was one of the great finds of the nineteenth century. It was this discovery that provided the key to the understanding of the entire Assyrio-Babylonian civilizations.

The precious tablets had been preserved by a fortuitous accident. When a fire, started by the attacking Medes, consumed the floor beams of the library building and the floor collapsed, the tablets, which had been stored in labelled baskets, cascaded into two basement rooms where they remained cocooned in debris until excavated over 2,500 years later. At the time of discovery, the tablets covered the floors of the basement rooms to a depth of 30 centimetres; and when finally counted, they represented a library of nearly thirty thousand "volumes". It was in this same library that George Smith found his famous tablets telling of the Flood.

In 1880 Bosanquet and Sayce published a new translation of the tablet known by its British Museum catalogue number as K 160 (K to identify it from its source Kuyunjik). It was recognized to be a series of sightings relating to the planet Venus and actually contained distinct groups of observations laced with astrological omens, for example: *In the month Sivan, on the twenty-fifth day Ninsianna [Venus] disappeared in the east ... she remained absent from the sky for two months six days ... in the month Ulul on the twenty-fourth day, Ninsianna appeared in the west ... the heart of the land is happy. ...*

This translation was of considerable interest. Because Venus is a planet closer to the Sun than the Earth, it appears from the Earth alternatively as an evening "star" in the west and then as a morning "star" in the east as it is carried round the Sun in its orbit in 225 days. Even the early Greeks had failed to recognize that the evening and morning stars (Hesperus and Eosphoros) were one and the same—namely Venus at different elongations of its orbit. It was not until the time of Parmenides or Pythagoras that the Greeks discovered this fact for themselves and believed it to be entirely new knowledge. This was a positive indication that the Babylonians had a more advanced astronomy than the Greeks, which some Greek scholars had long denied.

As is frequent with Babylonian tablets, there is often more than one source for a given text. Many of the tablets found in Assurbanipal's library were copies of much older tablets which the King had commissioned his agents to root out and then his scribes to copy. The K 160 tablet was actually a damaged Assyrian version. In 1906 the Italian astronomer G. V. Schiaparelli (the man to spark off the Martian-canal controversy in 1877) noticed what others had missed. In 1899 the tablet K 2321 + K 3032 had been published by Craig. Schiaparelli realized they concerned the same series as K 160 but provided a much longer series of observations. Yet another source, a tablet known as W 802, was excavated at Kish in the heart of Babylon in 1924.

The problem confronting the decipherment of these tablets is that all are damaged in some way, and the text has had to be reconstructed as a whole from the various portions. Collectively they are known as The Venus Tablets, or The Venus Tablets of Ammizaduga, and they refer to observations of Venus over a period of 21 years.

Only the top portion of W 802 has survived, but it gives the text for the first six years in legible form. On K 2321 + K 3032, the text can be read from Year 7 onwards. Between them, W 802 and K 2321 + K 3032 provide half the astronomical data.

The rest of the data comes chiefly from K 160. But this tablet has its top portion missing, and its surface is defaced. The observation sequence starts with Year 8, and if it all could be read, it would be otherwise complete. Although the omens can readily be identified, some of the astronomical data is illegible.

In spite of all the defects, however, the back of K 2321 + K 3032 gives additional information, and together the sources provide a complete 21-year check.

It is the actual dates for these Babylonian Venus observations B.C. that provide the great controversy about the tablets, and in addition they have a direct bearing on the pseudo-scientific (but influential) ideas of Immanuel Velikovsky.

Velikovsky c. 1950, in his book *Worlds in Collision*, put forward a theory—among many theories—which supposed that the planet Venus had earlier been a comet. Velikovsky, in this and other books, had much to say about the past, including the Earth's collision with a comet, the plagues of Egypt, the origin of coal and petroleum, ideas about faunal extinctions in the geological record, and the reasons for the parting of the Red Sea.

Putting aside for the moment the later Velikovsky controversy, scholars earlier recognized the Venus Tablets were important because they believed they might help sort out some of the confusing chronology in Babylonian times. This expectation was not without precedent, for two cuneiform astronomer-scholars had already helped sort out the chronology of the later Seleucid period *c*. 250 to 50 B.C. (below).

When Schiaparelli studied the problem in 1906, he assigned the content of the tablets to a period no earlier than the eighth century B.C. Next on the scene, in 1912, was the great Jesuit astronomer-scholar Franz Xavier Kugler (1862-1929) who examined the observations for Year 8 and noted that some of the observations for this year (in the 21-year period) were missing, and in their place, inserted between Years 8 and 9, was a passage that up to then had not been properly understood. Kugler now recognized this as the year-formula, the "Year of the golden throne". This was the year-formula that was known to have been used to refer to the eighth year of the reign of Ammizaduga, the next to the last king of the First Babylonian (or Hammurabi) dynasty that flourished in the early part of the second millenium B.C. Since it was also known that Ammizaduga reigned for exactly 21 years, the same span as that of the Venus Tablets, the identity seemed sure and complete.

These year-formula names were in use in Babylonia throughout the 300 years of the Hammurabi dynasty, but they were based on a custom derived from a much earlier period. Each year was designated by some significant or important event which had taken place. Occasionally it might also refer to an event of the previous year but more usually to something occurring in the year itself. In this way the year-formula names provide a compact and comprehensive history of the Hammurabi dynasty.

Although the relative chronology within the Hammurabi dynasty was well established, the absolute span of the dynasty itself—in terms of B.C. dates—was not certain. This was due to the shadowy Kassite period that immediately followed the Hammurabi dynasty, thirty-one years after Ammizaduga died.

It was now anticipated that Kugler's discovery would help pin-point exactly Ammizaduga's reign in B.C. dates, which in turn would fix the start and finish of the whole First dynasty. By use of established astronomical principles, it was hoped that astronomers could work backwards and examine the past movements of Venus for the period in the first half of the second millenium B.C. to find a time when the Venus-tablet observations were satisfied by a particular 21-year slot.

It was known too that the Babylonian astronomers had recognized that Venus appearances repeat themselves exactly after 5 synodic periods of the planet—a period equal to 8 years less $2\frac{1}{2}$ days, or equal to 99 Babylonian (lunar) months less 4 days. This period was of great use to check and then correct scribal mistakes made in copying the tablets from originals.

Kugler, on astronomical grounds, believed that Hammurabi's reign should be dated 2123 to 2081 B.C. based on the assigned period of 1977 to 1956 B.C. he found for Ammizaduga via the Venus observations. At the time this result was generally accepted, but soon doubts were cast because others discovered the astronomical method he had used offered alternative solutions. In 1917, E. F. Weidner offered dates for Ammizaduga of 1809 to 1788 B.C. In 1923, Kugler himself revised his figures for Ammizaduga to 1801 to 1780 B.C.

In 1927, S. Langdon of Oxford University requested the British astronomer J. K. Fotheringham to reassess the Venus Tablets dates, and subsequently a new set of dates, 1921 to 1900 B.C., was offered as a solution. In the same year F. Thureau-Dangin, Chief Conservateur of the Oriental Antiquities at the Louvre, offered dates spanning 1857 to 1836 B.C.

The problem had now developed into one like that which still besets absolute chronology in Mesoamerica over the correlation of Maya calendar dates to Julian dates which at present has nine suggested solutions.

Another attack was made by Langdon and Fotheringham, this time with the assistance of the German astronomer and mathematician Carl Schoch. It was Schoch's task to construct new, up-to-date astronomical tables and so eradicate earlier errors. The result was that Ammizaduga could not have lived in 1809 nor 1801 B.C. (Weidner's and Kugler's solutions), but the other dates still remained theoretically possible.

Another attack was made by examining legal documents of the period. Among these were found written contracts between landlord and tenant for the division of the date harvest. It was the practice for unripe dates to be counted before the harvest, and then a contract signed giving the terms by which the tenant undertook to supply his landlord a given quantity of ripe dates by a set day in the month designated Tesrit—or by the first day of the following month Arahsamna. Comparing times with later

Babylonian documents that could be fixed to the Gregorian calendar with certainty, and also present-day harvest conditions, it was worked out that the final delivery would not normally come before 14 October (Gregorian calendar).

Yet even this approach was not without its problems, and some worked solutions by this reckoning showed that the land-lord would have recieved his crop-share too early. Another method was also used in conjunction with the date-harvest method, and this hinged on a reconciliation with the Babylonian lunar calendar month. ... The problem with this particular calendar is similar to the one that was noted with Marshack's scratched bones (Chapter 2). Because the synodic lunar month is 29½ days, the Babylonian month usually alternated between 29- and 30-day intervals. For example, if the new crescent failed to appear when expected, that day was counted as the thirtieth day of the month. Occasionally in the Babylonian calendar two 29-day intervals follow and sometimes even three. Because 12 lunar months are about 11 days less than a true 365-odd-day solar year, the lunar calendar months move out of a proper seasonal sequence in the year. To prevent a complete breakdown, an extra intercalary month was introduced every few years to balance things up. ... The calendar approach rested on the fact that some documents were dated on the 30th day of the month, and from this it was inferred that those particular months *must* have contained 30 days.

Taken together, all the evidence assembled by Langdon-Fotheringham-Schoch indicated that Ammizaduga was a king of Babylon from 1921 to 1900 B.C. These results were finally published in a book (now very difficult to find) entitled *The Venus Tablets of Ammizaduga* (1928).

But this is by no means the end of the saga. Archaeological evidence was coming to light all the time. Interested scholars looked into accounts of neighbouring contemporaries of Hammurabi's, for example, Yarim-Lim, King of Alalak (a town on the Mediterranean coast on the route leading from the Upper Euphrates Valley). By taking into account objects of Egyptian origin found at Alalak and comparing them with periods in Egyptian history, it was seen that a date of round 1600 B.C. was indicated for the end of the First Babylonian dynasty. Thus Egyptian chronology, considered very reliable for this period, could now be used as a general guide to fix Babylonian chronology.

It was Sydney Smith, Keeper of the Department of Western Asiatic Antiquities at the British Museum, who first realized the significance of the Yarim-Lim evidence. In 1940 he published a booklet entitled *Alalak and Chronology*, setting out the accumulated evidence for a revision of the Hammurabi dynasty which resulted in a Venus-tablet solution of 1646 to 1625 B.C. The same solution was also adopted by the American archaeologist W. F. Albright.

Another, working quite independently of Smith, was the German scholar Arthur Ungnad who used a different method. Nevertheless, about the same time he reached the identical general conclusion as Smith—now known as the "short" chronology.

Solutions were coming thick and fast. Again in 1940, David Sidersky, a chemist whose hobby was ancient Oriental astronomy, mathematics and chronology, offered a solution of 1702 to 1681 B.C. The following year a Turkish scholar, Kemel Turfan, independently reached a similar conclusion.

In 1942, F. Cornelius, working solely on historical sources, set the date to an earlier time of 1582 B.C. for the year Ammizaduga began his reign.

In the digging season 1932–33 the Oriental Institute of Chicago uncovered an Assyrian king-list at Khorsobad which showed that Hammurabi was a *contemporary* of the Assyrian King Shamsi-Adad I, whereas previously it was believed that Hammurabi had lived two generations earlier. Since it was conclusive that Shamsi-Adad lived *later* than 1900 B.C., all the early chronologies for the Venus observations were ruled out by this discovery, disregarding any other reason for rejection. Nevertheless, all was not clear for the Khorsobad king-list tablet—preserved in almost perfect condition till the moment of its discovery —was damaged by the spade of the excavator. The result was that the length of five reigns was lost and the *exact* date of Shamsi-Adad can only be fixed to within ten years before or after 1734 B.C. On the evidence that Hammurabi was his contemporary, he must then have lived about that year.

According to Cornelius, Hammurabi reigned from 1728 to 1686 B.C.—in a period falling within the limits of the Khorsobad

o

king-list. Arno Phoebed of the University of Chicago re-examined the king-list and announced that Shamsi-Adad's reign must be 1726 to 1694 B.C. It was after this that Albright revised his own chronology to conform to the Cornelius dating of the Hammurabi dynasty.

In 1942, more support came for the Cornelius dating, this time from the Dutch scholar van der Waerden, another expert in ancient mathematics and astronomy.

By now it had become usual to discuss the dating problem of the Venus Tablets in terms of the merits of the three cited chronologies known as the "long", "middle" (or "medium"), and "short", viz:

a) Sidersky 1701 to 1681 B.C. (long)
b) Ungnad 1645 to 1625 B.C. (middle)
c) Cornelius 1581 to 1561 B.C. (short)

Although many now believed the Cornelius solution to be the best one, the arguments rolled on. Van der Meer of the University of Amsterdam published a solution in 1944 practically identical with the middle chronology of Ungnad (and Smith). In 1945, Smith dated Hammurabi's reign from 1792-1750 B.C.

By 1946, van der Waerden had developed his arguments further. He believed now that one might rule out completely Sidersky's long chronology, but one could not entirely dismiss out of hand the middle chronology of Ungnad. Although he felt the Cornelius solution to be the correct one, there were still problems with it. The chief difficulty was the niggling problem of the time of the date harvest. Fotheringham's work indicated that the landlord would have received his share too early. The only logical inference was that climatic conditions in Mesopotamia must have changed since Old-Babylonian times, for it seemed that the date and the barley crops ripened at least three weeks earlier in the first half of the second millennium B.C.

Evidence for possible climatic change is conflicting. There were marked changes in Europe from the time of the climatic optimum c. 4000 B.C., and from about 2500 to 1500 B.C. many Megalithic monuments were being rapidly smothered by peat because of increased rainfall. But how did this affect Babylonia? In 1962, M. A. Beek of the University of Amsterdam considered that the climate of Mesopotamia was almost static from about 5000 B.C. up to the present time. Nevertheless, new evidence is accumulating that changes of climate have occurred over very short cycles of a few hundred years in practically all parts of the world. Some of these are as dramatic as the changes that plunged Europe into the "Little Ice Age" in the period as recent as between the sixteenth and nineteenth centuries.

When Libby's radiocarbon method was applied to the Hammurabi problem in the 1950s, using a piece of charcoal recovered from a house in Nippur, the solution to Hammurabi's accession was given as the year 1756 B.C. plus or minus 106 years. Other radiocarbon experiments gave a spread of dates, but all favoured the short against the long chronology. Nevertheless, it has been seen that radiocarbon datings pertaining to this period are in error (too young) unless corrected by cross-calibration with tree rings.

At the present time a final and definitive choice between the middle and short chronologies is still awaited. However, it is absolutely certain that the tablets do refer to observations of Venus made by Babylonians sometime before 1500 B.C.

Schiaparelli (c. 1906) was the only one to assign a date no earlier than the eighth century B.C. and the only one to place them *after c.* 1500 B.C. We can be sure that had Schiaparelli lived long enough (he died 1910) to read Kugler's work and the work of those who followed him, he would have changed his opinion when confronted with the evidence not available to him in 1906. It is the acceptance of Schiaparelli's early date for the Venus observations which provides a key issue in the Velikovsky controversy—in particular about his so-called catastrophe theory.

Velikovsky c. 1950 proposed that two major catastrophes occured sometime in the past owing to the Earth's dynamical interaction with a comet and then Mars. The comet episode he claimed took place about 1500 B.C., and as a consequence the comet became transformed into the planet Venus; the later Mars encounter he claimed took place in 687 B.C. It was in both encounters Velikovsky maintained that the direction of the Earth's axial spin was switched plus the angle of tilt of the axis itself resulting in a *major* change in the obliquity of the ecliptic. A major change in obliquity would have a profound effect on the position in the sky we observe the apparent paths of the Sun, Moon and the planets.

These catastrophe theories were in fact only an updated and redacted interpretation of a fanciful seventeenth-century idea first thought up by Edmond Halley which he later revoked himself. It was then taken over and developed by William Whiston in his nonsensical book *New Theory of the Earth* (1696).

In support of his hypothesis, and to lend credence to the bizarre astronomical phenomena and terrible catastrophes which he believed coincided in various parts of the globe, Velikovsky cites Hindu, Chinese, Babylonian, Judaic, Mesoamerican and many other early "sources", including a host of biblical ones.

Now, if Velikovsky's arguments were correct, the proof of this would have far-reaching implications for the present, concerning the orientations and alignments of Megalithic monuments worldwide. The proof indeed *should* be forthcoming in Megalithic alignments—for it follows that Stonehenge and other Megalithic monuments constructed before *c.* 1500 B.C. would not *now* show positive alignments to the Sun and Moon if catastrophes had occurred after they were built and had brought about a major shift in the Sun's obliquity.

Also, if Venus was non-existent as a planet before 1500 B.C. (that is circling the Sun in its present-day orbit) as Velikovsky claimed, there could be no observations for the Babylonians to record in the Venus Tablets of Ammizaduga *before* 1500 B.C.!

How did Velikovsky and his suporters explain away this contradictory evidence? First they disclaimed all dates for the Venus Tablets, excepting Schiaparelli's obsolete one, and dismissed the learned arguments of all the other scholars, calling it "astronomers' dogma"—a term frequently applied by Velikovsky and Co. to any ideas which ran contrary to their own. Even Schiaparelli does not escape criticism and is sometimes accused of the self-same dogmatic thinking where parts of his argument conflict with those of Velikovsky.

In respect to the equally damning evidence provided by Megalithic alignments, Velikovsky claimed (shades of Fergusson *c.* 1870) that Stonehenge and other monuments were erected later than 687 B.C. In spite of the supporting calibration evidence of tree-ring dating, radiocarbon dates are cited by Velikovsky as completely unreliable. He also claims that all the archaeological data for Stonehenge has been wrongly interpreted, and that all the artefacts found there by excavation and attributed to the third and second milleniums B.C. might easily all have been placed there afterwards.

In atempts to damn the pre-1500 B.C. chronologies for the Venus Tablets, Velikovsky and his supporters have attempted to cloud the issue by manipulating the scribal errors contained in the tablets which for the most part have been cleared up and reconciled by scholars following Schiaparelli. Sometimes errors of several days—sometimes months—occur between tablet sources; often scribes in copying have added or subtracted "ten". Copyists also, it was noted, confused the cuneiform numbers six and eight. The first is denoted by two groups of three vertical wedges, one group above the other, while the latter was denoted by two similarly placed groups of four wedges. When the copyist's eye was tired and the vision blurred (no spectacles remember), the units would tend to merge into rectangular shapes and look very similar.

Velikovsky's theories have been damned from all sides, but the Velikovsky cult, like the cult of Pyramidology, still apparently thrives. In the 1960s the man himself was hailed as a kind of guru by some Western-World student bodies who saw him as an anti-establishment figurehead in the revolt against teaching authoritarianism. To others—because of his reliance on biblical sources to support his theories—he holds out a strong appeal in the fashion that Taylor's and Smyth's brand of Pyramidology appealed to god-fearing Victorians as an antidote to the unacceptable materialism of Darwin.

Prior to Kugler's interpretation of the Venus Tablets, the real breakthrough in understanding the scientific astronomy from Babylonia was made by the Jesuit fathers Joseph Epping and J. N. Strassmaier about 1881. When Epping died, it was Kugler who continued his labours and switched from his earlier scientific career in chemistry to devote the rest of his life to deciphering the astronomical content of Babylonian clay tablets.

Epping and Strassmaier were two brilliant scholars whose early work had provided the foundation stone to all subsequent decipherment of Babylonian astronomy and astrology. It was their first paper in the Catholic periodical *Stimmen aus Maria*

Laach in 1881 which provided (via astronomy) the correct determination of the zero point of the Seleucid Era and that of the
Parthian Era providing historians and archaeologists with a
proper chronological basis for the history of Mesopotamia after
Alexander the Great.

It was Epping and Strassmaier who finally exploded the myth
of the great antiquity of Babylonian scientific astronomy. . . .
While mathematical texts have been recovered on tablets from
the old Babylonian Hammurabi period (*c.* 1800 to 1600 B.C.),
which indicate wide knowledge at this period of square and cube
numeracy, and tablets are found that give "Pythagorean
theorems", nearly all these tablets seem to have been written to
help solve problems involving economic matters such as reckoning compound interest and calculating volumes of earthworks for
canals and other municipal constructions. None have been discovered that relate to the kind of scientific astronomy found in
the later Seleucid period *c.* 250 to 50 B.C.

The Venus Tablets of Ammizaduga belong to a series of tablets
known as "Enuma-Anu-Enlil" (so called because they refer
to the gods of Elam, Akkad and Amurra) and is a compendium
of astrology dating from about 1800 B.C. used by the court astro-
logers-cum-astronomers to decide which were favourable or unfavourable celestial omens. One early index of these tablets lists
seventy or more tablets comprising this series—the whole containing about 7,000 omens. The Venus Tablets are contained in
the 63rd tablet of this series.

Although the constellation figures had been mapped out round
2000 B.C. and the movements of the planets and the Moon were
well known, it was *not* until *c.* 700 B.C. under the Assyrian Empire that one finds Babylonian texts indicating true knowledge
of why eclipses occur, and it is not until *c.* 250 to 50 B.C. one
finds cuneiform ephemerides by which lunar eclipses might be
predicted satisfactorily. Before this, there existed rough and ready
methods—based on the 18-year cycle—used to predict lunar
eclipses, but even these were probably in existence only shortly
before the Seleucid period commenced.

Records of all eclipses were certainly kept by Babylonian
astronomer-priest scribes from the time of Nabonassor (*c.* 747
B.C.), and the actual names of a few of these scribes were recorded
by classical writers, and some appear to have belonged to scribal

guilds or families. Recognition of the 19-year Metonic cycle in Babylonia only dates from after *c*. 450 B.C., and it was about the same time that the concept of the zodiac as we know it today was invented.

Harking back to before Hammurabi's time to the earlier Sumerian period (the fourth millennium B.C. to *c*. 2000 B.C.), it always comes as something of a shock even to students of astronomy to be told that absolutely nothing is known about astronomy at this period. We can glean inferences, but that is all. Although the Sumerians had profound interest in the heavens and were star worshippers of a kind—much like the Egyptians in the same period—we can only conjecture their astronomical ideas from fragmentary evidence so far discovered. It has been estimated conservatively that a quarter of a million tablets and fragments of tablets of the Sumerian period are now in the hands of museums and private collections. Of these 95 per cent are strictly economic in character—contracts of sale, wills, testimonials, agreements, etc. The remainder consists of political, lexical, literary and arithmetical texts. But in Sumerian script we know that the picture of a star represents *an* (heaven), and the same sign signifies *dinger* (god). We can surmise too that the number seven—often considered a "magic" number in many cultures—was thematic in Sumerian astro-mythology *c*. 3000 B.C. It was significant to the ancients because the five planets plus the Sun and Moon provided the most significant cosmic number seven of all. But there are also seven bright stars in Ursa Major, Orion and in the Pleiades cluster. This concept of *seven* and *heaven* was still important to the late Babylonians, for the brick Ziggurat of Nabu, at Barsipki, was known as the "House of the Seven Bonds of Heaven and Earth" and was believed to have been painted in seven different colours. It was probably from the summit platforms of the ziggurats that the Babylonian priests made their observations of the sky.

The Sumerians were certainly a strongly religious people, and among the sky-gods and sky-goddesses, Venus was a very important deity. The planet, when it shone in the sky, was the visible manifestation of Inanna (later known as Ninsianna and Ishtar). In the same way the god Sin was directly visible at the Moon and the god Shamash as the Sun. Together these three formed a great triad of important deities that are shown on stelae and on the later period *kudurru*, or "boundary" stones (Plate 25). These stones—usually limestone—contained particulars about extent and boundaries of estates. They were probably not set to mark actual boundaries, as we find in Egypt bordering the Nile, but to contain title-deeds to properties—much like modern house deeds—to confirm the rights of some individual and his family. They all date from the Kassite period (following the Hammurabi dynasty) and usually contain depictions of the gods who, it is supposed, helped maintain a protective influence on the title-holders' rights. Occasionally they include a curse on anyone who interferes with the boundaries of the property. Below the triad of Venus, the Moon and the Sun, the other gods personify star asterisms, for example, the Scorpion, later to become an important sign among the twelve signs of the Babylonian Zodiac.

Venus, as Ishtar of the Accadian period, was very influential in astrology, but she was a battle goddess as well as a love, marriage and fertility goddess. In the "Enuma-Anu-Enlil" tablets we can read: *When Venus is at her post, there will be rebellion of hostile military forces, and abundance of wives. When Venus is high in the heaven there will be luck in copulation.*

It seems beyond doubt that the Sumerians understood the movements of the planets at this early date, and the old Sumerian poem about Inanna (Venus)—Queen of heaven—beautifully translated by the American scholar Samuel Noah Kramer, can be read directly that they understood that Venus was the evening star as well as the morning star and that the planet sometimes passed into the nether world (the period of invisibility).

From the "great above" she set her wind towards the great below ...
My lady abandoned heaven, abandoned earth,
  To the nether world she descended,
Inanna abandoned heaven, abandoned earth,
  To the nether world she descended. ...

This same poem remains thematic throughout the whole of Babylonian history, for we find it again when Inanna at a later period becomes Ishtar in Accadian ("Ishtar's Descent into the Nether World").

At the beginning of the twentieth century a cult, centred in Germany and known as Panbabylonism, did much to foster the idea of the great antiquity of Babylonian knowledge. They concluded with some plausibility that most of the extant mythological narratives have an astronomical basis. Most would go along with this basic thesis—as exampled by the Inanna poem, but the Panbabylonists went beyond this simple concept and believed that the myths contained highly elaborate and detailed astronomical information. They believed, too, that all astronomical knowledge could be linked back directly to the Sumerians who were attributed with possessing an amazingly advanced astronomical science. It was argued that only in Mesopotamia did one find the required mathematical background for astromythology to be expressed so precisely in mathematical cuneiform texts. The Panbabylonists were basically hyperdiffusionists who claimed unique world-wide similarities could *only* be explained by evoking widespread diffusion from ancient Sumerian sources. It was believed that every phenomenon in classical cosmogony, literature and religion might be traced back to the so-called cosmic philosophy of Babylonia.

Kugler was one of the few scholars in Germany who did not fall for this highly plausible but deceptive argument fostered by archaeologists such as Alfred Jeremias and the cuneiform philologist Hugo Winckler. Kugler maintained that similarities among world astro-mythologies—which the Panbabylonists cited as sure evidence for diffusion—could easily be explained by circumstances that all races witnessed the same events in the sky and these made like impressions on the human mind.

Yet the Panbabylonists were very influential in their time. Almost in scholastic isolation in Germany, Kugler—who knew more about Babylonian astronomy than any other living man—demolished the great edifice of Panbabylonism theory piece by piece, providing arguments to which there was no answer. When Hugo Winckler, the movement's controller, died in 1913, the cult of Panbabylonism became scientifically dead, and by the start of World War I it was banished for ever to the lunatic fringe of archaeology.

16 Quetzalcoatl and Calendar Stones

Only one god did they have. . . .
his name was Quetzalcoatl
The supreme guardian of their god,
his priest
his name was also Quetzalcoatl. . . .

An ancient Toltec hymn

One of the best known stories in history and travel is when Hernando Cortes arrived in the Aztec world of 1519 and his appearance was believed to be the return of the benevolent Quetzalcoatl of older Toltec times.

Quetzalcoatl by tradition was attributed with the invention of the arts. He stemmed from Mexico's "Golden Age" and was a white-bearded priest who took his name from the supreme god of the same name. It has been said that he who studies the life of this priest will not be surprised why some historians and scholars of the nineteenth century tried to see this man as an early Christian missionary or as a Buddhist monk who by accident arrived on the shores of the New World, for Quetzalcoatl is supposed to have lived an exemplary life and practised penance, abstinence, meditation and chastity. It was the divine nature of Quetzalcoatl and his legend which also led the early Spanish friars to formulate a myth that St. Thomas the Apostle once visited Mexico in the guise of a white-bearded god.

Much has been made by this legend and others like it, involving a god from across the water and his subsequent promise to return one day. A supposed relic supporting the factual nature of Quetzalcoatl is said to have been kept until after the Spanish conquest; and when it was opened, it was found to contain a quantity of fair hair. Others have seen Quetzalcoatl as the Irish Monk St. Brendan; a Norseman or, more bizarrely, as a survivor from the lost Atlantis. At least as an Atlantis culture-bearer he can be dismissed, for with the recognition of sea-floor spreading and the understanding of the New Geology of plate tectonics, the colourful sunken-continent-cum-Atlantis theories have been truly scuttled for all time.

In the culture and mythology of Mesoamerica, Quetzalcoatl is one of the most puzzling and confusing figures. He was the Feathered serpent, God of Civilization and Learning, but he was also identified with the planet Venus and the West. But just to confuse matters he is also depicted and interchangeable as a white Tezcatlipoca—the Smoking Mirror—and associated with the East as the morning star (Venus).

To confuse Quetzalcoatl more, the Toltec ruler Topiltzin was given the same title. Also a Mexican named Quetzalcoatl journeyed to the Maya people in Yucatan where he is said to have absorbed the higher civilization of the Maya before returning to Mexico to teach a version of their calendar.

It is a Toltec legend which recounts why Quetzalcoatl departed. Three sorcerers tried to persuade him to introduce human sacrifice, but Quetzalcoatl refused because he loved all his people dearly. Thwarted, the sorcerers deranged him and provoked his flight. Now Quetzalcoatl in exile gave himself up to all the pleasures of life he had long denied himself. Finally he decided to withdraw completely from the earth to find new wisdom, yet the belief of his immortality and his return one day lived on in a Nahuatl Indian text.

. . . the same Quetzalcoatl lives yet,
as yet, he is not dead,
he will come to rule.

If at first Cortes, in the guise of Questzalcoatl, was no surprise to the Mesoamericans, they were, nevertheless, a great surprise to the Conquistadores. Instead of finding India, they discovered a civilized world that paralleled their own. It has been said, wryly, that Europe has never got over its surprise. Many still find it difficult to believe that the civilizations of Mesoamerica and Peru were the result of several independent innovations or synocisms. To account for the presence of civilization in the New World, the hyperdiffusionists have in turn cited Greeks, Romans, Egyptians, Babylonians, survivors of the lost continent of Atlantis, Lemuria or Mu and, in particular, the Lost Children of Israel.

The Lost-Children-of-Israel hypothesis was the brain-child of the eccentric Edward King, Viscount Kinsgborough. Kingsborough's passion—his obsession—was the study of Mexican antiquities which in 1831 resulted in a seven-volume work (price £210 per set) of illustrated Mexican manuscripts. The book cost him £32,000 to produce, and then, heavily in debt, he was lodged in the debtors' prison in Dublin where he died of typhus fever aged 42 in 1837. Behind his passion for Mexican antiquities was his obsessive thesis that the civilized American Indians were descendants of the Ten Lost Tribes. Ironically, although today his thesis is relegated to the lunatic fringe, his magnificent seven-volume work, plus two published posthumously, are recognized as a vital source of material in the study of Mesoamerian antiquities and in the meantime have become priceless treasures.

Egyptian theories of Megalithic Mesoamerican civilizations have attracted many supporters including Thor Heyerdahl who made his famous, much publicized voyage to the Americas on his papyrus boat *Ra* (Re). Nevertheless, at present there is no reliable evidence which supports any other idea than that the pre-Columbian civilizations of America were self-willed innovations by earlier primitive peoples who had migrated from Asia via the once Bering-Strait landbridge sometime in a dim and distant early period B.C.

The pre-Columbian (pre-Hispanic) peoples of Mesoamerica from about the time of Christ onwards comprised the Maya, Mixtecs, Zapotecs, Otomis, Tarascs, Totonacs, Huaxtecs, Toltecs, Olmecs and the Aztecs. Among the best known are the Maya, Aztecs and Toltecs. It was the Toltecs before the tenth century who introduced into Mexico the worship of Quetzalcoatl and we later find him in Maya legends under the name Kukulkan, as the Green-feathered serpent, God of Air, the Wind and the Morning Star. It was the Aztecs who conquered the Toltec empire and then adopted a good deal of the conquered peoples' customs. It was the Aztecs too who finally subjugated the Otomis, Totonacs, Huaxtecs and the Zapotecs; and by the sixteenth century, when Cortes arrived, the Aztec empire comprised the greater part of Central Mexico. Thus the Aztecs were a dynamic composite of many cultural elements.

The Aztec rulers were a bloodthirsty, tyrannical lot. Their priestly class was the most powerful clan and worshipped a host of deities including Quetzalcoatl and Huitzilopochtli—God of War, to whom 20,000 prisoners of war were sacrificed at Tenochtitlán in 1487; they also worshipped the Sun (Tonatiuh) and the Moon (Meztli).

The Mesoamericans, like the Egyptians, became pyramid and temple builders and at great ceremonial centres erected clusters of grand and imposing structures. At Teotihuacan ("the place of the gods") they built the Pyramid of the Moon, rising to a height of 53 metres (175 feet). Even larger and grander was the Pyramid of the Sun, rising to a height of 66 metres (220 feet). This pyramid dwarfs all other buildings. The core of the Sun Pyramid was built in adobe brick, but the exterior was sheathed with blocks of volcanic stone and then rendered over with cement plaster. At its truncated summit was built a small temple-observatory dedicated to Tonacatecuhtli—God of Sun, Heat and Abundance.

The Aztecs, like all Mesoamericans, were obsessed with the passage of time—time past, time present and time future. This can be seen first hand in the various intricately carved calendar-stone sculptures of the late Aztec period. The largest of the Megalithic calendar stones, popularly known as "Montezuma's watch", was unearthed near the cathedral in Mexico City. It is 3·6 metres (12 feet) in diameter and is both a magnificent piece of art and a marvel of primitive calendrical science (Plate 26). The stone is cut from one large block of porous basalt and once took pride of place in a great Aztec temple. The carvings graphically shows the preoccupation with calendrical and life cycles, which was the obsessional *leitmotif* running through the whole of Mesoamerican astronomy. They believed that Nature operated in a series of rhythms or recurrences : night followed day; death relentlessly followed birth and maturity; and there were the recurring seasonal cycles of spring, summer, autumn and winter that went on without stop; and in the sky the eternal swings of the Sun, Moon and planets personified the rhythms of the cosmos. The preoccupation of the astronomer-priests was to discover all the rhythms and then study them; this led to a greater understanding of the purpose of all things; thus these rhythms were embodied in their calendar, and the stone itself reflected the whole of Aztec philosophy in its intricately carved face. According to Aztec belief, the world had passed through four or five ages, or Suns, and Quetzalcoatl himself was the divine ruler of the second era.

The great Aztec ceremonies took place in accordance with the rhythm dictated by the solar year consisting of eighteen months of twenty days and a five-day unlucky period. The preoccupation with farming and the agrarian life is plainly manifest for these Stonge-Age peoples, since all the months had names relating to farming activities, e.g. Tlaxochimaco (IX)—"the birth of flowers" (22 July—10 August); Xocotlhuetzi (X)—"the fall of the fruits" (11 August—30 August). Among the cycles depicted in the great Calendar Stone are lunar cycles and the cycle of the Venus year, which, as in Babylonia, had important ritualistic significance. The Aztec astronomer-priests also knew the Pleiades well; and when these stars reached their highest point in the heavens, the priests would declare it was a sign that the world would continue.

The Maya peoples first appeared in Guatemala, Honduras and Mexico early in the modern era. Without metal tools and beasts of burden and with poor communications they cleared the virgin forest lands and succeeded in building great palaces and temples and invented a calendar that is still the envy of scholastic Europe.

The Maya at one time had the image in history books of being peaceful primitive farmers whose priests practised their astronomical and calendrical skills in the remote fastness of the Central American jungles. Because the Maya were believed to be a race more interested in the liberal arts than in the martial arts like their neighbours the Aztecs, they were nicknamed the Greeks of the New World, while in the same analogy the Aztecs were likened to the Romans—more brutal, more mundane and less inventive. While this analogy is still part true, it has, nevertheless, now become clear that the Maya, and their immediate precur-

sors, were a vivid, warlike race, trading and raiding their neighbours with zest from about 500 B.C.

Maya history can be divided into two main periods. In the
Ancient Empire c. A.D. 300 to 900, their ceremonial centres,
monuments and cities of this epoch testify to extraordinary cultural skills. But this empire suddenly collapsed, and its decadence
was complete about the middle of the tenth century. However,
some survivors emigrated to the plains of north Yucatan and
took part in a brilliant renaissance known as the New Empire.
But this Empire in turn collapsed, and the population dispersed
in the region as nomadic tribes.

The cause of the earlier collapse in particular remains a mystery. To account for it hypotheses put forward include climatic
change, epidemics, wars, soil exhaustion and earth tremors. Certainly the Maya lived in a very active earthquake belt where the
great crustal plates of the Earth involved in continental drift
meet head on. But the traditional view was that it was the collapse of agriculture that spelt doom to the Maya empire, owing
to the believed practice of a primitive slash-and-burn technique
which finally exhausted the infertile tropical soil. This simplistic
view, however, can no longer be maintained. For the Maya
culture to have supported large towns such as Dzibilchaltún, in
northern Yucatan (probably a population of 40,000), agricultural techniques must have been advanced. Indeed this has
proved the case, for more recent archaeological research using
air photography has shown that the Maya employed elaborate
systems of raised fields and terracing not previously recognized on
the ground—indicative that irrigation and agriculture were practised on a much grander scale than previously thought possible.

Opinion has now shifted against agriculture as a prime cause
for collapse. It was more likely a widespread peasant uprising
against the demands of an elite class that finally became unbear-
able. History indeed has some good parallels to give credence to
this idea.

The view has been aptly expressed that Maya archaeology is
more than a dry catalogue of pots and pans—a situation which
is all too often the case with archaeology elsewhere. In spite of
the sparsity of documented "paper" evidence, Maya archaeology
is much more than a record assembled from the debris of the

ceramic evolution of a past culture. In the hieroglyphs that can be read we have the workings of the Maya mind with its insights preserved in symbols.

Why were the Maya so bound up with their calendars? And why did every building have its birth-date stamped on it? Almost every piece of Maya construction was part of a great calendar stone. It was probably the Maya or their immediate precursors who invented writing in Mesoamerica. The Maya system comprised about 350 main glyph signs, 370 affixes and about 100 glyphs portraying deities. Aztec writing is probably nothing but a degenerate derivative of the Maya script. Numbers and dates generally play a very important part in all pre-Columbian Mesoamerican writing. While much of the Maya hieroglyphic script is still undecipherable, the calendar and notation signs are understood. These latter are found engraved in stone sculptures and in the four remaining codices that escaped destruction.

The Maya codices are bark-cloth paper books in which the parts or pages are hinged together like folding shutters or blinds. Only four such codices belonging to the Maya have survived—the Dresdensis, Peresianus, Tro-Cortesianus and Grolier (a Toltec-Maya codex discovered in modern times). It is one of those ironies of history that the man chiefly responsible for the wholesale destruction of Maya manuscripts, Bishop Diego de Landa (1524-79), is also the main source of our knowledge of Maya history and civilization. It is known that in July 1562, twenty-seven codices and 5,000 inscribed stelae were destroyed at his direction. It is through de Landa—the second Spanish Bishop of Maya Yucatan—we can read the symbols of the days and months. It has been remarked that de Landa's description of the Maya calendar and his illustrations of the glyphs for the day and months signs is the closest we are ever likely to get to having a Rosetta stone for the Maya language. The Maya calendar and counting were more complex that those of the Aztecs, and we can deduce that the Maya priests were astronomers of the first order.

The Maya counted in a vigesimal system (20s) while the Old World counted in 10s or 12s. The use of 20s probably had a very early origin and stems from a primitive peoples' use of a natural number, viz. we have 20 toes and fingers.

The Maya had no knowledge of fractional numbers nor a decimal system, and all counts were finalized to the nearest whole number. In the face of such simple numerology, anyone who studies the Maya calendar and their astronomy is left in awe by their achievement with it.

There were two basic years running parallel, the solar (farmers') year of 360 plus 5 days (the *haab*) and the 260-day count of the sacred almanac (the *tzolkin*). The 260-day sacred count was divided into twenty periods of thirteen days, which were called by the names of the days of the solar month in the same order. In each period the glyph names were preceded by a number indicating their position from 1 to 13, the day *ik* ranking the start of the first period. Thus we find 1 *ik*, 2 *akbad*, 3 *kan*, etc. to 13 *ix*. The start day of the second period was 1 *men*, 2 *cib*, etc. In this scheme the recurrence of the numbering 1 *ik* did not repeat until the first day of the second *tzolkin*—that is after 260 days.

The solar year—the *haab*—had eighteen months of twenty days 20 × 18 = 360) plus an additional period of five days called *uayeb* giving a nearest whole-number year of 365 days. This solar year was often called the Vague Year. The usage of the 260-day year of the sacred almanac, or calendar, has given rise to several speculations to its origin. It seems unlikely to have been lunar-based, for it does not fit the cycle of 29-odd days. One suggestion has been that it spans the period of human pregnancy. An astronomical suggestion is that it relates to the interval in the year between passages of the Sun across the zenith (for the Maya lands), and still another astronomical explanation is that in Mesoamerica there was the belief of 13 heavens and 13 gods; and if we apply the vigesimal counting (20 fingers and toes), we arrive at 260.

When the Maya gave a date, it was denoted by its position in *both* years. How this intermeshed system worked is best understood by looking at a simple diagram first constructed by the American scholar Sylvanus Griswold Morley. It was Morley who—like an Alexander Thom of his day—visited almost every known site in the Maya lands in an insatiable quest for new hieroglyphic texts. The diagram (Fig. 18) shows two cogged wheels and demonstrates how the 365-day *haab* year (right) meshes with the 260-day *tzolkin* year. Each wheel has

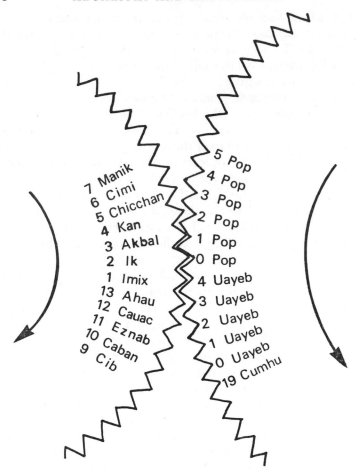

Figure 18   Cog-wheel calendar diagram devised by S.G. Morley to show how the Maya calendar of 365 days—the *haab* year—(right-hand side) intermeshed with the 260-day *tzolkin* year (left-hand side).

the number of cogs or spaces representing the number of days in each year. We can calculate that 73 complete revolutions of the *tzolkin* wheel and 52 complete revolutions of the *haab* wheel must occur before cog 2 *ik* is reinserted in the space between cogs 0 *pop* (Fig. 18). Thus 18,980 days will have passed, and during this period the *tzolkin* has occupied 365 possible positions of the *haab*. The latter period of 18,980 days (52 years) was of critical importance in Maya life and was known as the Sacred Calendar Round.

In addition the Maya had names and glyph signs for short, medium and long periods—from the *tun* of 360 days to the *alautun* of 23,040,000,000 days.

To write numbers under twenty the Maya usually used dots and horizontal bar-lines. The dot equalled one unit, the bar-line five units; thus 16 was written as three bars and one dot. Numbers could be written horizontally or vertically; if inscribed horizontally, the dots were placed above the bar-line; if vertically, alongside to the left.

In the extant literature containing Maya numerology and cycle counts, the most interesting example of the painted codices is that of the Dresden *Codex*—so named because it was found in Vienna by the director of the Library of Dresden in 1739. How it came to be in Vienna and its history before this time is not known. Fully opened, the *Codex* is 3·5 metres (11 feet 4 inches) long; it has thirty-nine leaves, or seventy-eight pages, of which four are blank.

The work is primarily an astronomical-cum-divinitary treatise and consists of various sections dealing with different subjects likened to chapters in a conventional book; nevertheless there are no obvious typographic devices to show change of topic, and the pagination is irregular. All the portraits of deities and the glyph signs are neatly executed in colours of red, black, bluish-green and light yellow and brown. The existing *Codex* is believed to be a twelfth-century edition copied from an earlier now lost original. This can be inferred because certain tables it contains were out of date when the copy was made—in much the same way as the Egyptian decans were out of date (owing to precession) when they were used on coffin lids.

Part of the Dresden *Codex* includes a calendar for the planet Venus covering a period of 384 years which shows that the Maya (like the Babylonians) knew that five synodic revolutions of the planet (2920 days) equalled eight solar years. Also like the Babylonian Venus Tablets the Maya Venus observations are loaded with astrological omens referring to danger periods. The planet, throughout Mexico, was considered particularly malignant at the moment of its rising as a morning "star" just before the Sun, and Mexicans supposedly shut all doors and windows so that the malignant light should not have chance to enter the house and introduce sickness. Yet Venus could also be taken as a good augury in certain parts of the sky.

The Dresden *Codex* also contains a lunar calendar of 405 consecutive lunations divided into sixty groups of six lunations and nine groups of five lunations. The duration of each lunation is made up of between 29 and 30 days. The group of six was calculated 177 days, sometimes for 178 days, and the group of five for 148 days. The 405 lunations give 11,960 days or 46 *tzolkin*. We can appreciate this particular Maya achievement in regulating the Moon's movement when we realize that in modern astronomy 405 lunations have been set precisely at 11,959·888 years. Therefore it can be seen that the Maya figure of 11,960 days is not a bad result for a Stone-Age people using counts to the nearest whole number; the difference in reckoning amounts to only one day in 300 years.

The Venus count was very important too in tying in with other cycles. The solar calendar of 365 days was essential for Maya agriculture. The Maya, or rather the proto-Maya peoples, must have been aware that the whole number count of 365 days, used as a guide-line for planting the maize crop, is short of the true solar year of 365·242 days, and as a consequence they made careful note of the accumulated error as time flowed. For example, after the 4th year of a 365-day solar calendar, the Sun would be one place (1 day) behind. They had no leap year, and to reconcile the various cycles of time and correct errors they looked for significant intervals when the various cycles coincided and could then be manipulated in grand large-number reconciliation schemes. One of the most beautiful of these Maya schemes was the interval of 37,960 days. This they discovered was the lowest common multiple of the 365-day solar year, the 260-day sacred year, *and* the 584-day (average) period of Venus's synodical revolution. The Maya Venus reckoning shows an error of only 0·08 days in the span of 481 years. This is a remarkable achievement taking into account that a Maya astronomer-priest would observe (presumably) standing at the top of some pyramid steps and would necessarily miss long periods of Venus risings because of cloud-outs caused by the long rainy season in Central America. The precise detail of how the Maya made their astronomical observations and with what instrumentation, if any, is not known. Nevertheless, it seems probable that they used their Megalithic architecture to provide alignments in much the same way as the Stone-Age astronomer-priests used the sarsens of Stonehenge.

We also find a similar achievement for the Maya estimate of the length of the year. Using the calendar in vogue in Europe before the 1585 reform, we find the year calculated Julian style to be 365·250,000 days; while the Gregorian reform of 1585 gives 365·242,500 days; the absolute reckoning of the year (sidereally) is 365·242,198 days and that provided by the Maya calendar 365·242,129 days. No wonder the scholars of Europe were left in awe at such precise numerology achieved by a Stone-Age people.

In the Dresden *Codex* we also find eclipse tables. Through painstaking scholarship Maya eclipse cycles have gradually been *partly* decoded. It can be inferred that by observing the Moon over long periods, the Maya priesthood discovered that eclipses fell into well-defined patterns; and in doing this they discovered the eclipse-important swing of the lunar nodes (in 18·61 years) without actually knowing precisely what it was they had discovered. It is the Maya eclipse reckoning using simplistic whole-number counts which provides insights into an exciting methodology that might also have been used at an earlier period by the Stone-Age astronomer-priests of North-West Europe.

But how *did* the astronomer-priests of the Maya and the other pre-Columbian American races make their observations to provide high accuracies in time-keeping cycles as demonstrated? The short answer is that at present their *modi operandi* are not clear. Nevertheless, there are indications that some buildings were purpose-orientated. Perhaps the most famous example is the ceremonial complex at Uaxactún in Guatemala where S. G. Morley demonstrated the accurate alignments for sunrise at the solstices and equinoxes. At the great ceremonial complex of Chichén Itzá, which was termed by Morley as the "Mecca of the Maya", several structures are supposed to be orientated in such a way that specific celestial bodies made alignments to walls and passages. The best known of these is the El Caracol (circular) Tower (the Snail). It has four outer doors facing the cardinal points of the compass and owes its name to its inner spiral staircase. Near the top of the structure is a flat area from where three rectangular horizontal shafts open. From this build-ing alignments suggested are for the extreme setting positions of the Moon and extreme Venus setting declinations for a date of *c*. A.D. 1000. It is also likely that this building was used as a point from which to judge the time of the equinoxes and solstices.

At Uxmal, another ancient ruined Maya city in northern Yucatan, most of the structures are strangely orientated 9° off the cardinal directions in the clockwise direction, and this is believed to have astronomical (or cosmological) significance. Some cited alignments are not very convincing—such as ex-ampled by Lockyer's second-hand interpretation, via Maudsley's work, that the temples of Chichén Itzá were purpose-orientated to the May Sun.

Maya "orientation theory" is yet in its infancy, and a great deal more field-work by responsible astro-archaeologists will be re-quired before any satisfactory general theory can be formulated about the manner in which the Maya made their observations.

In antiquity many cultures set a starting date for their chron-ology by some outstanding religious or cultural event, e.g. the Birth of Christ, the Foundation of Rome, etc. Likewise the Maya set their inception date to 3131 B.C., although this is about 3,400 years earlier than the oldest documentary evidence yet provided by the Maya culture. The Maya peoples kept a very accurate calendar—certainly more accurate than that kept in Europe spanning the period—but even so opinion has differed among scholars of how the Maya calendar should be correlated with Christian dates to obtain a precise time-fix between the two. It is an on-running contention much like the old problem previously alluded to with the Babylonian Venus Tablets. At present there are at least nine suggested correlation systems for the Maya calendar vying for acceptance. Nevertheless, many believe that the Goodman-Thompson correlation provides the best fit.

In the pre-Columbian Americas the Inca Stone-Age civil-ization is less revealing in its astronomical knowledge than its Mesoamerican counterparts, but they had a pantheon of gods, many of whom were celestial, and certainly Megalithic align-ments were important. In the lost city of Machu Picchu, dis-covered by Hiram Bingham in 1912, the traditional "hitching post of the Sun"—the *Inti-huatana*—was found intact. This was a stone artefact sculptured *in situ* from native rock which is believed to have indicated the times of the summer and winter solstices. Remains of such posts were found in all the major Inca sites, and their purpose was to regulate the farming calendar; but since the Conquistadors considered them central to the Inca's idolatrous Sun worship, they smashed them everywhere. But the one at Machu Picchu was fully preserved and is persuasive proof indeed that the Spanish invaders never penetrated as far.

The Inca also erected artificial markers to perform the same task. At Cuzco there were supposedly sixteen stone towers, eight in the west and eight in the east, arranged in groups of four. The two middle ones were smaller than the others, and the distance between the towers was 8, 10 or 20 feet (2·4, 3 or 6 metres). The space between the little towers, through which the Sun passed at sunrise and sunset, was the point of the solstices. For observations of the equinoxes, richly ornamented stone pillars were set up in an open space before the temple of the Sun. When the time approached, the shadow of the pillars was carefully observed. Long experience taught them where to look for the equinoctial point, and by the distance of the shadows from this point, they judged the approach of the equinoxes.

The Inca had no writing glyphs like their Mesoamerican contemporaries, but they did have the famous knotted cords—the quipus, or the "recipes of the devil" as the Spanish priests called them. Several theories and schemes have been put forward on how the quipus worked. The various colours were supposed to indicate the subject and the various knots numbers, arranged in a decimal counting system. From these knots one scheme put forward claimed they represented the "rhythms" of the Sun, Moon and the planets and kept the passage of time in the Inca calendar. The theory was based on evidence that the Inca needed to know the feast days when the Sun was highest or lowest in the sky (the summer and winter solstices). By manipulating the knots it is claimed the Inca astronomer-priests could keep account of the lunar months in relation to the passage of time in the solar year—a problem, we have seen, that has beset all calendarmakers since time immemorial. The quipus idea sounds plausible enough, for two of the most important Inca deities were *Inti*, the Sun god, and *Si*, the Moon-god, and it is known their festival

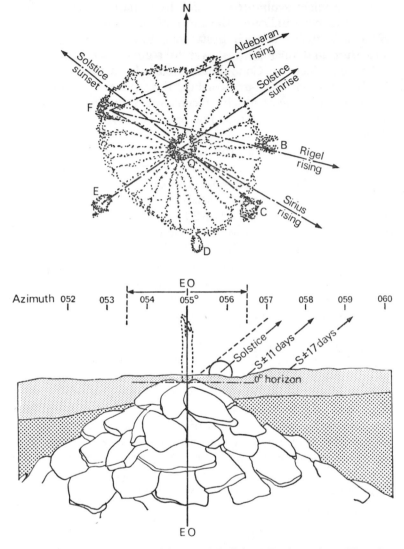

Figure 19   Two views of the Big Horn Medicine Wheel, northern Wyoming showing possible celestial alignments (azimuths) represented through various cairns (A; B; C; E; F; and O and the view in direction E–O (*see* plan). This 'wheel' consists of an imperfect circle of loose stones *c.* 25 metres (80 feet) in diameter. The central cairn is the hub from which twenty-eight unevenly spaced spokes are connected to the outer rim. The twenty-eight spokes may be a built-in lunar-month counter.

days were celebrated. Nevertheless, no one has yet demonstrated in a convincing *scientific* manner how in practice the Inca priests did reconcile the two time units, and until someone does so, the verdict on the quipus as a mnemonic device holding profound astronomical and/or mathematical truths must remain open.

Finally in the Americas, some of the most intriguing and fascinating Megalithic (and Megaxylic) monuments are the Medicine wheels of the Plains Indians. Some of these "wheels" are believed to have served as celestial calendar monuments—the ideas for which may have infiltrated from Mesoamerica. One of the most intriguing of the studied examples is the Big Horn Medicine Wheel in northern Wyoming. This has been subject to several alignment interpretations including the Sun's solstice rising and setting points and various seasonal star risings (Fig. 19).

17 Mystery of the Megaliths

It is now evident that back in prehistory, numbers were invented long before writing, and ancient races were manipulating them in relation to simple celestial phenomena soon after the onset of the Upper Paleolithic. Stonehenge was built by a Neolithic people who on present evidence had no writing but to whom numbers were already very important—and there can be little doubt about this. Yet among all those ancient cultures known to have manipulated numbers, the Megalithic culture of North-West Europe, which peaked sometime between *c.* 3000 to 1500 B.C., remains the most enigmatic simply because its believed achievements still defy a sure interpretation.

The chief difficulty in attempts to penetrate this particular veil of mystery is the total lack of any written back-up source material left by builders themselves. We know a great deal about the achievements of other ancient peoples, but without the sure decipherment of Egyptian hieroglyphs, Babylonian cuneiform and the part-decoded Mesoamerican glyphs, our knowledge of these cultures would still likely be on a par with that of the prehistoric folk of North-West Europe.

Nevertheless, by analogy we can justifiably speculate that the ancient folk of North-West Europe had traits in common with other peoples. From *all* ancient societies with source-texts we can glean unambiguous evidence that the sky and the celestial vault evoked an omnipotent power. What we read in Egyptian texts of the "welling-up" of a man's soul when confronted with the spectacle of the night sky can be equated with similar beliefs held by societies the world over both in ancient and modern times. We can be sure that man has been highly receptive to this "religious" mood since the rise of *Homo sapiens* in the Upper Paleolithic some forty millenniums back—and a natural evolutionary consequence of this germinal sky religion is the later development of a true astronomy.

In North-West Europe there can be little doubt that the dolmens and the various designs of passage and chambered structures were built to hold the remains of the dead. While there is certainly strong evidence that some of these structures were often purpose-orientated, nevertheless, they were funerary chambers *primarily* and there is no escaping this conclusion.

But what about other Megalithic structures of North-West Europe—the long stone avenues; complex and simple circles often with outlying stones set at specific orientations; the isolated single stones; and those especially enigmatic Men-an-tol stones? If all these designs were not built for astronomical, directional or calendrical use as some claim, what purpose were they built for?

Archaeologists would like to dismiss them all simply as ceremonial or religious structures, yet the evidence for this belief is no more convincing than the evidence for their involvement with a numerical-celestial or directional use.

And what do the woodhenges represent in the Megaxylic culture which preceded and then overlapped with the culture of stone? Are they observatories, temple sanctuaries or dwelling places for priests? What cultural ideas shaped their layouts? What supreme purpose was played by that great Neolithic mound of dirt, Silbury Hill, overlooking Avebury, which Flinders Petrie once believed was a British pyramid : memorial to a chief, observatory, temple platform, sacrificial site to a Sun-god, or a special beacon site? Excavation through it has revealed nothing, except the method and the various stages in which it was built. What about these strange earthwork features the so-called causewayed camps, the ringed ditches, and the long straight hollowed cursuses? In spite of all the excavations and the speculations, these features which were contemporary and associated with nearby Megalithic structures remain as inscrutable as they were when first noticed by the enlightened men of the seventeenth century.

The absence of recognizable permanent dwellings on the British landscape contemporary with the Megaliths has suggested that the Neolithic farmers were chiefly nomadic pastoralists who herded cattle and kept them on the move. Perhaps—but no one can be sure—all the causewayed camps, cursuses and ring ditches are nothing more sophisticated than surviving traces of practical man-made features utilized in some way in a pastoralist economy. Perhaps even the long stone avenues and the simpler stone circles also had a primary mundane use. . . .

A search of the southern British landscape for signs of the activities of the earlier Brits is made that much more difficult because erosion has shaved off at least 60 centimetres (24 inches) of the upper surface during the last 4000 years. This erosion process is due to rainwater charged with carbon dioxide (producing a weak solution of carbonic acid) dissolving the underlying chalk rock. It can be recognized in the field where an ancient stone monument has protected the surface of the bedrock and thus preserved it at a higher level than the surrounding level— a phenomenon known as differential weathering, which in some instances can be put to good use as a rough method for dating a monument.

Standing stone monuments without reliable back-up evidence from texts as to their prime use are vulnerable to the wildest speculations, especially among the lunatic fringe. Yet one plausible suggestion once put forward that cannot be refuted by contrary evidence is their involvement with fertility cults. The concept of fertility has been thematic *in all cultures* since Upper Paleolithic times, and the Neolithic agricultural revolution, which most societies later passed through, gave rise to fertility concepts that provided a dominant background cultus for day-to-day living. Out of the ancient fertility beliefs was created a link between the living and the dead, and woven into it was the mystical drama of birth, ripening, death and the ingrained idea of seasonal rebirth. Going back to the pre-Neolithic period of Marshack's scratched bones, we already find fertility symbols of various kinds widespread in Upper-Paleolithic art—particularly in the form of the so-called Venus or "Mother Earth-cum-Nurse" figurines. In appearance most are plump little creatures with exaggerated female characteristics : large breasts, thighs and buttocks. Many are carved from mammoth tusks. Many are so grotesquely distorted that it is concluded they were not intended as true-to-life sculptures but objects venerated in the cults of fertility, for their modellers purposely exaggerated the parts of the female form relevant to childbirth and seem to have regarded the rest of the female figure as irrelevant.

In all times human and animal birth and the seasonal sprouting of the crops have been one of the great mysteries, and the Venus figurines might be concluded to be works of man made to reflect in some way the biological miracle of birth and rebirth. This concept was likely terrestrial and cosmical, for ancient man saw for himself the Moon reborn each month. One of the bas-reliefs cited by Marshack in his lunar-month studies is of a face-less Venus from Laussel holding a bison horn inscribed with thirteen lines (Plate 28). The number thirteen is astronomically significant, for it represents the "round count" of lunar months in the solar year. Significant too is that the Moon and fertility are closely connected in several later cultures.

Views have been expressed that standing stones of the Neolithic period may represent directly a continuation and a cultural development of earlier fertility concepts. There is plenty of evidence to connect standing stones to fertility fetishes. The arrangement of the Men-an-tol monuments, particularly, are highly suggestive of this. Near-contemporary Megaliths found in Assam are certainly associated with a fertilty and a phallic cult, and alignments there have representations of male and female stones. It is significant too that these Megaliths had a multi-purpose use and were sometimes involved with the dead and symbolic of the vital essence of an enemy as well as that of a deceased clansman. It is of interest too that in the same area the Cherama clan in the Nago Hills determined the calendar of their agricultural year by careful observation of the Sun rising along a distant range of jagged peaks which enabled them to fix the horizon points of the solstices.

More than once the great stone-laid Avenue at Avebury has been given a plausible sexual/fertility interpretation. The Megaliths forming the Avenue *do* suggest selective pairings (male and female)—each being of contrasting shape. A relatively upright "phallic" pillar is often opposed by a diamond-shaped "Venus" stone, erected with one of its points in the ground (Plate 29 abc). Stonehenge (disregarding for the moment the astronomical evidence) is perhaps one of the most suggestive of the more elaborate and less ambiguous of the Megalithic fertility sites. The Heel Stone, as a phallic symbol, perhaps marks the point where the power of the rising Sun at midsummer is at its greatest to rekindle life or stimulate birth. In the same vein it has been suggested that the trilithon and bluestone horseshoes are symbolic of the womb (of the Great Earth Mother?) with their openings directed towards the Heel Stone and the Sun—the propagators of life; and that other egg-shaped circles or rings are built so to represent eggs—the most original symbol of fertility and birth.

These ideas, like the astro-archaeological ideas, are, of course, only speculative. Nevertheless, ethnologists and anthropologists are only too aware that growth and human fertility have been a preoccupation of mankind since the Upper Paleolithic. Earlier we have seen that the Megaliths of Brittany were used as fertilty/fetish symbols in the nineteenth century, and symbols of all kinds have been used in such a way. . . . Even the dust scraped from particularly significant standing stones was at one time swallowed as a fertility potion by sterile women. Stone dust from church walls was also an important element in Teutonic folklore. Stone again is cited in a church in Brandenburg where two sandstone blocks were built into a wall so that people might carve small holes in them at weddings to bring good fortune to the bridal couple and guarantee fecundity.

Among the most bizarre of the fertility/fetish objects was an old Dutch shore-defence cannon—the Holy Cannon, Kyai Satoma—at Bantam, to which local women flocked offering flowers and prayers for fertility. This may perhaps raise a wry smile in us modern people, but in 1976 the Dallas public library reported that the hottest thing in their collection since *Lady Chatterley's Lover* was a wooden sculpture which could be borrowed in their sculpture-loan section. This was a doll that women of the Ashanti tribe had carried round on their backs if they wished for a child. Word got round; and when a local newspaper reported that several Dallas women became pregnant one month after borrowing the statue, the librarian was subsequently inundated with loan requests.

We can be sure, by inference, that the culture of the Megalithic peoples of North-West Europe was motivated by an elitist class of the kind we find clearly demonstrated in Egypt, Babylonia and Mesoamerica. It seems likely too that the various kinds of funerary chambers in North-West Europe were reserved for the elitist-class families, for it was a privilege to be so buried. Archaeological field-evidence strongly supports this idea.

What happened then to the fellahin division of society, and what kind of a peasant society was it that was exploited by the Megalithic overlords? Here the record is a total blank; but clearly the master-builders required a large labour-force, for apparently the only tools used were antler picks, oxen bones and stone implements.

And what kind of labour-force was required to excavate great Neolithic earthworks as, for example, the great bank-and-ditch feature round Avebury? Atkinson made such a calculation and estimated it took a total of 1·5 million man-hours to complete— yet Avebury was only one among several henges with similar bank-and-ditch constructions.

Among the elitist class—perhaps at the very top of the hierarchy—would be the astronomer-priests. Without writing, how then did they record observations and keep tally of the various complex astronomical cycles? Perhaps Stonehenge itself (even disregarding the built-in alignments) was a kind of recording machine, a prehistoric memory bank or a central government mnemonic device. And we have already seen how one might keep tally of the Moon's motion by a simple stone-counting method.

Were the astronomer-priests of Neolithic time the predecessors to the Druids of the Iron Age as Lockyer and others believed? It was Pliny, remember, who tells us that the Druids took twenty years to acquire their education and that it was considered unlawful to commit their knowledge to writing. Could then an astronomer-priesthood class, without writing and with only stones to use in counting numbers, develop a sky science and evolve a calendrical astronomy and an eclipse-prediction method like that of the Maya? The answer must be a guarded *yes*—although this does not prove they did. But no longer is it possible for archaeologists to say that this was culturally impossible as once they maintained.

But what happened in prehistory to these peoples of the great Megalithic cultures of North-West Europe? Why did these cultures decline as decline they did in the Early Bronze Age?

Was it that following the climatic optium which occurred around 4000 B.C. the landscape changed and triggered a late Neolithic agricultural collapse? Or was it partly, or wholly, the same cause that some believe brought about the Maya collapse—a peasants' revolt? Evidence for such a peasant uprising is totally lacking, but evidence for climatic change and declining soil fertility, and then a farming collapse is very positive. Was it that overgrazing of the British uplands, in conjunction with climatic change and overpopulation, did bring about a radical transformation of the British scene?

We know that when Neolithic farming first began in Britain around 4000 B.C. or earlier, Britain was covered by a great primeval forest which extended to a height of 540 metres (1,800 feet). Today, particularly in Ireland and Scotland, there are remains of trees much larger and higher than now found in the neighbourhood. But apart from the secular change in climate, it does seem likely it was the long-term effect of Neolithic over-grazing that tipped the ecological balance and helped the metamorphosis of woodlands to create today's British upland "deserts" of bleak heathlands and peatland moors. In prehistoric times, as the climate deteriorated and rainfall increased, the man-made Megalithic landscape slowly became smothered in a thick blanket of peat. Today, in Europe generally, excavation down through peat to the old forest level reveals the lost world of the Neolithic landscape. Excavation through the peat has brought to light the complex nature of the long-buried Megalithic landscape, which has lain cocooned for over three millenniums. The realization that many stone circles in Britain are lost or part buried below the present-day landscape holds out a prospect that one day excavators may still come across some exciting artefactual evidence which will shed a brighter light on the great Megalithic cultures that once flourished throughout North-West Europe. Perhaps, too, still buried and preserved below the peat level is direct geometrical evidence of how the ancient Brits measured the sizes and shapes of their peculiar circles. Discovery of this kind of evidence might certainly tell us whether Alexander Thom's thesis is correct or false.

In finding intellectual solutions to the mystery of the Megaliths, those involved need to be ever wary of the set attitude of scholars or pundits whose obsessive attitude is almost indistinguishable from delusion. In hindsight the case is only too familiar where someone's set belief—occasionally heralded as "a great natural truth"—is nothing more than a farrago of unsound reasoning, manipulated fact and mistaken assumption. The nub of the problem was once summed up by the archaeologist-scholar R. A. S. Macalister who wrote: "Let an archaeologist once become obsessed with an idea that a defaced inscription must be read in a particular way . . . and he is lost, his eye will follow the dictates of his mind." For Macalister's archaeologist, one may substitute engineer, astronomer, surveyor, mathematician or whatever other specialologist with an obsessive bee in his bonnet is appropriate to the situation. In the long term the best critical tool of both researcher and reader to any new idea is healthy scepticism.

John Aubrey freely admitted that his research at Stonehenge was "a gropeing in the Dark". Few scholars and researchers today would be generous enough to be so candid, yet their theories and even whole books are sometimes based on tenuous *a priori* assumptions. Looking back to past schemes claiming a particular metrology involved in an archaeological monument, one is set wondering too about Alexander Thom's equally beguiling "Megalithic yard" and his intriguing ideas about how particular shapes of certain stone circles came about. It would be doing Thom an injustice to summarily dismiss them out of hand as some are inclined to do. Thom's ideas concerning solar and lunar alignments—similar to those cited for Stonehenge by others—are certainly more convincing than the "measures" he so readily manipulates to form his geometric constructions. This part of his work carries overtones of Stukeley's "Druid cubit", Smyth's "Pyramid inch" and Petrie's "Etruscan foot". In looking at this aspect of Thom's work, the cautionary yesteryear warning of Macalister echoes repeatedly.

Certainly, those who maintain a very necessary sceptical approach have strong doubts about several claims made for Megalithic man's achievements, and at present there remain several puzzles. For example, it would be expected that these Megalithic astronomers would also be regular observers of Venus. This planet, after the Sun and Moon, is the most striking "regular" object in the sky—discounting the spectacular falls of large meteorites and appearances of the brilliant Sungrazer comets.

Q

We have seen how important Venus was to the Babylonians and the Maya—proven stargazers of considerable abilities. She was important too to the Egyptians and many other cultures. She was known on sight to all primitives and figured strongly in the traditional astro-myths of peoples as divorced in geographical distance and climate as the Greenland Eskimo and the Australian Aborigine. It is an intriguing thought that still hidden in the complex arrangements of Stonehenge—or in the horizons round-about—may be stone-counts and alignments used by the astronomer-priests to track Venus which then enabled her period to be determined with the accuracy we know was achieved by the Maya and the Babylonians.

As often happens in the field of scientific endeavour, perhaps some key piece of evidence that is obvious to all in hindsight has so far been overlooked. Our knowledge of the intellectual record of the Megalithic past of North-West Europe is yet a preliminary sketch plan. Hopefully, in the future, in the light of fresh evidence, we can anticipate that uncommitted minds will re-examine the whole problem, and, basing their work on a more solid foundation of proven fact, start to draw up the definitive blueprint.

Select Bibliography

Atkinson, R. J. C., *Stonehenge*, London, 1956

Atkinson, R. J. C., "Decoder Misled?", *Nature*, Vol 210, 1302

Atkinson, R. J. C., "Moonshine on Stonehenge", *Antiquity*, Vol 40, 215

Baity, E. C., "Archaeoastronomy and Ethnoastronomy So Far", *Current Anthropology*, Vol 14, 389. (In this very useful contribution the author includes the most comprehensive bibliographical compilation of Megalithic astronomy source-material yet published).

Borst, L., "English Henge Cathedrals", *Nature*, Vol 224, 335

Brugsch, K. N., *Thesaurus Inscriptionum Aegyptiacarum*, Leipzig, 1883–91 (photo-reprint Graz 1968).

Colton, R. and Martin, R. L., "Eclipse cycles and Eclipses at Stonehenge", *Nature*, Vol 213, 476

Emmott, D., "The Mystery of Hole G", *Yorkshire Post*, 16 March 1963

Frazer, J. G., *The Golden Bough* (Abridged Edition), London, 1922

Hawkes, J., "God in the Machine", *Antiquity*, Vol 41, 174

Hawkins, G. S., "Stonehenge Decoded", *Nature*, Vol 200, 306–8

Hawkins, G. S., "Stonehenge : A Neolithic Computer", *Nature*, Vol 202, 1258

Hawkins, G. S., *Stonehenge Decoded*, London, 1966

Hoyle, F., "Stonehenge—An Eclipse Predictor", *Nature*, Vol 211, 127

Hoyle, F., "Speculations on Stonehenge", *Antiquity*, Vol 40, 262

Hawkins, G. S., Atkinson, R. J. C., Sadler D. H., Thom, A., Newham, C. A., Newall, R. S., "Hoyle on Stonehenge : Some

Comments", *Antiquity*, Vol 41, 91

Kellaway, G. A., "Glaciation and the Stones of Stonehenge", *Nature*, Vol 233, 30

Kendall, D., "Megalithic Lunar Observatories: Review", *Antiquity*, Vol 45, 310

Kramer, S. N., *Sumerian Mythology*, New York, 1961

Lancaster Brown, P., *Measuring Length: The History of Methods and Units*, London, 1971

Lancaster Brown, P., *What Star Is That?*, London and New York, 1971

Lancaster Brown, P., *Comets, Meteorites & Men*, London, 1973; New York, 1974

Lockyer, J. N., *The Dawn of Astronomy*, London, 1894

Lockyer, J. N., *Stonehenge and Other British Stone Monuments*, London, 1909 (2nd Edition)

Long, W., "Wiltshire Archaeological Magazine", Vol 16, 1876

Marshack, A., *The Roots of Civilization*, London, 1972

Michell, J., *The View Over Atlantis*, London, 1973

Morley, S. G., *The Ancient Maya*, Stanford, California, 1946, 1947, 1956

Neugebauer, O., "Tamil Astronomy", *Osiris*, 10, 252

Neugebauer, O. and Parker, R. A., *Egyptian Astronomical Texts* (4 vols), London, 1960, 1964, 1969

Neugebauer, O., *The Exact Sciences in Antiquity* (2nd Edition), New York, 1969

Newall, R. S., *Stonehenge, Official Guide Book*, London, 1959

Newham, C. A., *The Enigma of Stonehenge and its Astronomical and Geometrical Significance*, Leeds, 1964

Newham, C. A., "Stonehenge: A Neolithic 'Observatory'", *Nature*, Vol 211, 456

Newham, C. A., *Supplement to the Enigma of Stonehenge*, Leeds, 1970

Newham, C. A., *The Astronomical Significance of Stonehenge*, Leeds, 1972

Patrick, J., "Midwinter sunrise at Newgrange", *Nature*, Vol 249, 517

Renfrew, C., *Before Civilization*, London, 1973

Rose, L. E., "Babylonian Observations of Venus", *Pensee* Vol 3, Number 1, 18–22

Sadler, D. H., "Prediction of eclipses", *Nature*, Vol 211, 1120

Smyth, Piazzi, *Our Inheritance in The Great Pyramid*, London, 1864

Smyth, Piazzi, *Life and Work at The Great Pyramid*, London, 1867

Stevens, F., *Stonehenge: Today and Yesterday*, London, 1929

Thom, A., *Megalithic Sites in Britain*, Oxford, 1967

Thom, A., *Megalithic Lunar Observatories*, Oxford, 1971

Thom, A. and A. S., "The Astronomical Significance of the Large Carnac Menhirs", *Journal for the History of Astronomy*, Vol 2, 147

Thom, A., A. S. and A. S., "Stonehenge", *Journal for the History of Astronomy*, Vol 5, 71; Vol 6, 19

van der Waerden, B. L., *Die Anfänge der Astronomie*, Groningen, 1966

Velikovsky, I., *Worlds in Collision*, London, 1950

Watkins, A., *The Old Straight Track*, London, 1925

see also text, *passim*

Index

Note: Figures in italics refer to the page number of a relevant text figure.